Mapping the Trail
of a Serial Killer

Mapping the Trail of a Serial Killer

HOW THE WORLD'S MOST INFAMOUS MURDERERS WERE TRACKED DOWN

BRENDA RALPH LEWIS

The Lyons Press

Guilford, Connecticut
An imprint of The Globe Pequot Press

Editorial and design by:
Amber Books Ltd
Bradley's Close
74-77 White Lion Street
London N1 9PF
United Kingdom
www.amberbooks.co.uk

Project Editor: Sarah Uttridge
Design: Zoë Mellors
Picture Research: Terry Forshaw and Natascha Spargo

Library of Congress Cataloging-in-Publication Data is available on file.

ISBN 978-1-59921-813-7

Printed in Thailand

10 9 8 7 6 5 4 3 2 1

Contents

Introduction

A serial killer is much more than a killer who murders a minimum of two – or by most definitions three – people within a certain length of time. For what statistics can never take into account is the extreme fear serial killing generates. Its premeditated, predatory nature is horrifying, and spreads a particular type of terror among the community in which it occurs. Where will the killer strike again? Who will be the next victim? Are we secure in our homes, on the streets, at night, when we are alone? The answer to all these questions is a resounding No, for serial killers upset normal concepts of security. In imagination at least, and at worse in reality, they lay everyone open to the risk of sudden, terrible death.

Mutant Beings

The serial killer is a type of mutant, a being for whom the normal rules of human behaviour do not apply. As the killers featured in this book reveal, many of them have no sense of pity, no idea of guilt or any of the other qualities – love, friendship, self-discipline, decency – that motivate the rest of us. Many serial killers are sexual perverts driven to rape, sodomy or necrophilia – sex with the dead – and sometimes all three. Schizophrenia or misogyny have accounted for the dark deeds of other killers. So has the curious syndrome in which the fame craved by Andrew Cunanan was sublimated by murdering someone – in his case, the Italian fashion designer Gianni Versace – who was himself famous.

Quite a few serial killers glory in their exploits and even become disturbed at the thought that

Detectives gather at the bleak scene where a victim was left by Peter Sutcliffe, 'the Yorkshire Ripper'. He created fear throughout North England from 1975 to 1980.

someone else may score more murders than they have themselves managed to accomplish. Some blame outside influences for their crimes, notably voices ordering them to kill, or an irresistible urge to wipe out people they see as social undesirables, such as prostitutes or beggars. More than once,

The body of the serial killer Andrew Cunanan is removed after he committed suicide in Miami in 1997. He had earlier killed the fashion designer Gianni Versace.

serial killers have named demands from God as the motive behind their crimes.

> **'Some blame outside influences for their crimes, notable voices ordering them to kill, or an irresistible urge to wipe out people they see as social undesirables, such as prostitutes or beggars.'**

On the Loose

Another aspect of serial killing which increases the horror it inspires is that many of these killers can be uncaught for years. For example, Gary Ridgway, the Green River Killer, murdered 90 victims but remained at liberty for 20 years. Randy Steven Kraft murdered 16 people and was suspected of killing even more over a period of 12 years. How did these and other serial killers manage to remain at large for so long? In some cases, killers remained free to operate because of the inability of the authorities to recognize and tie up similarities in their murders. There was also the charm and affability which some serial killers, like Ted Bundy, employed to mask their dangerous nature. But as the 25 killers featured in this book demonstrate, the geography of their murders also served to cover up the trail they might otherwise have left behind.

This is where *Mapping the Trail of a Serial Killer* differs from other books on the subject. Each of the

'By moving on, a serial killer could be many miles away by the time the bodies were discovered. They often travelled light, leaving few, if any, clues to guide the police.'

murderers featured in these pages travelled between killings as the maps which accompany each chapter show. These maps, which indicate where some of the bodies were found – not all the locales are known – also demonstrate the great distances that lay between each murder scene. By moving on, a serial killer could be many miles away by the time the bodies were discovered. These killers often travelled light, leaving few, if any, clues to guide the police and almost nothing connected with anyone local people could easily recognize. Truck drivers whose job kept them constantly on the road were particularly favoured by geographical serial killing, as it might be termed, but railroad travel, Angel Maturino Resendez' preferred method, accomplished much the same task.

Monsters on the Rampage

Serial killers have often been called 'monsters', suggesting that they are not really human, but luckily, the murderers in this book were human enough to commit the errors that finally put them behind bars. Sometimes, they were pulled up on some petty crime, like drunken driving or theft. In other cases, a witness was in the right place at the right time. Or they were caught by sheer coincidence, in Volker Eckert's case, he was eventually caught after being photographed on CCTV. But however it was accomplished, another reign of terror was, thankfully, over.

America's mass murderer Ted Bundy did not fit the image of a killer, being educated, articulate and charming. On trial, he even acted as his own lawyer.

Randy Steven Kraft

The Southern Californian Strangler

FULL NAME:
Randy Steven Kraft

DOB:
19 March 1945

NUMBER OF VICTIMS:
Convicted of 16 but suspected
of many more

SPAN OF KILLINGS:
1971–1983

LOCATION OF KILLINGS:
Along the freeways of California

DATE OF ARREST:
14 May 1983

SENTENCE:
Sentenced to death, he remains on
Death Row

Randy Steven Kraft was born in Long Beach, California on 19 March 1945 and had an IQ of 129, which placed him in the 'highly intelligent' category. He was scholarly, scored brilliantly in aptitude tests, earned a university degree in economics and seemed destined for a high-achieving future. Except that he never got there. His chances were scuppered by the fact that he was gay at a time when this was not as acceptable as it later became. After 'outing' himself in 1969, he was dismissed from the US Air Force, took a job as a bartender and then began to show an alarming propensity – for serial killing – chiefly, though not exclusively, in California.

The first sign that Randy Steven Kraft had turned to murder was discovered on 5 October 1971, when the naked body of Wayne Joseph Dukette, a 30-year-old gay bartender, was discovered beside the Ortega Highway. This is a section of State Route 74 that runs through the Santa Ana Mountains of southern California. The corpse had been there for some time, to judge by the degree of decomposition, and neither Dukette's clothes nor his belongings were ever found. Nevertheless, the police concluded that there was nothing to suggest that Dukette, who had been missing for two weeks, had met his death by foul play.

That was surprising to say the least, for California freeways like the Ortega were well-known dumping grounds for dead bodies, many of them hidden in shallow graves and most quite evidently tortured and sexually assaulted. The writer Dennis McDougal called the Ortega Highway a 'kind of unique strip of remote, undeveloped and primitive real estate for people of ill intentions. It gained this dark reputation as a place where evil could be done with impunity.'

Dukette, however, was probably not Kraft's first victim. Kraft began in March 1970 with Joseph Alwyn Fancher, a 13-year-old runaway whom he encountered at Huntington Beach on the coast of Orange County, California. Kraft took the boy home, plied him with marijuana and wine and showed him photographs of men having sex with each other. Then he sodomized the boy and threatened him with dire punishment if he ever breathed a word of what had happened.

Joseph survived and, after Kraft went to work the next day, he escaped to a nearby bar, where the staff called an ambulance. His stomach was pumped out, and he afterwards led police back to Kraft's apartment, where they found illegal drugs and photographs of Kraft fornicating with several men. No arrest followed because the search had been done without a warrant and no case based on the evidence found would stand up in court. Even so, the episode did mean that the police were now aware of Kraft.

The Killings Continue

Randy Steven Kraft, they discovered, drove a forklift truck at a bottled water plant in Huntington Beach.

Huntington Beach Pier, where Kraft picked up victims and left the remains of one. Other corpses were found on different California beaches.

'Moore had been beaten and strangled and there were bite marks on his genitals. To judge by the state and posture of the body, Moore had been thrown out onto the road from a moving vehicle.'

By night, he cruised from one gay bar to the next, seeking out partners for sex. Kraft had a penchant for Marines and some time before 26 December 1972, he found what he wanted. In the early hours of that morning (1.45 a.m.), the body of a 20-year-old Marine, Edward Daniel Moore, was found by a motorist lying beside the 405 Freeway in Seal Beach in the westernmost corner of Orange County near the resort of Long Beach. Moore had been beaten and strangled and there were bite marks on his genitals. To judge by the state and posture of the body, Moore had been thrown out onto the road from a moving vehicle.

This discovery was followed by another on 6 February 1973, when a young man about 18 years of age was found strangled on the Terminal Island freeway in the Wilmington district of Los Angeles. He was a 'John Doe', or unidentified victim, and so were the next two bodies discovered in the following five months – a corpse found with genitals missing on Huntington Beach, and another discovered in pieces across two California counties: his head in Long Beach; torso, right leg and arms in San Pedro; and left leg on Sunset Beach.

At various freeways and other locations – Seal Beach, the San Bernardino Mountains, and Laguna Beach golf course among them – similar victims were found during the rest of 1973 and on into 1974 and 1975. If anything, the murders accelerated, and so, on 24 January 1975, detectives from several districts in California – Sheriff's officers from Orange County, Imperial County and San Bernardino County and police from Los Angeles and Long Beach, Seal Beach,

Irvine and Huntington beaches – convened at Santa Ana. Their purpose was to form a task force dedicated to finding the serial killer.

Suspicions Aroused

A profiler, Dr E. Mansell Patterson of the University of California, Irvine, was called in to assess the sort of man the task force was looking for. He concluded that this was a man 'who desires to be masculine, but does not feel masculine, gnawing the nipples and genitals of his prey to symbolically make the victim a female.'

The Task Force set to work, and it was not long before they encountered Randy Steven Kraft. On 8 May 1975, three young boys looking for starfish near the Long Beach Marina discovered a head. It was the head of 19-year-old high school dropout Keith Daven Crotwell, who was last seen alive at Long Beach on 29 March. Crotwell was travelling south, thumbing rides along the way, and one of the vehicles seen to pick him up was a black and white Mustang. The Mustang was located a few days after the head was found and, on checking out the registration, police found that the owner was Randy Kraft.

Kraft was questioned on 19 May, and told police that he had given Crotwell a ride, but had left him at an all-night café. Some detectives wanted to charge Kraft with murder there and then, until it was pointed out that Crotwell's head was not enough evidence in the absence of a body and a certain cause of death.

This close shave unnerved Kraft for a while and no more killings took place for nearly six months, until Larry Gene Walter, 21, was murdered in Los Angeles County on 31 October 1975. The series of killings that followed in 1976 revealed a switch to younger victims, aged between 13 and 19 years, whose remains were found dumped on Manhattan Beach, Inglewood, Los Angeles, Redondo Beach, and further south towards the Mexican border near Calexico. Yet, despite the best efforts of the Task Force, clues to the culprit remained hard to find and those they *did* manage to obtain failed to match any known suspect.

Even more embarrassing, dead bodies were still turning up, many of them with genitals horribly mutilated or cut out. The victims had been stabbed, bludgeoned, strangled, raped and were frequently

The Trail of Murders

Long Beach Marina, California, 8 May 1975:
Greater Los Angeles provided Kraft with the urban maze needed to pick up victims, kill them and dispose of their bodies. They were left beside highways and in seaside communities, such as Redondo Beach. Three boys found one severed head near the Long Beach Marina.

Orange County, California, August 1974–June 1978:
Kraft would often chose Orange County, California, as a final resting place for his victims' remains. Several were left throughout the large area from August 1974 to June 1978, and the killer was finally apprehended there five years later with a corpse in his car.

Oregon, July 1980–December 1982:
During his travels as a data-processing consultant, Kraft left five bodies in Oregon from July 1980 to December 1982. The first of the mutilated victims was a hitchhiker discovered near Salem. Kraft deposited three others in the Portland area and one near Goshen.

Michigan, 9 December 1982:
Kraft, visiting as a freelance consultant in the Midwest in December 1982, murdered two cousins near Grand Rapids, Michigan, where he was attending a computer conference. The victims were last seen in the bar at his hotel, and their bodies were found in Plainfield Township.

Key Randy Kraft's victims

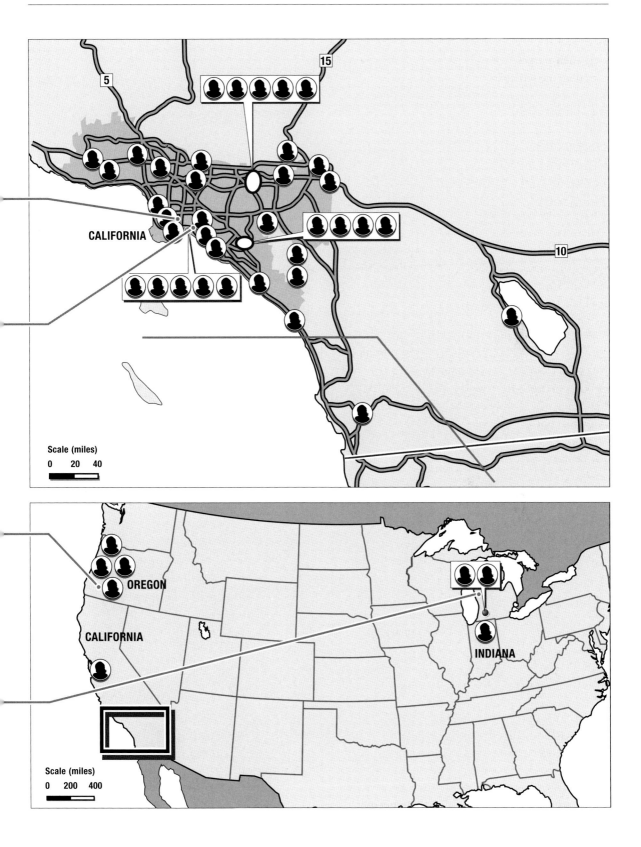

RANDY STEVEN KRAFT

The following victims or suspected victims of Randy Steven Kraft are those whose names have been established. There were several more victims who have never been identified.

Victim/Suspected victim (Named)	Age	Body found	Body found in California unless otherwise stated
Wayne Joseph Dukette	30	5 October 1971	Ortega Highway
Edward Daniel Moore	20	26 December 1972	Seal Beach
Ron Wiebe	20	28 July 1973	Seal Beach
Vincent Cruz Mestes	23	29 December 1973	San Bernardino Mountains
Malcolm Eugene Little	20	1 June 1974	Salton Sea
Roger Dickerson	18	22 June 1974	Laguna Beach
Thomas Paxton Lee	23	3 August 1974	Orange County
Gary Wayne Cordova	23	12 August 1974	Orange County
James Dale Reeves	19	29 November 1974	Irvine
John Leras	17	December 1974	Long Beach
Craig Victor Jonaites	21	17 January 1975	Long Beach
Keith Daven Crotwell	19	8 May 1975	Long Beach
Larry Gene Walter	21	31 October 1975	Los Angeles County
Mark Hall	22	3 January 1976	Cleveland National Forest
Oliver Peter Molitor	13	21 March 1976	Manhattan Beach
Kenneth Buchanan	17	7 April 1976	Inglewood
Larry Armendariz	14	19 April 1976	Los Angeles
Michael Craig McGhee	13	11 June 1976	Redondo Beach
Randall Lawrence Moore	16	October 1976	Highway 80, east of El Cajon
Paul Fuchs	19	10 December 1976	Vanished from Redondo Beach
Scott Michael Hughes	19	16 April 1978	91 Freeway, Orange County
Roland Young	23	11 June 1978	Irvine
Richard Keith	23	20 June 1978	Orange County
Keith Klingbell	-	6 July 1978	Mission Viejo
Michael Inderbeiten	21	18 November 1978	Seal Beach
Donald Harold Crisel	-	16 June 1979	405 Freeway, Irvine
Thomas Lundgren	13	29 May 1979	Agoura
Marcus Grabbs	17	6 August 1979	Ventura Freeway
Donald Hayden	15	27 August 1979	Liberty Canyon
David Murillo	17	11 September 1979	Highway 101
Michael Shaun O'Fallon	17	17 July 1980	Salem, Oregon
Robert Loggins, Jr	19	25 August 1980	El Toro Marine Airbase, Irvine
Michael Duane Cluck	17	April 1981	Goshen, Indiana
Raymond Davis	13	29 July 1981	Echo Park, Los Angeles
Robert Avila	16	29 July 1981	Echo Park, Los Angeles
Christopher Williams	17	20 August 1981	San Bernardino Mountains
Brian Witcher	26	26 November 1982	Portland, Oregon
Dennis Alt	-	9 December 1982	Plainfield Township, Michigan
Christopher Schoenborn	-	9 December 1982	Plainfield Township, Michigan
Lawrence Trenton Taggs	19	9 December 1982	Portland, Oregon
Anthony Joseph Silveira	29	18 December 1982	Hubbard, Oregon
Eric Church	21	28 January 1983	605 Freeway
Geoffrey Nelson	18	13 February 1983	Claremont College
Rodger de Vaul, Jr	20	13 February 1983	Claremont College
Terry Gambrel	25	14 May 1983	Orange County

naked. By 1979, the death toll had reached slaughter proportions and California's gay community was now seriously alarmed. Warning posters went up in gay bars, accompanied by photographs of unidentified victims in the hope that someone, somewhere, would realize who they were – or rather, had been.

Meanwhile, Randy Steven Kraft appeared to be thriving. In July 1979, he set himself up as a freelance data-processing consultant, and did well enough to afford a house in Long Beach, which he shared with his lover, Jeff Seelig. The two of them travelled widely, to Mexico and Lake Tahoe, and on an east coast tour from New York City to Key West. By 1980, Kraft had become a consultant for Lear Sigler Industries with regional offices in San Diego, Michigan and Oregon. By 1981, he was earning around $50,000 a year and seemed, at last, to be fulfilling the intellectual promise he had shown in earlier years.

Yet there was a grim undertow to Kraft's success: he claimed more victims wherever he went. During the early 1980s, corpses were discovered in Salem, Oregon, near El Toro Marine airbase at Irvine, California, at Goshen, Indiana, Echo Park, Los Angeles, on a road in the San Bernardino Mountains and near Portland, Oregon, and Plainfield Township, Michigan. The police were able to discern a pattern in the killings. Besides the sexual abuse, many of the victims had been drugged and strangled, recalling the unsolved murders that had taken place in Southern California over the previous decade. In an effort to link a name to the sequence, police trawled computer records of airline, hotel and rental car bookings and found 18 references to Randy Steven Kraft.

And then fate intervened.

On 14 May 1983, Kraft was arrested in Orange County for drunk driving. He was travelling along the San Diego freeway in Mission Viejo, and there was a man in the passenger seat. On closer investigation, the police found that the man was dead. Terry Gambrel, a 25-year-old Marine, had been strangled and was slumped in the seat with empty beer bottles at his feet. The car also contained tranquillizers, alcohol and, most incriminating of all, clothes and other items that had belonged to some of the young men found murdered on various freeways since the early 1970s. There were also numerous photographs of the murder victims, either dead or unconscious. A search of Kraft's garage produced a torn jacket from one of his killings and his fingerprints were found at one of his crime scenes. At last, the police had the evidence they had long sought to link with Randy Steven Kraft.

Justice Postponed

Kraft was arrested and charged with 16 homicides, but this was only a fraction of his likely toll. Kraft had kept a list of his victims. It was in code, and Terry Gambrel had not yet been added to it, but the list suggests that

Kraft may have have been responsible for as many as 67 murders.

The trial began on 26 September 1988, after five postponements and a series of legal arguments that cost the taxpayers of California $10 million. Kraft was accused of 16 murders – and pleaded Not Guilty to all of them. The court proceedings were lengthy, for the prosecution called over 157 witnesses and brought 1052 exhibits into evidence. The defence then took its time, presenting Kraft as a respectable 'homeowner, taxpayer and hard worker' who had 'killed no one', and the trial did not end until 1 May 1989. The jury delivered a Guilty verdict on 11 August, and recommended the death penalty. A few months later, on 29 November, Judge Michael McCartin formally sentenced Kraft to death.

But thanks to the tortuous US legal system, with its multiple appeals, Randy Steven Kraft was still alive on 11 August 2000, when his sentence was upheld by the California Supreme Court. However, the lawyers were not yet done, and 20 years after he was first admitted, on 30 November 1989, he remains on Death Row in San Quentin prison, near San Rafael in California – something of a record in the US prison system.

During Kraft's trial, former colleagues testified that he was normal and friendly. Kraft presented a calm image, but jurors were not impressed.

Joachim Kroll
The Duisburg Maneater

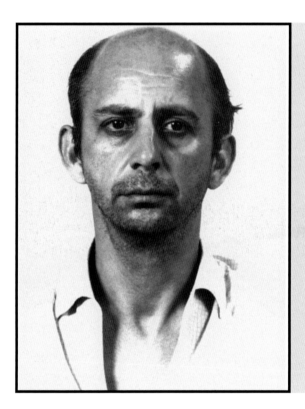

FULL NAME:
Joachim Kroll

DOB:
17 April 1933

DIED:
1 July 1991

NUMBER OF VICTIMS:
Convicted of eight murders but confessed to several more

SPAN OF KILLINGS:
1955–1976

LOCATION OF KILLINGS:
Duisberg, Germany

DATE OF ARREST:
3 July 1976

SENTENCE:
Nine life sentences

Known as both the Ruhr Cannibal and the Duisburg Maneater, Joachim Kroll was one of several killers at large in the Duisberg district of the Ruhr Valley in Germany between 1955, when he killed his first victim, and 1976, when he raped and strangled his last. This multiplicity of murderers helped him escape detection for more than 20 years. But Joachim Kroll was different from the rest. As his nicknames suggest, he ate human flesh. When he was at last detained, his latest meal of body parts was simmering on the stove.

Joachim Kroll was born on 17 April 1933 in the east German city of Hindenberg. He was a weak, sickly child with an IQ that was later calculated by psychiatrists at 76, very much below average. He was a loner and had difficulty forming relationships, particularly with women, though he liked children and was in turn liked by them. But a clue to his personality lay in the collection of inflatable dolls he kept secretly in his small, three-room apartment. He used them principally for sex, but also practised strangling them – sometimes performing the two acts at the same time. Inevitably, the day came when Kroll started playing his secret sex games for real. He always knew when he was about to stalk a victim, for what he described as a 'tingling feeling' came over him and the urge to kill became irresistible.

The trigger that first set him off on his killing spree was the death of his mother in late January 1955, when he was 21 years old. Though he was well past the age at which his brothers had left home,

Kroll was still living with his mother when she died. It may be that her demise set him free to express his sinister sexual desires. Certainly, he committed his first murder three weeks later, on 8 February 1955, when he raped 19-year-old Irmgard Strehl and stabbed her to death with a long-bladed folding knife. To make sure she was dead, Kroll strangled her and then used his knife to disembowel her body, which he left in a barn at Lüdinghausen on the Dortmund-Ems Canal, some 24km (15 miles) southwest of Münster. Her ghastly remains were discovered five days later.

Taking Precautions

In 1957, Kroll moved to Duisburg, where he worked as a lavatory attendant and lived in the Laar district of the town. He knew enough about police methods to avoid killing too often in the same district or killing again too soon after his last murder. Instead, he visited towns round Duisburg where he was not well known, looking for victims and choosing wooded areas where their bodies could be more easily hidden.

Kroll picked Kirchhellen as the scene of his second killing, in 1958. There, he raped and murdered a 12-year-old girl, Erika Schuletter.

The Ruhr area city of Duisburg and its suburbs were a hunting ground for Kroll. He moved there in 1957, two years after killing his first victim.

In March of the next year, he followed a 23-year-old homeless woman named Erika from a Duisburg tavern to Rheinhausen, one of the city's suburbs, and assaulted her, knocking her unconscious. Kroll normally made sure his victims were dead, but Erika managed to survive. Soon afterwards, he attacked and killed two more women in different towns. He then returned to Duisburg, where, on 16 June 1959, he murdered 24-year-old Klara Frieda Tesmer in the meadows at Rheinhausen not far from the River Rhine. Tesmer, it seems, struggled so hard as Kroll tried to remove her clothing that the two of them fell to the ground and rolled down the embankment towards the water. He grabbed her by the throat to silence her and when he was convinced she was dead, he raped her corpse. Subsequently, a mechanic called Heinrich Ott was charged with Tesmer's murder: the experience was so traumatic that he eventually hanged himself in prison. Poor Ott was only the first of five men falsely accused of committing Kroll's murders:

'The corpse was in such a fearful state when they found it that police first believed that the 16-year-old had been attacked by an entire gang. No one, as yet, imagined that the killer had turned cannibal.'

three of them committed suicide as a result. One even confessed to murder in order to to silence neighbours who were baying for his blood.

Becoming a Cannibal

On 26 July that same year, Kroll murdered 16-year-old Manuela Knodt. She was strangled in woods inside a park in Essen, but this time Kroll also masturbated over the dead girl's face and pubis and sliced flesh off her buttocks and thighs. The corpse was in such a fearful state when they found it that police at first believed that the 16-year-old had been attacked by an entire gang. No one, as yet, imagined that the killer had turned cannibal.

Thus far, Joachim Kroll had managed to kill six women but remain undetected. This, naturally, gave him a sense of invincibility. He now began to widen his area of operations: he would take a bus or train to an isolated area, then disembark and walk around until he spotted a woman or girl on her own. By this means, Kroll was able to stalk and seize his victims and rape and kill them without witnesses. Kroll needed the leisure and the secrecy this *modus operandi* afforded. Although he strangled his prey quickly, the rest of his crime took time. He would strip the corpse naked, have sex with it and masturbate over it. Once satisfied, Kroll then proceeded to mutilate the body, and remove pieces of flesh to cook and eat later.

Out of three murders committed by Joachim Kroll in 1962, the fate of two followed this pattern. Petra Giese, 13, was murdered in the City Park at Essen, near the River Ruhr on 23 April, and Monika Tafel,

The Trail of Murders

Munster, 8 February 1955:
Kroll's first murder occurred in 1955 near Munster when he raped, stabbed and strangled 19-year-old Irmgard Strehl, leaving her body in a barn. Police were baffled by this seemingly motiveless crime, and Kroll waited until 1957 before striking again.

Duisburg, 1958–1976:
Duisburg and its surrounding area provided Kroll with many of his victims. He murdered them there from 1958 until 1976, when police caught him cooking the flesh of 4-year-old Marion Ketter on the stove in his Duisburg flat.

Essen, 26 July 1959:
The first time Kroll resorted to cannibalism was in 1959 in Essen, where he murdered 16-year-old Manuela Knodt. He would later tell authorities that he was motivated by the cost of meat and his desire to taste human flesh.

Breitschied, 21 May 1970:
Breitschied in the German state of Hesse was the site picked by Kroll for the 1970 murder of 10-year-old Jutta Rahn. He watched her leaving a train alone and followed as the girl walked home through woods where he attacked and strangled her.

Key   Joachim Kroll's victims

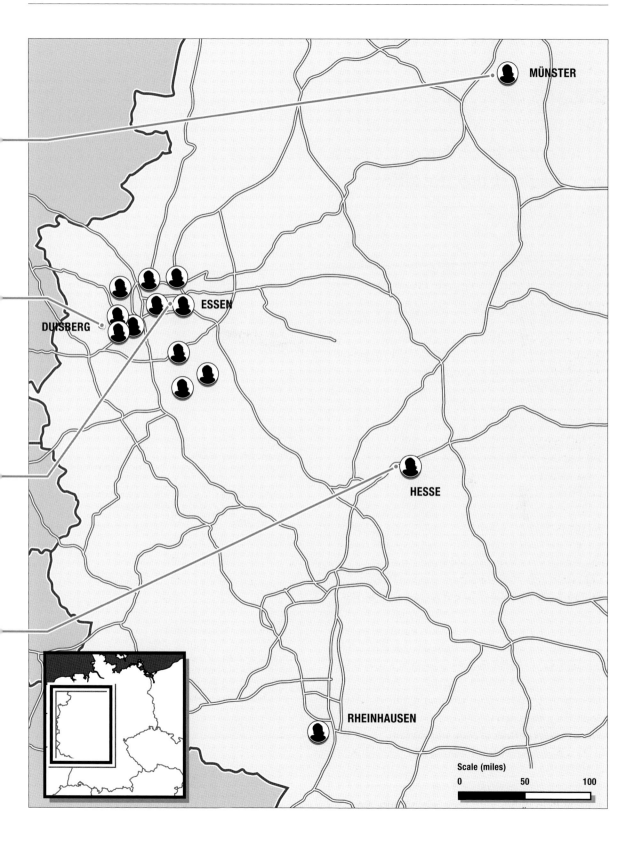

MÜNSTER

ESSEN

DUISBERG

HESSE

RHEINHAUSEN

Scale (miles)

0　　　50　　　100

Kroll (right) consults a lawyer during his trial in Duisburg, where it became a worldwide sensation. He received nine life sentences.

12, was killed at Walsum, a suburb of Duisberg, on 4 June. Walter Quicker, a 34-year-old paedophile, was arrested for killing Tafel, but was afterwards released. Nonetheless, neighbours hounded him so viciously that he took shelter in nearby woods and hanged himself. Kroll carved flesh out of the bodies of Petra Giese and Monika Tafel. His favourite 'cuts' appeared to be taken from the buttocks and thighs, although he also removed Petra's left forearm and hand.

Unusually for a killer of established habits, Joachim Kroll changed his pattern on 22 August 1965, when he attacked a couple who were 'necking' in their Volkswagen near a lake outside Duisburg. Kroll aimed to get rid of 25-year-old Hermann Schmitz first, then concentrate on Schmitz's girlfriend, Marion Veen. Kroll used his knife to stab one of the Volkswagen's tyres. Schmitz leapt out of the car and ran straight into Kroll's blade, receiving several strikes in the heart. As Schmitz fell dead, Kroll made a grab for Marion, but instead of cowering in terror, as he doubtless expected, she jumped into the driver's seat, sounded the horn several times and plunged her foot onto the accelerator. The Volkswagen jerked forwards,

almost hitting Kroll and so scaring him that he fled for the safety of the surrounding woods.

After that, Kroll lay low for more than a year and did not emerge to kill again until 13 September 1966, when he strangled and raped Ursula Rohling, 20, in Foersterbusch Park near Marl in the Ruhr region of western Germany. Once again, another man paid the price of this murder: Ursula's boyfriend, Adolf Schickel, was accused of the crime and was soon being so cruelly pressurized by police and public opinion that he drowned himself in the River Maine.

New Tactics

Three months later, Kroll became interested in a new method of disposing of his victims: what would it be like, he wondered, to drown somebody? On 22 December 1966, he took the first step towards satisfying his curiosity by luring 5-year-old Ilona Harke onto a train in Essen. They disembarked at Wuppertal, east of Dusseldorf, where they went for a walk. Kroll was looking for a ditch with enough water in it to drown a small child. When he found it, he forced the little girl's head into the water and held it there until she ceased struggling. Afterwards, he reverted to type: he raped the girl and sliced flesh from her shoulder.

Kroll's next victim was a woman of 61 – Maria Hettgen, who was murdered at Hückeswagen on 12 July 1969 – but afterwards he specialized in children whose flesh, it has been presumed, tasted sweeter than an adult's. The last of three young girls killed by Kroll in the 1970s was 4-year-old Marion Ketter, who was kidnapped from a Duisburg playground and murdered on 3 July 1976. When it was discovered that the girl was missing, police searched the area around the playground, but finding nothing, resorted to a house-by-house search. At this point, Oscar Muller, who lived in the same apartment block as Joachim Kroll at 11, Friesenstrasse, Duisburg, came rushing out of the building and buttonholed one of the police officers.

Muller had a terrifying story to tell. The tenants at 11 Friesenstrasse shared toilet facilities, and Muller was on his way to use them when he met Kroll. Kroll told him that the lavatory was blocked and out of order. When Muller asked what was blocking it, Kroll told him 'Guts!' Muller thought this was a joke, but when he looked into the toilet, he was horrified to see that the water in the bowl was blood-red and whatever was floating in it did indeed resemble guts. In addition, the toilet cubicle gave off a disgusting smell.

Muller's first thought was that the mess in the toilet was meat scraps, but the police were less sure. There had been several child murders in the area, and they feared that here was evidence. The contents of the toilet were examined, and their fears were confirmed: these were the lungs, kidneys, intestines and heart of a child together with odd pieces of flesh.

Kroll, who seemed to know what the bowl contained, was questioned by police and told them that he had killed a rabbit to make a stew and had thrown its internal organs into the toilet. The police knew perfectly well that the remains did not come from a rabbit, although they were able to smell something cooking in Kroll's kitchen. It was a stew all right, but the small hand that was found in it told

another, utterly horrifying story. So did the contents of plates found in Kroll's refrigerator and the neatly parcelled packages of 'meat' stored in the freezer.

Kroll put up no resistance when he was taken to the police station for questioning. His interrogators soon realized that they had caught a sex killer who could boast the longest run of crimes ever committed in Germany. Kroll confessed to the murder of Marion Kettner and also admitted 14 other killings, adding that he had sliced pieces of some of his victims to economize on his grocery bills. He was under the impression that he could be 'cured' of his compulsion to kill and cannibalize, and would then be released, to live a more normal life. He was soon disabused of that fantasy when he was put on trial, charged with eight murders and one attempted murder. The trial lasted 151 days and ended with his conviction on all counts and nine life sentences. He served a little over eight years before he died of a heart attack in Rheinbach prison, near Bonn, on 1 July 1991. He was 58.

JOACHIM KROLL TIMELINE

17 April 1933: Joachim Kroll born in Hindenberg, eastern Germany.

8 February 1955: Three weeks after his mother's death, Kroll commits his first murder: he rapes and kills 19-year-old Irmgard Strehl in Lüdinghausen, 24km (15 miles) southwest of Münster.

16 June 1959: After killing 12-year-old Erika Schuletter in 1958, assaulting a homeless woman in Rheinhausen (March 1959) and subsequently killing two more women in different towns, Kroll murders 24-year-old Klara Frieda Tesmer in Rheinhausen. Heinrich Ott, a mechanic who was falsely accused of killing Tesmer, commits suicide.

26 July 1959: Manuela Knodt, 16, is murdered by Kroll in a park in Essen. Afterwards, he slices flesh from her buttocks and thighs.

23 April 1962: Petra Giese murdered in the City Park at Essen. Vinzenz Kuehn, a 52-year-old sex offender, is convicted of the crime and spends six years out of a 12-year sentence in jail.

4 June 1962: Monika Tafel, 12, killed at Walsum, a suburb of Duisberg. A 34-year-old paedophile, Walter Quicker, is arrested for killing Tafel, but is released. Quicker is hounded by neighbours into committing suicide. Also murdered by Kroll in 1962: Barbara Bruder, 12, kidnapped by Kroll in Burscheid. Her body is never found.

22 August 1965: Kroll attacks a couple near a lake outside Duisburg, first killing Hermann Schmitz, 25. He aims to assault Schmitz's girlfriend, Marion Veen, but she escapes.

13 September 1966: Kroll strangles and rapes Ursula Rohling, 20, at Marl, western Germany. Her boyfriend, Adolf Schickel, is accused of the crime and commits suicide.

22 December 1966: Kroll drowns 5-year-old Ilona Harke in a ditch at Wuppertal and rapes her corpse.

12 July 1969: Maria Hettgen, 61, is raped and strangled at Hückeswagen.

21 May 1970: Jutta Rahn, 10, is strangled by Kroll at Breitschied, in Hesse, western Germany. Jutta's neighbour, Peter Schay, is arrested. Though afterwards released, he nevertheless confesses to the murder six years later, after being hounded by his neighbours.

3 July 1976: After killing Karin Toepfer, 10, in Voerde, Kroll claims his last victim in 4-year-old Marion Ketter in Duisburg. Parts of Marion's body are found simmering on Kroll's stove after police investigate a blocked-up toilet in the building where he lives.

7 October 1979: The trial of Joachim Kroll begins.

8 April 1982: After a 151-day trial spread over two and a half years, Kroll is convicted of eight murders and one attempted murder and is given nine life sentences.

1 July 1991: Joachim Kroll, 58, dies of a heart attack in Rheinbach prison near Bonn.

Pedro Lopez
Monster of the Andes

FULL NAME:
Pedro Alonso Lopez

DOB:
8 October 1949

NUMBER OF VICTIMS:
Accused of killing more than 300 women

SPAN OF KILLINGS:
1978–1980

LOCATION OF KILLINGS:
Colombia, Peru and Ecuador

DATE OF ARREST:
April 1980

SENTENCE:
Guilty of three murders, 16 years in prison

DATE OF RELEASE:
January 1999

Pedro Lopez, who was born in Tolima, Colombia on 8 October 1949, was known to the media as the 'Monster of the Andes'. But he had a very different view of himself and his own importance. By his own admission, he sexually abused and then killed up to 300 women, and believed that he was 'the man of the century. No one will ever forget me.' The reality lay somewhere between these two extremes. Lopez suffered horrendous experiences early in life: the son of a prostitute, he was the victim of a paedophile who repeatedly sodomized him, and the target while in prison of a gang of rapists, all of whom he later killed. It may have been no coincidence, therefore, that his career as a serial killer began soon after his time in prison came to an end in 1978.

Pedro Lopez was the seventh of 13 children, and his birthplace, Colombia, was one of the most violent places in the world. Its crime rate was 50 times greater than any other country in the world. Riots, political assassinations, a civil war that killed over 200,000 people in 10 years, and human rights abuses of every conceivable kind were everyday events in Colombia. From a very early age, Lopez was witness to many of them.

He was already living on the streets by the age of 8, when his domineering mother threw him out after finding him fondling the breasts of his younger sister. He slept in alleys and doorways, always at risk from predators, perverts and criminals. In order to survive, he scavenged around dustbins and begged on the streets. Eventually, a kindly American couple took him into their home where he had a room of his own and plenty of food to eat. They also sent him to school, but there he was molested by one of the teachers and responded by stealing money from the school office. Before long, Lopez was back on the streets, begging again and committing petty thefts.

Apprentice to Murder

Lopez began to specialize, and when he was around 15 years old he became a car thief. He was well paid for his efforts by the 'chop shops' that dismantled stolen vehicles and sold the parts or used them for repairs. Lopez was such a consummate thief that he was soon well respected in the 'trade'. Unfortunately, he also became well known to the police, who arrested him in 1969 and put him in jail for seven years.

When Lopez made himself a crude knife and killed the four-man gang who raped him in prison, the authorities judged this to be a case of self-defence rather than murder and gave him only an extra two years in jail. But by this time, Pedro Lopez was already irreparably damaged by the hardships and suffering he had endured in life. When he was released from prison in 1978, he was not a little mad, with a range of resentments – fear and hatred of women, inability to socialize, a taste for extreme violence – that led him inexorably to serial murder.

> **'… he was not a little mad, with a range of resentments – fear and hatred of women, inability to socialize, a taste for extreme violence – that led him inexorably to serial murder.'**

Lopez chose Peru, next door to Colombia, as his hunting ground. He travelled widely through the high Peruvian Andes, where society was still essentially 'Indian' and tribal and his targets, chiefly young girls, were easily available. Here, in 1979, he took to stalking these girls and, he afterwards claimed, murdered around 100 of them. But in northern Peru, Lopez fell foul of the Ayacucho tribe, when they caught him trying to abduct a 9-year-old Ayacucho girl. Vengeance was rough and immediate in these remote regions. Lopez himself described what happened next: 'Indians in Peru had me tied

San Juan de Ambato, Ecuador, was the end of the road for Lopez. He murdered several victims there but was caught taking a girl at a local market.

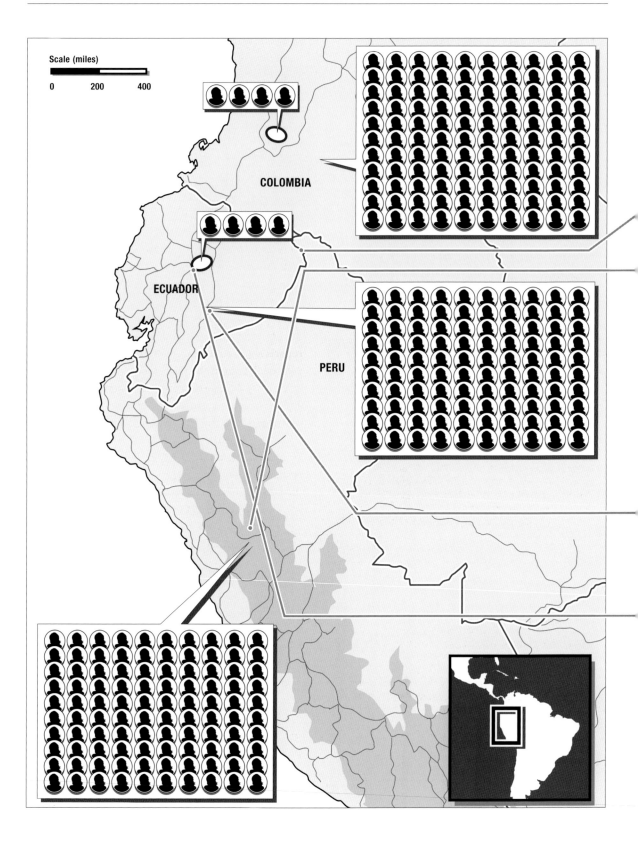

The Trail of Murders

Colombian border, January 1999:
Lopez was born in Colombia. After years of living and killing in Peru, he made frequent visits to Colombia and left a trail of death. When he was freed from prison, Lopez was driven to the Colombian border and simply released onto his native soil.

Peru, 1979:
Peru's high Andes were Lopez's main hunting ground, where he claimed he murdered at least 100 young girls. It was here that the Ayacucho people nearly killed him after they caught him abducting a girl. Handed over to the Peruvian police, he was deported to Ecuador.

Ecuador, 1980:
Although eventually imprisoned there, Ecuador was Lopez's favourite source of victims. He travelled the country after being deported from Peru and killed about three girls each week. Later Lopez said he preferred the girls of Ecuador because 'they are more gentle and trusting, more innocent'.

San Juan de Ambato, April 1980:
The bodies of four female children were revealed in April 1980 by a raging flood in San Juan de Ambato in central Ecuador. Murder seemed probable but unproven. Within days, Lopez was chased down trying to abduct a 12-year-old girl from her mother.

Key   Pedro Lopez's victims

up and buried in sand up to my neck. They placed syrup on me and were going to let me be eaten by ants.'

Just then, good luck intervened. An American missionary came by and somehow managed to convince the Ayacucho that murder was ungodly. What they needed to do, the missionary told them, was to turn Lopez over to the authorities and let them deal with him. The missionary must have been impressive, for the Ayacucho agreed, though reluctantly, and Lopez was saved. He was duly delivered to the Peruvian police, who regarded him more as an inconvenient nuisance than anything else, and promptly deported him to neighbouring Ecuador.

The Prison Cell

After his lucky escape, Lopez began travelling around Ecuador, with frequent visits to Colombia. Soon, reports about young girls going missing started to escalate. However, the police did not believe a serial killer to be the cause, blaming the increasing South American sex slave trade. But then, in April 1980, a flash flood near San Juan de Ambato in central Ecuador revealed some disturbing evidence. When, eventually, the waters subsided, they revealed the remains of four girls. There were no clues as to how they had met their deaths but if it had not involved foul play, the police reasoned, why would anyone have bothered to conceal their bodies?

A few days later, in San Juan de Ambato, Carvina Poveda was shopping in the local market with her 12-year-old daughter Marie, when they were approached by a man who tried to abduct the girl. The man swept Marie into his arms and started to run away with her when her mother began screaming. Nearby market traders rushed to the rescue, chased after the man and, catching up with him, pinned him to the ground until the police arrived. It was, of course, Pedro Lopez, who appeared to be rambling wildly as he was taken into custody, so much so that the police concluded that they had a madman on their hands.

When the questioning began, Lopez refused to answer. This went on for some time until the police, growing impatient, decided on a ruse. They called in a priest, Father Gudino, dressed him up in prison clothes and put him in the same cell as Lopez. Before long, Father Gudino succeeded where the police had failed. Lopez began to talk, and continued to talk, telling stories of such horrific brutality, in such graphic detail, that the priest begged to be removed from the cell.

All the same, the facts were out. Lopez had admitted to the murders of 110 young girls in Ecuador, 100 more in Colombia and a great deal more than 100 in Peru. Lopez also revealed why he had gone in for serial killings.

'I lost my innocence at the age of eight,' he told Father Gudino 'so I decided to do the same to as many young girls as I could.'

According to an interview with Ron Laytner, published in the *National Examiner Magazine* on 12 January 1999, Lopez' method was to haunt village markets for girls with 'a certain look of innocence.' He preferred to seek and seize this 'look of innocence' in full daylight rather than at night, so that when he raped and then strangled his victims, he could stare into their eyes. As he watched their lives ebb away, Lopez confessed to feeling a surge of excitement and sexual pleasure at the death throes he was observing. Nor did his activities stop there. Lopez

would prop up the corpses of the girls and then 'invite' them to have tea with him while he did all the talking.

Official Doubts

Lopez' story struck the police in Ecuador as so outlandish that they hesitated to credit it. This belief was reinforced when their colleagues across the border were unable to confirm his professed activities in Peru and Colombia. Lopez decided to give them proof and offered to lead them to the places in Ecuador where he had buried the bodies. The police agreed. They took Lopez, who was wearing leg irons, to a police caravan and toured the sites he named in forest country around Ambato. Their scepticism vanished very quickly when the remains of 53 young girls aged between 8 and 12 were discovered. At 28 other sites named by Lopez, nothing was found, but the police believed that the remains must have been scattered, probably by foraging animals and flooding. Nevertheless, the evidence that *had* been found was indisputable: Pedro Lopez was a serial killer on a major scale.

After that, the police lost no time in charging Lopez with 57 murders – the 53 young girls just discovered and the four found at San Juan de Ambato

---

PEDRO LOPEZ TIMELINE

8 October 1949: Pedro Alonso Lopez born in Tolima, Colombia, the seventh of the 13 children of a prostitute.

1957: Aged 8, Lopez is thrown out by his mother for fondling his younger sister's breasts, and is forced to live on the streets.

1964: The 15-year-old Lopez becomes a car thief, selling stolen vehicles to 'chop shops' which use them for their spare parts.

1969: Lopez is jailed for car theft. While in prison he is raped by four of the other inmates. Later, he kills them in revenge.

1978: Lopez is released from jail and travels to neighbouring Peru.

1979: Lopez begins raping and killing young girls. After attempting to abduct a 9-year-old Ayacucho girl, he is seized by members of the tribe, tortured and almost killed. Lopez is rescued by an American missionary. Afterwards, he moves to neighbouring Ecuador.

April 1980: Flash floods near San Juan de Ambato in central Ecuador reveal the remains of four girls. A few days later, Lopez is prevented from abducting a young Ecuadorian girl. He is arrested by police, but refuses to answer when questioned. Eventually, though, he confesses to murdering more than 300 girls in Ecuador, Colombia and Peru.

1980: Police do not believe Lopez, but he

leads them to the graves of 53 girls he claims to have murdered.

27 January 1981: Lopez is sentenced to 16 years in prison on three counts of murder.

January 1999: There is public outrage when Lopez is released from prison at the end of his sentence and taken across the Ecuadorian border into Colombia.

2001: Despite fears that Lopez may kill again, there are no reports of young girls missing in Ecuador, Colombia and Peru over the previous two years. There is speculation that someone, somewhere has taken up one of the many rewards offered for killing him.

in April. This already stunning figure was boosted to 110 killings, based on part of Lopez' confessions. But Lopez had admitted 300 and given the circumstances, Victor Lascano, the director of prison affairs in Ecuador, thought that this even more greatly increased number was 'very low'.

'If someone confessed to 53 (killings, which) you find, and hundreds more' Lascano explained, 'you tend to believe what he says.'

Pedro Lopez went on trial in San Juan de Ambato on 27 January 1981, where the judge, Jose Roberto Cobos Moscoso, pronounced him guilty on three counts of murder, and sentenced him to 16 years in prison, the maximum permitted by Ecuadorian law.

Nearly 20 years later, in 1999, when Lopez was interviewed by Ron Laytner, of *National Examiner Magazine,* he elaborated on his method of luring young girls into remote places, where he killed them.

'I would take (them) to a secret hideaway where prepared graves waited,' Lopez told Laytner 'Sometimes there were bodies of earlier victims there. I cuddled them and then raped them at sunrise.... I forced the girl into sex and put my hands around her throat. When the sun rose I would strangle her. It took the girls five to 15 minutes to die.... I would spend a long time with them making sure they were dead. I would (use a) mirror to check whether they were still breathing. Sometimes I had to kill them all over again.... My little friends liked to have company. I often put three or four into one hole. But after a while I got bored because they couldn't move, so I looked for more girls.'

A Killer Released

A few days after the Laytner interview, Pedro Lopez was released from prison at the end of his sentence. He was bundled into a prison van, which drove through the night towards the border between Ecuador and Colombia. Dawn was breaking as the van pulled off the road. It stopped at the frontier line, its back doors were opened and Lopez was unceremoniously dumped onto Colombian soil.

Lopez was released in this furtive fashion, under cover of darkness, to prevent vigilante mobs gathering outside the prison and possibly attempting to lynch

Lopez was 50 when released from prison in 1999. He said this was for 'good behaviour' and that being released was as exciting as watching someone die.

him as soon as he appeared. But the authorities could not prevent intense public outrage in all three countries where the killings had taken place. The prospect of the Monster of the Andes being let out of jail, possibly to kill again, was too much.

'God help the children!' remarked Victor Lascano. 'He is unreformed and totally remorseless. This whole nightmare may start again.'

The families of the victims, however, had already made their own arrangements to prevent a repeat of the nightmare. While Lopez was still in prison, they had joined together to raise a $25,000 reward, payable to anyone willing to kill him. This was not the only bounty offered for the death of Pedro Alonso Lopez, and it is possible that someone, somewhere took up the offer and claimed the reward. For it was reported in 2001 that in the previous two years, there were no reports of young girls going missing in Ecuador, Colombia or Peru, nor of any more ghastly finds in remote places where the Monster of the Andes preferred to leave his victims.

Charles Sobhraj

The Bikini Killer

FULL NAME:
Hatchand Bhaonani Gurumukh Charles Sobhraj

DOB:
6 April 1944

NUMBER OF VICTIMS:
At least nine, some predict several more

SPAN OF KILLINGS:
1975–1976

LOCATION OF KILLINGS:
He preyed on Western tourists throughout Southeast Asia

DATE OF ARREST:
19 September 2003

SENTENCE:
Life imprisonment

Hatchand Bhaonani Gurumukh Charles Sobhraj, born in Saigon (Ho Chi Minh City) on 6 April 1944, was the illegitimate son of a Vietnamese mother and an Indian father. Charles Sobhraj, as he was usually known, went to prison for virtually every felony it was possible to commit. He began his career in crime with burglary and went on to forgery, fraud, car, passport and jewel theft, smuggling, armed robbery and drug dealing. Sobhraj's great ambition was to create a crime family similar to the clan surrounding the notorious American murderer Charles Manson: it was this that led him to the first of his serial killings.

Charles Sobhraj was a man of powerful personality and extraordinary *chutzpah*, who found it easy to attract others to connive with his scams and other schemes that were designed to exploit them and enrich himself. Essentially, he was a con man: when he was only 10 years old, Sobhraj told his mother that he could 'always find an idiot' to do what he wanted.

Useful Idiots

Later on, he was always able to recruit 'idiots' into his crime family by befriending English- or French-speaking tourists on holiday in exotic venues like India, Thailand or Nepal and using them as couriers to smuggle stolen goods for him. Alternatively, Sobhraj salted them as a source of income, stealing their money, traveller's cheques, passports or travel tickets. He attracted young men to his side by wining and dining them and generally showing them the high life, complete with alluring women and the promise of riches to come. Once, Sobhraj even went so far as to poison a French boy named Dominique. Afterwards, to make him grateful and dependent, he administered an antidote to help him recover.

But not all Sobhraj's 'idiots' were as gullible as he liked to imagine. It was when they saw behind the mask or baulked at the crimes he wanted them to commit that the ruthlessness of the psychopath was revealed: it was then that they started to disappear or turn up dead.

The First Corpse

Sobhraj's first known murder victim was an American girl named Jennie Bollivar. An idealist, she came to Thailand in 1975 seeking a new, more spiritual

'He attracted young men to his side by wining and dining them and generally showing them the high life, complete with alluring women and the promise of riches to come.'

meaning to her life, hoping to find it in the country's religion, Buddhism. Instead she encountered Charles Sobhraj, who apparently attempted to persuade her to join his 'family's' smuggling activities. According to the Dutch diplomat Herman Knippenberg, who spent two decades tracking the activities of Sobhraj, Jennie refused. Sobhraj responded by killing her so that she would not be able to reveal his smuggling operations to anyone else. Her corpse was found in a

Police surround their infamous prisoner, Sobhraj, when he was arrested in New Delhi in June 1976. Also taken into custody were his three female 'family' members.

tide pool of the Gulf of Thailand. She was wearing a flowered bikini.

Initially, it was believed that Jennie had fallen into the water and drowned after spending a night imbibing a deadly mixture of beer and drugs. It was several months before an autopsy was performed and when it was, it refuted the beer and drugs story: instead, it was revealed that Jennie's head had been pushed under the surface and held there until she drowned.

A Fatal Charm

Sobhraj's second murder victim, a young Jew named Vitali Hakim, came to Thailand during 1975. Like Jennie, he was on a spiritual quest. Instead, Hakim encountered Charles Sobhraj. Before long, Hakim joined the 'family' and was so trustful that he gave his passport and traveller's cheques to Sobhraj, who promised to keep them safe for him. When Sobhraj and his Indian 'lieutenant' Ajay Chowdhury, a vicious young criminal, travelled to Pattaya, a glamorous resort on the Gulf of Thailand, Hakim went with them – and promptly disappeared.

A few days later, a badly burned male corpse was discovered on the road leading to Pattaya. There were obvious signs that the victim had been severely beaten and, worse, had been still alive when gasoline was poured over him and set on fire. There were several gangs at work in the area, and the Pattaya police assumed the victim was one of their prey.

But Charmayne Carrou, a French friend of Hakim's, was not satisfied with that explanation. In December 1975, she arrived in Thailand to search for him. She learned from a hotel where he had stayed that Hakim had checked out some weeks earlier but never returned. Carrou took up the trail from there and, it seems, traced him to Charles Sobhraj and his 'family', who were staying at Pattaya. It is not precisely known when news reached Sobhraj that the French girl was asking too many questions, but it was not long before she was found drowned in the Gulf of Thailand. Like Jennie Bolliver, she was wearing a flowered bikini. The subsequent autopsy revealed that Carrou had been strangled so forcefully that the bones in her neck had disintegrated.

The Trail of Murders

Various continents, 1975–1976:
Sobhraj moved easily between continents in order to steal and murder without facing justice. His vicious trail went from Thailand to Nepal, returning to Thailand, then periods in India, Singapore, Thailand again, Malaysia, India once more, France and lastly Nepal, where he was imprisoned for life.

Thailand, 1975:
Thailand was where Sobhraj began his long odyssey of death. His first five victims died in 1975, with two found in the Gulf of Thailand and the others in Pattaya. Twice the following year, Sobhraj and his 'family' fled Thailand after the police became suspicious.

Nepal, 18 December 1975:
Sobhraj and his female Canadian companion, Marie-Andrée Leclerc, entered Nepal. They soon met an American man there to climb Mount Everest and a Canadian woman. Four days later their stabbed bodies were found in Kathmandu, the latest victims of Sobhraj.

India, 1976:
Sobhraj left corpses on both coasts of India in 1976. In March, he murdered an Israeli in Calcutta and, with two new women companions, killed a Frenchman in Bombay (Mumbai). Four months later, Sobhraj was caught in New Delhi and convicted of the latter crime.

Key Charles Sobhraj's victims

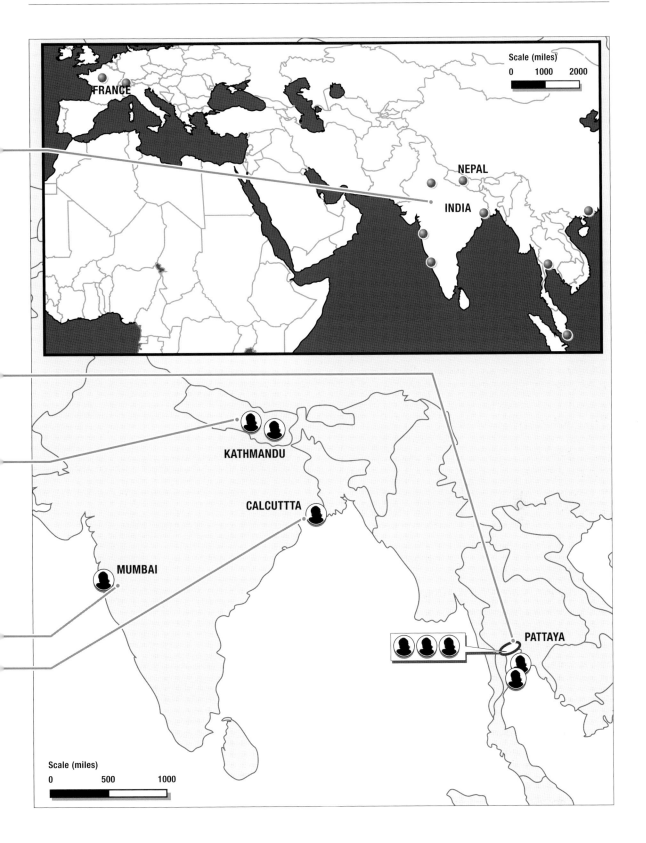

Scale (miles)
0   1000   2000

FRANCE

NEPAL

INDIA

KATHMANDU

CALCUTTTA

MUMBAI

PATTAYA

Scale (miles)
0   500   1000

Even as a prisoner, Sobhraj maintained a positive outlook. Bribery helped win the goodwill of his guards, who allowed him the easy lifestyle of a celebrity.

The same month, a Dutch couple, Henricus Henk Bintanja, 29, and Cornelia Cocky Hemker, 25, who were travelling round southeast Asia, encountered Charles Sobhraj in Hong Kong. Posing as Alain Dupuis, a dealer in jewels, Sobhraj befriended Henk and Cocky but told them that he had to leave soon for Bangkok, the Thai capital. Why not follow him there, he suggested, and spend time at his luxury villa? Henk and Cocky accepted the invitation and when they arrived in Bangkok, Alain Dupuis was there to meet them. Like so many others who were dazzled by Sobhraj's charm, they entrusted him with their

passports and valuables – and soon after that, they disappeared. Shortly afterwards, on 16 December 1975, they were found strangled and burned.

Two days later, Charles Sobhraj entered the Himalayan kingdom of Nepal, using Henk Bintanja's passport. Travelling with him and using Cocky Hemker's passport was another member of the Sobhraj 'family', Marie-Andrée Leclerc, a French-Canadian girl from Quebec. In Kathmandu, the Nepalese capital, Sobhraj and Leclerc met 26-year-old Laurent Ormond Carrière, 26, a Canadian, and Connie Bronzich, 29, from California, neither of whom survived the encounter for long. They were found murdered on 22 December 1975, but before they could be identified, Sobhraj and Leclerc returned to Thailand using the dead couple's passports. Once back in Bangkok, where he arrived in March of 1976, Sobhraj sold jewels that had been stolen from Carrière.

Allowed to Escape

But in Bangkok, Sobhraj received a nasty surprise. While he was away in Kathmandu, three 'family' members had come to realise that they were consorting with a psychopathic killer. The three were all Frenchmen – Yannick and Jacques, both former policemen, and Dominique Rennelleau. This they discovered after breaking into Sobhraj's apartment and finding dozens of passports that had once belonged to tourists who had disappeared or been found dead. The trio fled to Paris, first telling the Thai police about Sobhraj and his sadistic activities.

It was clearly time for Sobhraj and 'family' to leave Thailand. Leaving everything behind in their haste to

'Like so many others who were dazzled by Sobhraj's charm, they entrusted him with their passports and valuables – and soon after that, they disappeared.'

get away, including their money, the fugitives headed for India and made their way to the eastern city of Calcutta. There, they blended into the ragged poverty-stricken masses that inhabited the streets of one of the world's poorest and most overcrowded cities. Soon, Sobhraj encountered his next victim, an Israeli scholar named Avoni Jacob, whom he drugged and strangled in his hotel room. Stealing Jacob's passport and $300 in traveller's cheques, Sobhraj made his way to Singapore posing as the dead Israeli scholar. He was accompanied by Ajay Chowdhury and Marie-Andrée Leclerc.

The three of them remained in India long enough for the furore in Thailand to die down – or so they thought. Then they returned to Bangkok. It was a risky move and nearly ended in disaster. Against their expectations, the Bangkok police had not forgotten about the 'bikini' killings of Jennie Bollivar and Charmayne Carrou and the trio were brought in for questioning. But somewhere along the line, it occurred to the police that a widely publicized murder

scandal was not good for the tourist trade. They backtracked and the investigation began to falter.

At the Dutch embassy in Bangkok, Herman Knippenberg insisted on a thorough enquiry. This, he was sure, would reveal Charles Sobhraj to be the killer of the two Dutch tourists Henk Bintanja, and Cocky Hemker. Knippenberg was out of luck, however. Charles Sobhraj was well aware of how easy it was to grease palms in Asia and, literally in his case, get away with murder. A payment of $18,000 to a suitably venal Thai police official sufficed to let Sobhraj off the hook and enable him to escape from Thailand with his two companions.

Their first stop was Malaysia, where Ajay Chowdhury was sent on a series of jewel-stealing expeditions. Chowdhury returned with stones said to be worth some $40,000. Soon afterwards, he disappeared and was never found. It is believed that Sobhraj decided Chowdhury had outlived his usefulness and murdered him before he left Malaysia with Marie-Andrée, bound for Geneva, Switzerland.

CHARLES SOBHRAJ TIMELINE

6 April 1944: Charles Sobhraj born in Saigon (Ho Chi Minh City), Vietnam.

1963: Sobhraj is sent to prison for the first time, after being found guilty of burglary.

1975: After committing a long series of crimes, Sobhraj murders his first victim, Jennie Bollivar in Thailand. Sobhraj's second murder victim, Vitali Hakim, is killed in Pattaya, Thailand.

16 December 1975: A Dutch couple, Henricus Henk Bintanja and Cornelia Cocky Hemker, meet Sobhraj in Hong Kong. Sobhraj invites them to Pattaya where they are later found murdered.

December 1975: Charmayne Carrou, a friend of Vitali Hakim, arrives in Thailand to search for him. She is found drowned in the Gulf of Thailand.

18 December 1975: Sobhraj uses Henk's passport to enter Nepal. His accomplice, Marie-Andrée Leclerc, uses Cocky's passport.

22 December 1975: Laurent Ormond Carrière and Connie Bronzich encounter Sobhraj in Kathmandu, Nepal and are subsequently found murdered.

March 1976: Sobhraj and Leclerc arrive back in Bangkok, using Carrière's and Bronzich's passports. The Thai police are alerted to Sobhraj's activities by three members of his 'family' and he hastily departs Thailand for Calcutta, India. In Calcutta, Sobhraj murders Avoni Jacob, an Israeli scholar, and steals his passport and traveller's cheques. Sobhraj travels to Singapore with accomplices Ajay Chowdhury and Leclerc.

1976: Sobhraj, Chowdhury and Leclerc return to Bangkok, Thailand. There Dutch diplomat Herman Kippenberg tries to persuade the police to investigate Sobhraj's murderous activities – but fails. Sobhraj, Chowdhury and Leclerc leave Thailand for Malaysia. Chowdhury vanishes after stealing gems – his body is never located. Sobhraj sells the gems in Geneva, Switzerland. He subsequently returns to

India and kills Jean-Luc Solomon in Bombay (Mumbai).

July 1976: Sobhraj, Leclerc and two new female 'family' members move to New Delhi, where they trick French students into hiring them as tour guides. Sobhraj's attempt to drug the students goes wrong and he and the three women are arrested. Sobhraj is charged with killing Jean-Luc Solomon and is sentenced to 12 years in prison.

March 1986: Sobhraj escapes from Tihar prison, New Delhi, but is caught in Goa and receives an additional 10 years in prison.

17 February 1997: Sobhraj is released from prison and departs for France.

19 September 2003: Sobhraj is arrested in Kathmandu, Nepal and is sentenced to life imprisonment for murdering Laurent Carrière and Connie Bronzich in 1975. After a failed appeal, the sentence is confirmed in 2005.

Sobhraj sold the jewels in Geneva, but soon returned to Asia, heading for Bombay (Mumbai), where he set about rebuilding his by now depleted 'family'. He was soon back to his old routine, this time staging a robbery that led to another murder: a Frenchman, Jean-Luc Solomon, was doped with poison to keep him quiet while the robbery was in progress, but died as a result.

Moving on to New Delhi, the Indian capital, in July 1976, Sobhraj and his new 'family' – Leclerc and two other women, Barbara Sheryl Smith and Mary Ellen Eather – posed as tour guides. They attached themselves to a group of French students but instead of showing them the sights, they drugged them with bogus anti-dysentery pills. The pills had such a dire effect that some of them collapsed unconscious within seconds. Three of the students, fortunately unaffected, realized what was happening. They seized Charles Sobhraj, and hung onto him long enough for the police to arrive and arrest him, together with the three women.

On trial in Nepal in August 2004, Sobhraj was followed by the international media. He had been arrested after a journalist recognized him and tipped off police.

Under interrogation, Smith and Eather soon broke down and admitted everything. Charles Sobhraj, by contrast, denied everything and for two weeks stuck to his story that he was a prominent French merchant. All the same, he was charged with killing Jean-Luc Solomon and together with Leclerc, Smith and Eather, he was taken to the Tihar prison outside New Delhi.

Despite the filth, the squalor and the rats and insects that infested Tihar, Sobhraj contrived to live a life of ease, even luxury while he was there. For one thing, he was able to bribe the guards to obtain anything he wanted. He had entered Tihar with 70 carats of precious gems concealed in his body and used them to acquire a television set, gourmet foods and luxury goods of all kinds. His outlandish lifestyle and notoriety made him something of a celebrity, and he was in regular demand for newspaper and magazine interviews. Similarly, Sobhraj bribed his way to occasional freedom, paying prison guards to look the other way when he slipped out of Tihar for a few hours.

Tihar also served as a safe haven for Sobhraj, for he was wanted by the police forces of other countries for his crimes. The Nepalese were anxious to get hold of him and the Thais had a warrant for his arrest, which would remain in force for 20 years. But as long as Sobhraj remained in Tihar prison, no one else could get their hands on him and it was, of course, the Indian judicial system that had first pick at putting him on trial. The backlog of cases awaiting hearings was so long that two years passed before Sobhraj appeared in court. He was found guilty of the manslaughter of Jean-Luc Solomon and sentenced to 12 more years in prison.

Sobhraj scans the news in Paris after his release from prison in India in 1997. While in the French capital, he became rich selling his life story.

> **'Despite the filth, the squalor and the rats and insects that infested Tihar, Sobhraj contrived to live a life of ease, even luxury while he was there.'**

This, though, was not long enough for Sobhraj. The 20-year Thai warrant was due to expire in 1996 and his projected release date from Tihar would occur in 1990. What Sobhraj needed was more time in jail to enable the Thai warrant to run out. To this end, in March of 1986, he organized a lavish party for the guards and other prisoners in Tihar, plied them with sleeping pills and then escaped. He headed for Goa, where he was pleased to be quickly apprehended. As punishment, his sentence in Tihar prison was extended by another 10 years.

The Profits of Crime

On 17 February 1997, when the Thai warrant and most other evidence and witness statements against him had long since lapsed, Charles Sobhraj was released from Tihar prison. He departed for France, where he earned another fortune in fees for interviews and photographs and, in 2002, the sale of rights to a film based on his outlandish life.

But Sobhraj became too confident. He returned to Nepal, where a journalist recognized him walking down a street in Kathmandu. Two days later, on 19 September 2003, Sobhraj was gambling in the casino at the Yak and Yeti Hotel when Nepalese police arrested him.

On 20 August 2004, in the Kathmandu district court, Sobhraj was sentenced to life imprisonment for the murders of Laurent Ormond Carrière and Connie Bronzich in 1975. Hermann Knippenberg's efforts to nail Sobhraj were justified at last, for the Dutch diplomat provided most of the evidence against him. Sobhraj appealed against his conviction, but the life sentence was confirmed by the Kathmandu Court of Appeals in 2005. The luck of Charles Sobhraj had run out at last.

Ted Bundy

Notorious Sociopath and Multiple Killer

FULL NAME:
Theodore Robert Cowell
(changed to Bundy when he was adopted)

DOB: 24 November 1946

DIED: 24 January 1989

NUMBER OF VICTIMS:
37 according to his own estimate

SPAN OF KILLINGS:
1974–1978

LOCATION OF KILLINGS:
Washington State, Utah, Colorado,
Idaho and Florida, USA

DATE OF ARREST:
15 February 1978

SENTENCE:
The death penalty (electric chair)

No one could have guessed that Ted Bundy was anything but the handsome, intellectually brilliant, charming young man he appeared to be. Yet behind this agreeable façade lurked a sociopath fascinated by images of sex and violence. Bundy himself regarded this aspect of his character as a separate personality, naming it 'The Entity'. The Entity fed a merciless drive to kill and keep on killing until Bundy's toll of victims reached, by his own estimate, 37 girls and young women.

Ted Bundy's first killing ground was the University of Washington State. On 1 February 1974, a 21-year-old student and part-time radio announcer, Lynda Ann Healy, went missing. The first sign that something was amiss came from Lynda's alarm clock, which went off at 5.30 a.m. every day to enable her to reach the radio station in time to start work. The alarm hadn't been switched off and kept ringing until one of her housemates got out of bed to investigate.

She found Lynda's room empty and presumed that Lynda was on her way to work. Then the telephone rang. It was the radio station, asking where she was. From there on, disturbing evidence began to accumulate. The front door to the house, normally secured at night, was found to be unlocked. Small bloodstains had been discovered on her pillow and the bottom sheet on her bed. The top sheet was missing. More blood was found on Lynda's nightdress, which was hung up in the cupboard.

Even so, the police did not, at first, suspect foul play. Ultimately, they worked out what must have happened: someone had entered the house, broken into Lynda's room in the basement and knocked her unconscious. He then took off Lynda's nightdress, hung it up, and dressed her in a pair of jeans and a shirt. Still unconscious, she was wrapped in the missing top sheet and carried out into the street. It was all done so quietly that no one was either disturbed or alerted.

A Man With a Cast

Before long, though, another kind of evidence started to emerge. On 12 March 1974, another university student, Donna Gail Manson, aged 19, was kidnapped and murdered at Olympia, the Washington State capital. Another four weeks, and another university student, 18-year-old Susan Rancourt, vanished from the university campus at Ellensburg on 17 April.

By this time, there were eyewitnesses to suspicious happenings, which indicated that the killer was fishing for more victims. Soon after the disappearance of Susan Rancourt, two students from Rancourt's college, Central Washington State, reported meeting a man with a heavy cast on his arm. On the night of 17 April, the first student was asked for help in carrying a load

> **'Behind this agreeable façade lurked a sociopath fascinated by images of sex and violence. Bundy himself regarded this aspect of his character as a separate personality, naming it "The Entity".'**

of books to his car, a Volkswagen Beetle. Three days later, the second student was asked to do the same thing. Neither came to harm but, tragically, the same could not be said of Roberta Parks, who was last seen alive at Oregon State University campus at Corvallis on 6 May 1974, or of Brenda Ball, who disappeared on 1 June after leaving the Flame Tavern in Burien,

Bundy listens intently during his second court case in Florida. A year earlier, he had acted as his own lawyer, being articulate but overcome by the evidence.

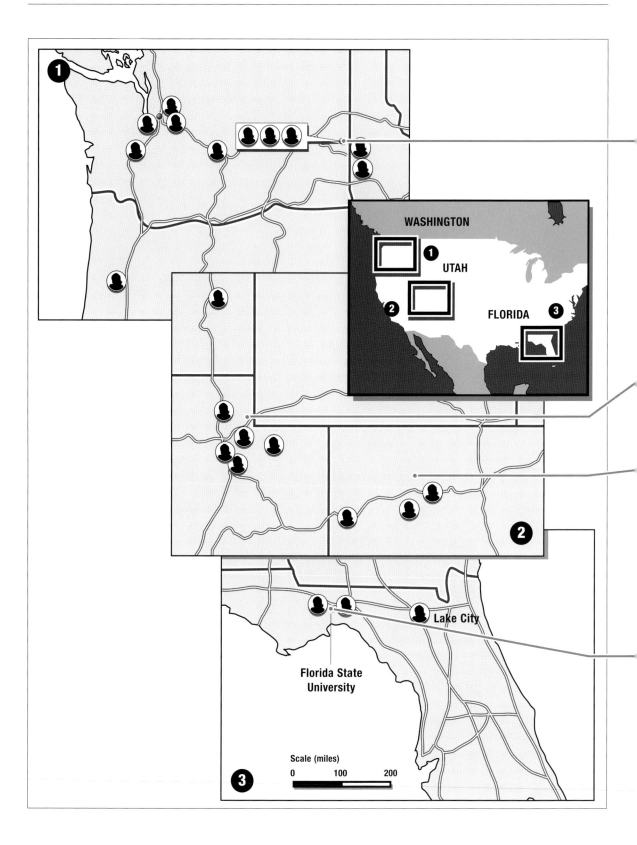

WASHINGTON

① UTAH

②

FLORIDA ③

Lake City

Florida State
University

Scale (miles)

0   100   200

③

The Trail of Murders

Washington State University, 4 January 1974:
Bundy's reign of terror began in 1974 at Washington State University in Pullman, Washington, where he assaulted and nearly killed one student in January and a month later murdered another student. He returned to the campus in June to kill a sorority member.

Salt Lake City, October 1974:
By October 1974, Bundy had moved to Salt Lake City, Utah. He had previously killed a teenaged girl there and during the year added four more victims and unsuccessfully tried to abduct a fifth. He was arrested and convicted in the city in August 1975.

Colorado, 12 January 1974:
Colorado was Bundy's next choice in his search for victims. He went to top ski resorts to meet attractive women, first killing a nurse who was skiing in Snowmass and then a ski instructor in Vail. Bundy then murdered a woman bicycling to Grand Junction.

Florida, 1978:
Bundy travelled to Florida in 1978 to find his last victims. In a brazen attack on a sorority house in Tallahassee, he murdered two students and attacked three others. A month later, he drove east to Lake City to murder a 12-year-old girl.

Key Ted Bundy's victims

Washington State. Sometime in the early hours of 11 June, Georgeann Hawkins died after leaving her boyfriend's dormitory to return to her own accommodation. Later, a man with a cast, this time on his leg, was seen carrying a suitcase in the same area. Afterwards, yet another student said that the same man had asked for her help in taking the briefcase to his car, a Volkswagen Beetle.

On the Trail of a Serial Killer

Typically, it has been said, a serial killer becomes more confident, in fact over-confident, as murder becomes easier and he remains uncaught. This may have occurred with the handsome young man who called himself Ted and was seen on 14 July by eight different people – five women and three men. All of them noted that he had his left arm in a sling and the five women were asked for help to unload a sailboat into his Beetle car. One woman accompanied Ted to his car, but when she realized that there was no sailboat she left in a hurry.

She was wise to do so. Earlier on 14 July, two more students, 23-year-old Janice Ott and 19-year-old Denise Naslund, were seen walking with Ted from the beach at Lake Sammamish State Park, in Issaquah, Washington. Both women were later murdered. Their remains were discovered on 7 September 1974 at Issaquah, 1.6km (1 mile) from the State Park. On 3 March 1975, the skulls of four other victims – Lynda Anne Healy, Susan Rancourt, Roberta Parks and Brenda Ball – were uncovered in a nearby area, Taylor Mountain, east of Issaquah.

If the police did not know there was a serial killer on the loose before this, they certainly knew it now. A possible ninth victim, 20-year-old Carol Valenzuela, vanished on 2 August 1974: her remains were discovered together with those of an unidentified woman south of Olympia on 12 October. With her long dark hair parted down the middle, she fitted the general description of the girls known to have been killed by Bundy, who usually bludgeoned and strangled his victims and sometimes indulged in rape, sodomy and necrophilia.

One more girl, Nancy Wilcox, aged 16, was murdered on 2 October 1974 before Ted Bundy left

TED BUNDY TIMELINE

4 January 1974: Ted Bundy attacks and sexually assaults 18-year-old Joni Lenz, a student at Washington State University, beating her with a metal bar torn from her bedframe and leaving her brain-damaged.

1 February 1974: Washington State University student Lynda Ann Healy goes missing.

12 March 1974: Donna Gail Manson is kidnapped and murdered at Olympia, the capital of Washington State.

17 April 1974: Student Susan Rancourt vanishes from the university campus at Ellensburg. That same night, also at Ellensburg, a man with a plaster cast on his arm asks a girl student for help to carry a load of books to his car, a Volkswagen Beetle.

20 April 1974: The same man with a plaster cast asks another student for the same help.

6 May 1974: Roberta Parks is last seen alive on the Oregon State University campus at Corvallis.

1 June 1974: Brenda Ball disappears after leaving the Flame Tavern in Burien, Washington State.

11 June 1974: Student Georgeann Hawkins vanishes after leaving her boyfriend's dormitory in the early hours. Later, a man with a cast on his leg asks a student for help in taking a briefcase to his Volkswagen Beetle.

14 July 1974: Students Janice Ott and Denise Naslund are seen walking with a man who calls himself Ted near the beach at Lake Sammamish State Park, Issaquah, Washington. Janice is later murdered. Denise disappears without trace. Later, Ted is seen by five women and three men with his left arm in a sling. The women are asked for help in carrying a load from a sailboat to Ted's car. One accompanies Ted to the car, but flees on finding there is no sailboat.

2 August 1974: Carol Valenzuela vanishes in Washington State.

7 September 1974: The remains of Janice Ott and Denise Naslund are discovered at Issaquah.

2 October 1974: Nancy Wilcox, 16, last seen riding in a Volkswagen Beetle at Holladay, near Salt Lake City, Utah, is murdered.

12 October 1974: The remains of Carol Valenzuela are found south of Olympia. That same fall, Ted Bundy leaves Washington State for Utah, where he enrolls at the State University as a law student.

18 October 1974: Melissa Smith, 17, is raped, sodomized and strangled by Ted Bundy. Her mutilated body is discovered in a canyon nine days later.

31 October 1974: Laura Aime, 17, vanishes from a Halloween party in Lehi, Utah. A month later, she is found naked and strangled on a river bank in American Fork Canyon.

8 November 1974: Debbie Kent, 17 years old, disappears from Viewmont High School in Bountiful, Utah. Around the same time, a man is seen behaving suspiciously behind the school auditorium. The same day, Carol DaRonch narrowly avoids being abducted by 'Officer Roseland' – Ted Bundy in disguise – in Murray, Utah.

12 January 1975: Bundy's first victim in Colorado, Caryn Campbell, disappears from the Wildwood Inn at Snowmass, Colorado. Her body is found on 17 February.

3 March 1975: The skulls of Lynda Ann Healy, Susan Rancourt, Roberta Parks and Brenda Ball are found at Taylor Mountain, east of Issaquah.

15 March 1975: Julie Cunningham, 26, a ski instructor at Vail, Colorado, disappears after being approached by Ted Bundy for help in carrying ski boots to his car. He later strangles her.

6 April 1975: Denise Oliverson vanishes from Grand Junction, Colorado, while on her way to visit her parents.

6 May 1975: According to a confession made while on Death Row, Bundy rapes Lynette Culver and drowns her in a bathtub at the Pocatello, Idaho, Holiday Inn.

28 June 1975: Shortly before his execution in 1989, Bundy confesses to murdering

Susan Curtis in Utah on 28 June 1975. Her body is never found, nor are those of Julie Cunningham, Lynette Culver or Denise Oliverson.

16 August 1975: Arrested in Salt Lake City, Bundy is linked to the attempted kidnapping of Carol DaRonch and the fate of Nancy Wilcox, Melissa Smith, Laura Aime, Debbie Kent, Caryn Campbell, Julie Cunningham and Denise Oliverson. He is later identified as the fake Officer Roseland by DaRonch and witnesses from the Bountiful, Utah, high school.

1 March 1976: Bundy is convicted of kidnapping Carol DaRonch and sentenced to 15 years' imprisonment.

7 June 1977: Extradited to Colorado, Bundy escapes from a pre-trial hearing for the murder of Caryn Campbell in Aspen. He is recaptured on 13 June.

30 December 1977: Bundy escapes again, this time reaching Chicago by plane.

8 January 1978: Bundy travels to Tallahassee, Florida.

15 January 1978: Bundy murders students Lisa Levy and Margaret Bowman at the sorority house of Florida State University, and attacks Karen Chandler, Kathy Kleiner and Cheryl Thomas.

9 February 1978: Bundy rapes and murders 12-year-old Kimberly Leach at Lake City, Florida.

15 February 1978: Bundy is stopped while driving a stolen Volkswagen through Pensacola by police officer David Lee, who identifies the car as stolen.

25 June 1979: On trial in Florida for the murders of Margaret Bowman and Lisa Levy, Bundy is found guilty and sentenced to death. Afterwards, in 1980, he is tried for murdering Kimberly Leach and receives a second death sentence. He is put on Death Row.

24 January 1989: After exhausting all appeals, Ted Bundy goes to the electric chair. He is pronounced dead at 7.13 a.m.

Washington State and enrolled at the University of Utah as a law student. Shortly afterwards, the trail of serial killings resumed in Utah and neighbouring Colorado, where there were seven more murders in the next six months. By the time the last of them occurred, on 6 April 1975, the police had built up a dossier of valuable information.

More than a dozen witnesses had helped build up a picture of the good-looking, clean-cut young man, and this accorded with several identifications – from a friend of Ted Bundy's sometime girlfriend Elizabeth Kendall, from his professor at Washington State University, and from Ann Rule, a crime writer who knew Ted well and later wrote *The Stranger Beside Me* (2000), a book describing Bundy's 'career'. All this helped police put together a drawing of the suspect which, when publicized in the media, produced up to 200 fresh tips a day.

A Victim Escapes

The most graphic was an account given by Carol DaRonch, who encountered Ted Bundy face to face at Murray, Utah, on 8 November 1974. Bundy, who claimed to be a police officer named 'Roseland',

> **'Bundy enrolled at the University of Utah. Shortly afterwards, the trail of serial killings resumed in Utah and neighbouring Colorado, where there were seven more murders in the next six months.'**

approached Carol and told her that someone had attempted to break into her car. He asked her to accompany him to the local police station. She got into his car, but Bundy had driven only a short way before he tried to handcuff her, then attempted to hit her on the head with a crowbar. Carol managed to catch the crowbar in mid-air inches from her skull,

The testimony of forensic experts helped identify Bundy as a murderer. His teeth matched a bite mark found on a recent victim in a university sorority house.

then she opened the passenger door and threw herself out onto the road.

Tragically, none of the information gathered by the police in Utah had served to save the lives of three 17-year-olds who were murdered by Bundy during October 1974 or to prevent his move to Colorado, where he began another reign of terror in January 1975. He killed Caryn Campbell on 12 January and two more young women in the next three months before an unexpected stroke of fortune intervened.

On 16 August 1975, Bundy was flagged down by a police officer while driving 'erratically' through Salt Lake City in a a Volkswagen Beetle. Bundy tried to drive on, but was halted and arrested. A search of the Volkswagen revealed several items that looked like burglary tools: a crowbar, handcuffs and an ice pick. But one of the State detectives went further, suspecting a connection between Bundy's car, the attempted kidnap of Carol DaRonch and the girls who were missing in Utah. Bundy was placed in a line-up. Police brought in Carol and several witnesses who had seen a strange man behaving suspiciously at a Bountiful, Utah, high school during the staging of a play. All of the witnesses identified Bundy as 'Officer Roseland'.

The Convict Escapes

Seven months later, on 1 March 1976, Ted Bundy was sentenced to 15 years in Utah State Prison for the kidnapping of Carol DaRonch. However, he was extradited to Colorado, where the authorities were planning murder charges against him. On 7 June 1977, Bundy appeared at a hearing for the murder of

'Bundy became an authority on the serial killer mentality, giving police and psychiatrists his own "insider" advice. He was still doing so the night before his execution, when he was interviewed on television.'

During his second trial in 1980, Bundy consults his attorneys. He soon began to lose his confidence and became agitated, even standing to shout at a witness.

Caryn Campbell at Pitkin County Courthouse in Aspen. During a recess, he jumped to freedom from the second floor window of the law library. He was apprehended six days later and taken back to jail at Glenwood Springs, Colorado, but escaped again on 30 December. This time, he got clean away and boarded a plane bound for Chicago.

Eight days later, on 8 January 1978, Ted Bundy arrived by bus at Tallahassee, Florida, where he embarked on a series of petty thefts – shoplifting, stealing cars, snatching purses. Bundy also purloined a set of identification papers belonging to one Ken Misner.

By this time, Bundy's killing instincts had been on hold for over two years and his murderous drive soon reasserted itself. At around 3 a.m. on 15 January, Ted Bundy broke into a sorority house at Florida State University. Within just 30 minutes, he had murdered two women, Margaret Bowman, 21, and Lisa Levy, 20, whom he raped before strangling. He also injured two more students, Kathy Kleiner and Karen Chandler. That done, Bundy moved on to another sorority house, where he attacked and badly injured another student, Cheryl Thomas.

Bundy's next port of call was Lake City, Florida, where he arrived on 9 February 1978. There, he raped and killed his youngest – and last – victim, Kimblerly Leach, aged 12, and hid her corpse under a pig shed. Bundy headed west in a stolen Volkswagen, only to be stopped around 1 a.m. on 15 February by a Pensacola police officer, David Lee. His suspicions aroused, Officer Lee checked out the Beetle's licence plate: the car came up as stolen.

When Lee moved to arrest him, Bundy put up a brief, but futile, fight and was taken to jail. There, he gave police the name Ken Misner, producing Misner's stolen papers to prove it. But the false identification did not last long. Bundy was fingerprinted and his real name was revealed. Back in Tallahassee, he was formally charged with the killings of Margaret Bowman and Lisa Levy.

The Defence Fails

Ted Bundy's trial opened at Dade County Circuit Court, Miami, on 25 June 1979. He acted as his own

defence attorney, but his legal skills did him scant good. Bundy was identified by a Florida University student, Nita Neary, who saw him leaving the sorority house after the murders and by a bite mark he had left on Lisa Levy's body, which matched a plaster cast of his teeth taken by police. He was sentenced to the electric chair, but his execution was postponed so that he could be tried, in 1980, for the murder of Kimberly Leach. He was found guilty and again he was sentenced to death.

There followed a long series of appeals, which kept Bundy alive on Death Row for the next nine years. During that time, Ted Bundy confessed to several till then unsolved murders, including eight killings in Washington State in 1974. Ironically, Bundy became an authority on the serial killer mentality, giving police and psychiatrists his own 'insider' advice. He was still doing so the night before his execution, when he was interviewed on television and warned against the violence on TV that encouraged boys to emulate him. His last appeal having failed, Ted Bundy died in the electric chair at 7.13 a.m. on 24 January 1989.

Bundy's body is removed after his execution. He was originally scheduled to die three years earlier, but the date was postponed to allow a series of appeals.

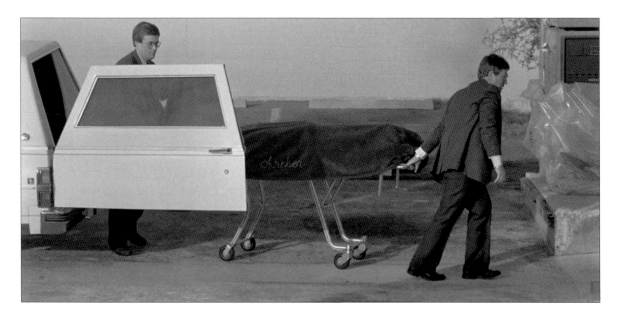

Volker Eckert

Truck Driver and Serial Strangler

FULL NAME:
Volker Eckert

DOB:
1 July 1959

DIED:
2 July 2007

NUMBER OF VICTIMS:
Confessed to the murder of six women
but is suspected of many more

SPAN OF KILLINGS:
1974–2006

LOCATION OF KILLINGS:
Germany, France, Spain and Italy

DATE OF ARREST:
17 November 2006

SENTENCE:
Committed suicide whilst awaiting trial

Arrested on a Spanish warrant in 2006, German truck driver Volker Eckert, 47, confessed to murdering five young women – two in France, three in Spain. Alerts subsequently went out to police forces all over Europe. For Eckert was an international killer, whose job took him to several countries where police had unsolved murders on their books. The Spanish police, who led the investigation, asserted that Eckert 'killed for pleasure' and, though the alert covered his killings only since 1999, he may have been a serial murderer for as many as 30 years.

Volker Eckert's career as a serial killer began in 1968, when he became obsessed by a doll belonging to his sister Sabine. Eckert, who was 9 years old at the time, was fascinated by the doll's long hair, which he habitually stroked and, even at that early age, found sexually arousing. His next discovery encouraged the fetish: he found a hairpiece belonging to his mother and added it to his secret sex games with the doll. This went on for about three years until he tired of artificial hair and switched his affections to the real thing: he would sit in class at school, gazing at the long hair worn by the girl in front of him and aching to touch and stroke it. Her name was Silvia Unterdorfel and she was, of course, inaccessible. But Eckert soon formulated a plan to solve that problem: for several months, Eckert practised strangling his doll before running his hands through its long hair. In May 1974, he was ready.

On 7 May, when he was still only 14 years old, Volker Eckert went to the flat where Silvia lived, and

knocked on the door. Silvia, who was alone in the flat at the time, opened the door, recognized him and let him in. Within minutes, Eckert had Silvia by the throat with his thumbs on her windpipe. Silvia soon collapsed unconscious, and Eckert was able to act out a fantasy he had been rehearsing for many months: he buried his hands in her hair. At this juncture, Silvia was still alive, but Eckert realized that she could get him into big trouble if he allowed her to survive. There was a clothesline nearby, so he tied one end of it to a doorknob, probably to make it look as though the girl had committed suicide, and drew it tight around her neck. When he was sure Silvia was dead, Eckert returned to his own flat, where he was so aroused by what he had done that he masturbated.

Silvia's stepfather was an officer in the *Volkspolizei*. He did not believe his daughter had killed herself, but there was no evidence of foul play, either. The file on Silvia's death was closed. Eckert had got away with murder – and would keep on doing so.

Although of average intelligence, Volker Eckert was largely uneducated and had no skills. His first job was as a house painter and cleaner. But in 1999, when

Finally in custody, Eckert confessed to his crimes. German and Spanish authorities argued over who should take charge of the enquiry; the Germans were given control.

he was 40 years old, he qualified for a job that fitted perfectly his ongoing obsession with long hair: driving tanker trucks on international routes across Europe gave him the privacy he needed to kill his victims, enabled him to make a quick getaway from the murder scene, and left behind no clues at the site that could reveal his identity.

The First Adult Victims

According to his later confession, his venture into serial killing began in 1999, when he murdered an unknown prostitute at Bordeaux in southwest France. He continued on 21 June 2001, when he was driving back to Germany from Spain. On the way, he stopped his truck near a railway station in Bordeaux, where he picked up a 21-year-old Nigerian prostitute called Sandra Osifo. She had long hair, although it later turned out to be a wig. Nevertheless, Eckert lured her into the cab of his lorry, where he proceeded to strangle her. When he had finished with her, Eckert threw her dead body into a ditch by the roadside some 90km (56 miles) north of Bordeaux. After she was found four days later, on 25 June, the police at Poitiers managed to identify her, but they had no leads and no idea of who had killed her.

No Clues for the Police

The following August, Volker Eckert went back to Spain. There, he picked up Isabel Beatriz Diaz in Lloret del Mar, a popular tourist resort on the northeast coast. As Eckert tried to strangle her in the cab of his truck, she fought back hard, but could not prevent him from raping her. After she died, Eckert threw out her body at the motorway junction at Maçanet de la Selva, near Gerona in northeast Spain. Two months passed before she was found, but no one had reported her missing and police in northeastern Spain had no luck discovering who had killed her.

A year later, in August 2002, police were no more successful in France, where 23-year-old Benedicta Edwards, from Sierra Leone in West Africa, was murdered in the town of Troyes, near Paris. Her naked corpse was found on a footpath. Subsequently, it was discovered that Volker Eckert had been driving through Troyes and had withdrawn money with his credit card shortly before Benedicta was discovered.

Police in the Czech Republic were equally baffled over the body of a woman who had been strangled and thrown out, naked, near the motorway close to Pilsen in western Bohemia in June of 2003. Again, as was later proved, Eckert was in the area at the time, although he never confessed to killing either this woman or Benedicta Edwards. This, though, did not prevent police from strongly suspecting that he was responsible. But Eckert was not content merely to kill his victims and then dispose of them. He collected souvenirs, cutting off their hair, stealing clothes, handbags and even cosmetics. He also kept a record of his crimes, by photographing the bodies with a Polaroid camera.

Since no one had yet found clues to Eckert's identity or evidence that could place him at the venues or times at which the murders took place, he was able to range across Europe, killing at will.

The Trail of Murders

Plauen, 7 May 1974:
Eckert began killing in East Germany where he grew up in the small town of Plauen. The first to die was his teenaged schoolmate, Silvia Unterdorfel, murdered in her home in 1974. Eckert then waited 13 years before killing again, outside the town in 1987.

Bordeaux, France, 1999 and 2001:
Eckert took the lives of two prostitutes. Soon after qualifying as a long-distance truck driver, he murdered the first in 1999 and two years later killed a Nigerian woman. His three other French victims were found in the north of the country.

Gerona, Spain, 2001, 2005, 2006:
Eckert's travels to Gerona, Spain, led to three murders. Isabel Beatriz Diaz was killed in August 2001, Mariy Veselova, a Russian, in February 2005, and Miglena Petrova Rahom, a Bulgarian, in November 2006. When Eckert left Rahom's body near Gerona, CCTV led to his arrest.

Northeast Italy, 2003 and 2004:
Thirty years after Eckert committed his first murder, he killed Ahhiobe Gali, a Ghanaian woman, in September 2004 in northeast Italy. The previous year, he strangled a woman in the Czech Republic, tossing her naked body from his truck just off a motorway near Pilsen.

Key   Volker Eckert's victims

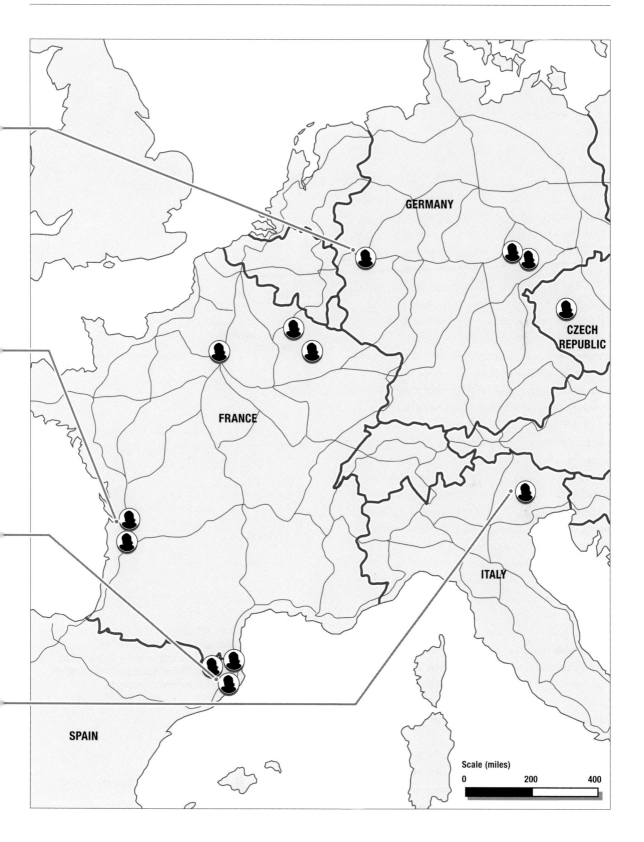

GERMANY

CZECH REPUBLIC

FRANCE

ITALY

SPAIN

Scale (miles)

0   200   400

Ahhiobe Gali, a Ghanaian woman, was murdered in northeast Italy in September 2004; Mariy Veselova, a Russian, in Figueras near Gerona in February 2005; and Agneska Bos, a Pole, in northeastern France in October 2006. Subsequently, evidence was found of three other murders committed by Eckert – an unknown woman in France in February 2005 and two others in the Czech Republic in the mid-1990s, murdered by Eckert before he began driving trucks.

Volker Eckert's last known murder took place in November 2006, when he killed Miglena Petrova Rahom, a 20-year-old from Bulgaria, at Sant Julia de Ramis, a small town near Gerona. The circumstances that finally trapped him depended on pure chance. Eckert had parked his truck outside the football stadium at Sant Julia de Ramis and remained there,

'There were three Polaroid photographs between the two front seats, one showing a dead woman with a noose around her neck, others depicting women tied up or mutilated.'

The above victims of Eckert display features he sought in women: a pretty face and long hair. He collected hair and various other trophies after murdering them.

waiting for nightfall to dump Rahom's body. There was a factory nearby, where a technician was fixing a CCTV camera on the wall. As he was adjusting it so that it faced the factory gate, the technician accidentally switched on the camera and scanned the stadium car park. The camera also photographed Eckert's truck, which had its owner's logo painted on one side.

Later on, Eckert got rid of Miglena's body and returned to his employer's premises in Cologne, Germany, unaware that he had been photographed. Back at Sant Julia de Ramis, the local police discovered the corpse and checked the CCTV footage. Eckert's truck was easily identifiable, and it was just as easy for the police to trace it back to Cologne. The police arrived in Cologne on 17 November 2006, intending to interview the driver of the truck as a witness or a murderer. They soon recognized which of the two Eckert was and arrested him. Eckert resisted police questioning for a full hour, asserting that he knew nothing about the body. Then, unexpectedly, he gave himself away. He complained of a headache, and said that he wanted medicine from his truck to cure it.

Possibly Eckert thought he might be allowed to fetch the medicine himself, but a police officer was sent instead. In the cab, he found much more than he had been sent to find. There were three Polaroid photographs between the two front seats, one showing a dead woman with a noose around her neck, others depicting women tied up or mutilated. On searching further, the officer discovered handwritten notes in which Eckert described other killings, together with two lengths of rope.

A Lack of Co-operation

Faced with this evidence, Volker Eckert soon confessed to the murders of six women. Afterwards, he was transferred to his home town, Hof, in southern Germany, where the police proceeded to investigate Eckert's movements, using the satellite tracking device installed in the cab of his truck. A horrifying picture emerged of serial murder in Spain, Germany, Italy, France and the Czech Republic. They even traced Eckert's killings back to the death of the 14-year-old schoolgirl, Silvia Unterdorfel, while uncovering more than 50 other murders and attempted murders. These included the killing of Heike Wünderlich, 18, in April 1987. Her body was left by Eckert in woods outside Plauen, 96km (60 miles) from Leipzig in eastern Germany. Eckert himself provided details of 30 attacks on women in Plauen, girlfriends he had throttled and assaults in 1988 on two young women who identified him: as a result, Eckert was arrested and sentenced to prison for 12 years, half of which he served.

But though Eckert confessed to six murders, he refused to give information about any of the others he is thought to have committed. He knew, of course, that the German media had cast him as a monster. But he had not expected Sabine, his favourite sister, to agree. She refused to visit him in prison at Hof, where he was awaiting trial. According to his lawyer, Alexander Schmidtgall, her rejection left Eckert deeply depressed and his black mood was increased when he spent his 48th birthday alone in jail on 1 July 2007. At some time during the night, he hung himself from the bars of his cell and was found dead the next morning. German police closed the Eckert case five months later, leaving many of Eckert's killings uninvestigated and many of his victims unidentified.

VOLKER ECKERT TIMELINE

1 July 1959: Volker Eckert born in what was then the Democratic Republic of Germany (East Germany).

1968: Eckert, aged 9 years, first develops a fetish for long hair.

7 May 1974: Aged 14 years, Eckert murders Silvia Unterdorfel, a girl from his school, and afterwards fondles her long hair.

April 1987: Eckert murders 18-year-old Heike Wünderlich outside Plauen, near Leipzig, eastern Germany.

1988: Eckert assaults two young women in Plauen and goes to prison for six years.

Mid-1990s: Two women are killed by Eckert in the Czech Republic.

1999: Eckert qualifies as a long-distance tanker truck driver. The same year, he kills a prostitute in Bordeaux, southwest France.

21 June 2001: Eckert kills 21-year-old Nigerian prostitute Sandra Osifo and throws her body into a ditch 90km (56 miles) north of Bordeaux. She is found four days later.

August 2001: In Lloret del Mar, northeast Spain, Eckert kills Isabel Beatriz Diaz and throws her body onto a motorway junction near Maçanet de la Selva, near Gerona, northeast Spain.

August 2002: Benedicta Edwards, 23, is murdered in Troyes, near Paris.

June 2003: The body of a woman who has been strangled is found near the motorway close to Pilsen in the Czech Republic.

September 2004: Ahhiobe Gali, from Ghana, is murdered in northeast Italy.

February 2005: Mariy Veselova, a Russian, is killed in Figueras near Gerona, Spain. An unknown woman is killed in France.

October 2006: Agneska Bos, a Polish woman, is murdered in northeastern France.

November 2006: Eckert murders Miglena Petrova Rahom, 20, from Bulgaria, and dumps her body near a football stadium at Sant Julia de Ramis, near Gerona. By chance, he is photographed by CCTV cameras. This enables the Spanish police to track him to his employer's premises in Cologne, Germany, where he is arrested and confesses to six murders.

1 July 2007: After being transferred to prison in his home town, Hof, in southern Germany, Volker Eckert spends his 48th birthday alone in his cell.

2 July 2007: Eckert commits suicide by hanging himself from the bars of his cell.

Henry Lee Lucas

America's Most Prolific Serial Killer

FULL NAME:
Henry Lee Lucas

DOB:
14 August 1936

DIED:
13 March 2001

NUMBER OF VICTIMS:
4–213

SPAN OF KILLINGS:
1960–1982

LOCATION OF KILLINGS:
Virginia, Texas and possibly Florida, USA

DATE OF ARREST:
11 June 1983

SENTENCE:
Life imprisonment; he died whilst
in prison

Henry Lee Lucas once earned the name of the World's Most Dangerous Killer after he confessed to committing 600 murders in Canada and in 27 US states. Later, Lucas recanted, insisting 'I am not a serial killer'. He was, however, a serial liar, so no one really knows how many victims he killed. Between four and 213 have been suggested. But one fact is known for certain: Lucas began his murder spree at home, for his first victim was his own mother.

Henry Lee Lucas was born in a one-room log cabin in Blacksburg, Virginia on 14 August 1936. He had very little chance to form a proper relationship with his mother, Viola, or, indeed with his alcoholic father, Anderson Lucas, who died when Henry was 13.

Lucas used to describe his mother as a 'violent prostitute', who forced him to watch her as she 'serviced' her clients.

Life with mother was a life of almost continual abuse: Lucas endured regular maternal beatings, and she once neglected an eye injury he suffered at the hands of his brother for so long that the eye became infected and had to be removed. Lucas, aged 14, ran away from home in 1950, soon after his father's death, and became a drifter in his native Virginia. He lived on the proceeds of petty thefts and burglaries in places around the state, and it was not long before he was arrested for his crimes in Richmond. On 11 June 1954, Lucas was sent to prison for the first time, when he was sentenced to a four-year term. In fact, he served five and was released on 2 September 1959.

At the end of the same year, Lucas was staying with his half-sister, Opal, at Tecumseh, Michigan, when their mother arrived to stay over Christmas. By this time, Lucas was engaged to be married, but his mother disliked his fiancée and the two of them quarrelled fiercely throughout the holiday. Viola wanted her son to return home to Blacksburg and look after her in her old age. But Viola never reached old age. Their argument escalated to such intensity that on 11 January 1960, Viola struck her son with a broom and he responded by seizing a knife and plunging it into her neck.

'After that,' Lucas later recalled, 'I saw her fall and decided to grab her. But she fell to the floor and when I (picked) her up, I realized she was dead. Then, I noticed I had a knife in my hand and she had been cut.'

Viola was not, in fact, dead, but, according to the police, died later in an ambulance from a heart attack brought on by her son's assault. Afterwards, Lucas returned to Virginia, but later set out again for Michigan and was arrested on the way, in Ohio. At his trial for his mother's murder, Lucas claimed self-defence, but his plea was rejected. Found guilty of

'Lucas endured regular maternal beatings, and she once neglected an eye injury he suffered at the hands of his brother for so long that the eye became infected and had to be removed.'

second-degree murder, he was given a prison sentence of up to 40 years. He was released after only 10 years, in June 1970, when the prison became overcrowded.

After that, Henry Lee Lucas drifted around the southern United States, sometimes working at short-term jobs. After he reached Florida in 1976, he encountered Ottis Elwood Toole and Toole's

Lucas guides investigators to a rural site in Georgetown, Texas, where he buried the 'Orange Socks' victim. By then, he had confessed to being a serial killer.

'According to Lucas, the police placed him in a small cell in Montague County Jail in Montague, Texas, stripped him, refused to let him have cigarettes and prevented an attorney from seeing him.'

15-year-old niece, Frieda Becky Powell, an escapee from a juvenile detention centre. Despite their 25-year age difference, Lucas and Powell started an affair. Between 1978 and 1982, according to Lucas, he and Toole collaborated in a series of 108 murders. In 1982, Lucas, Toole and Powell left Florida for a religious commune, The House of Prayer, in Stoneburg, Texas, where Lucas and Powell occupied a small apartment. Later, the couple took to travelling on their own and in Ringgold, Texas, in May 1982, stayed with an 82-year-old widow, Kate Rich. Subsequently, Lucas and Powell split up after an argument at a truck stop in Bowie, Texas, and Powell went off with a trucker. Neither Kate Rich nor Powell was seen alive again.

An Extraordinary Confession

Then, on 11 June 1983, Henry Lucas was arrested by a Texas Ranger, Philip Ryan, for the unlawful possession of a firearm: as a convicted felon, Lucas was not allowed to carry a gun. The arrest was something of a blind. The Texas Rangers were really interested in the disappearance of Kate Rich and Becky Powell and it seems that they were resolved to get the truth out of Lucas by any means.

According to Lucas, the police placed him in a small cell in Montague County Jail in Montague, Texas, stripped him, refused to let him have cigarettes and prevented an attorney from seeing him. Again according to Lucas, he confessed to murdering Rich and Powell in order to obtain better treatment. When he was arraigned at the Montague County Courtroom on 21 June 1983, the court took him at his word and

The Trail of Murders

Tecumseh, Michigan, 11 January 1960:
Lucas's first murder occurred in 1960 at Tecumseh, Michigan, when he killed his 74-year-old mother. After drinking heavily, he argued with her about a woman he wanted to marry. Lucas stabbed his mother in the neck and was convicted of second-degree murder.

Stoneburg, Texas, 1982:
In a bizarre move, Lucas and his lover, Frieda Becky Powell, went to Stoneburg, Texas, in 1982 to check out a religious commune, The House of Prayer, but they soon left. The following year, Lucas was arrested there for the unlawful possession of a firearm.

Denton, Texas 1982:
When they left the religious commune on 24 August 1982, Lucas and Powell hitchhiked to Denton, Texas. They argued and after she slapped him, Lucas, who was drinking beer, stabbed her fatally in the chest. He later said she had reminded him of his mother.

Georgetown, Texas, 1979:
The crucial evidence against Lucas was the body found near Georgetown, Texas. He led police to the watercourse site where the corpse's orange socks gave a name to the case. Lucas testified that she was a hitchhiker he had picked up and murdered in 1979.

Key Lucas's victims

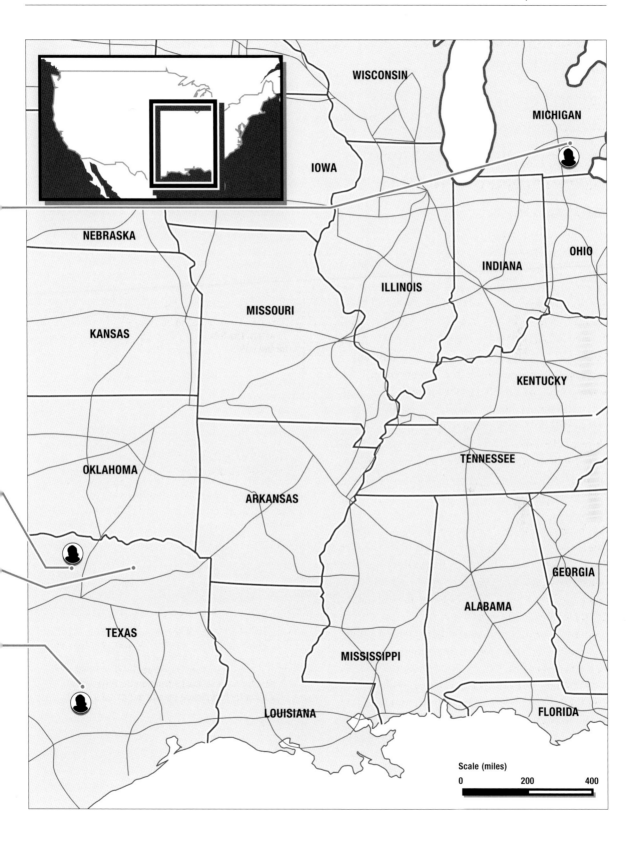

HENRY LEE LUCAS TIMELINE

14 August 1936: Henry Lee Lucas born in a one-room log cabin in Blacksburg, Virginia.

1950: Lucas, aged 14, runs away from home after years of being abused by his mother, Viola.

11 June 1954: Lucas is sent to prison for petty theft and burglary.

2 September 1959: Lucas is released from prison.

11 January 1960: Lucas kills his mother after an argument over his fiancée. At his trial for the killing, he is sentenced to 40 years in prison for second-degree murder, but is released after 10 years, in June 1970.

1976: After drifting around the southern United States for several years, Lucas meets Ottis Elwood Toole and his 15-year-old niece, Frieda Becky Powell, in Florida. Lucas and Powell begin an affair.

1979: Lucas kills a woman near Georgetown, Texas, in what is later called the Orange Socks murder.

1978–1982: Lucas and Toole collaborate in what Lucas claims were 108 murders.

1982: Lucas and Toole part company and Lucas goes with Powell to The House of

Prayer in Stoneburg, Texas. Subsequently, in May 1982, the couple stay with an 82-year-old widow, Kate Rich, in Ringgold, Texas. Neither Kate Rich nor Powell are seen alive again.

11 June 1983: Lucas is arrested for unlawful possession of a firearm but is questioned over the disappearance of Kate Rich and Becky Powell. He confesses to murdering both of them.

21 June 1983: Lucas is charged with the murders of Kate Rich and Becky Powell. The Texas Rangers question him about unsolved murders on their books. Seven of these cases prove to have been his doing, including the Orange Socks murder. But Lucas also confesses to killings for which he is not suspected or charged.

2 August 1983: Lucas is charged with the Orange Socks murder.

12 August 1983: The Orange Socks murder trial is halted when Lucas withdraws his confession to the Becky Powell killing. He is, however, convicted in September of murdering Kate Rich, and is sentenced to 75 years in prison.

7 December 1983: By this time, Lucas has been credited with 126 murders, and on 7 December a conference of the Henry Lee

Lucas Task Force (formed in November by the Texas Rangers) meets to connect Lucas with 35 of these killings.

January 1984: A second conference takes place at the Holidrome, in Monroe, Louisiana, attended by 107 police officers from 18 US states, all of them with unsolved murders on their books. By this time, 72 murders have been ascribed to Lucas and his one-time collaborator Ottis Elwood Toole, who are suspects in another 71.

March 1984: The Orange Socks murder trial resumes in San Angelo, Texas. Lucas is found guilty and is sentenced to death. But the verdict is challenged by former Attorney General investigator Michael Feary, who has gathered information demonstrating that Lucas was elsewhere, in Florida, at the time of the killing.

1996: Twelve years after the Orange Socks murder verdict, Feary's investigation earns Lucas a stay of execution.

1998: George W. Bush, then governor of Texas, commutes Lucas's death sentence to life imprisonment.

13 March 2001: Henry Lee Lucas dies of heart failure in prison, aged 64.

---

charged him with the murders of both women. Lucas provided some grisly evidence – decomposed fragments of Becky Powell's body, which he said he had burned in a wood stove, and a confession that he had stabbed Kate Rich to death.

'I killed Kate Rich!' Lucas announced to a stunned courtroom, 'and at least one hundred more.'

Next day, on 22 June, the name of Henry Lee Lucas was plastered all over newspaper headlines coast to coast as he was widely touted as the most prolific serial killer in US history. Lucas's confession was music to the ears of the Texas Rangers, for besides Rich and Powell, they had several other unsolved cases on their books. Their hope was that Henry Lucas would be able to fill in at least some of the gaps. The news spread far beyond Texas, to states where Lucas had

been active over the years: they, too, had unexplained deaths on their records.

The Orange Socks Murder

The problem was that Lucas was such a habitual liar, no one could be sure of the truth. The fact that he was remarkably forthcoming with information about the killings he claimed to have committed did not make the search for truth any easier. He signed detailed statements about some murders and even offered to provide drawings depicting 70 corpses of his victims. Around seven of the cases involved were proved to be his doing. One of them became famous as the 'Orange Socks' case. This involved a woman whom Lucas claimed to have murdered in 1979 and buried in a watercourse off Interstate 35, north of

Georgetown, Texas. Lucas took police officers to the spot, where the woman was duly found, wearing nothing but a pair of orange socks.

Lucas even gave details of murder cases for which he was neither suspected nor charged. One of these was a double killing, of a husband and wife in Texas who owned a liquor store. Other cases concerned murder for the sake of robbery, the killing of witnesses or simply the sensation of power that Lucas experienced as he extinguished a life. He also confessed to killing girls and women for necrophiliac purposes, for Lucas preferred to have sex with a corpse. 'To me,' he admitted in an interview, 'a live woman ain't nothin.'

'I had no feelings for the people themselves or any of the crimes,' Lucas confessed on another occasion. 'I'd pick them up hitchhiking, running and playing, stuff like that. We'd get to going and having a good time. First thing you know, I'd killed her and throwed her out somewhere.' Such insights into his killer's

'I'd pick them up hitchhiking, running and playing, stuff like that. We'd get to going and having a good time. First thing you know, I'd killed her and throwed her out somewhere.'

mind and the welter of information he willingly provided made Lucas notorious countrywide, a status he clearly enjoyed. He also relished telling the media about his methods of fooling the authorities by not leaving evidence at murder scenes. One way was to

During his trial, Lucas wept over the murders he had committed and also when a psychiatrist described his mental problems, labelling him a schizophrenic.

vary his style of killing – strangling, knifing – so that he left no pattern for the police to follow up. This often meant that the only proof of a killing available was Lucas's own confession. And his persistent lying meant that his confessions were not always believed.

But the Orange Socks murder, unlike most of Lucas's other, putative, killings, came complete with a burial site and a corpse. This enabled the police to

'One way was to vary his style of killing – strangling, knifing – so that he left no pattern for the police to follow up. This often meant that the only proof of a killing available was Lucas's own confession.'

Ottis Toole, who collaborated with Lucas, was in jail for arson when tried for the murders. He received life but died in prison in 1996 of natural causes.

charge him with homicide, on 2 August 1983. But 10 days later, the trial was thrown into disorder when Lucas withdrew his confession to the murder of Becky Powell. In September, he pled guilty to killing Kate Rich and was sentenced to 75 years in jail. The authorities, for their part, refused to let the Becky Powell killing go unanswered and Lucas was put on trial for it in November 1983. In yet another turnaround, he admitted murdering Becky, who died from a single thrust in the chest with a meat-carving knife. Lucas turned tearful in the dock and told the court that he did not know how he had managed to kill her. He was found guilty just the same and received a life sentence.

At this point, Lucas had been credited with 126 murders. The Henry Lee Lucas Task Force was formed by the Texas Rangers in late November, and on 7 December 1983 it met in conference in an effort to connect Lucas with 35 of these killings. Another meeting, attended by 107 police officers from 18 US states, took place over three days in January 1984 at the Holidrome in Monroe, Louisiana. By this time, 72 murders had been ascribed to Lucas and his one-time collaborator Ottis Elwood Toole, and they were suspects in 71 more.

This was progress, but none was so dramatic as the Orange Socks murder, which remained pending from August 1983. The trial resumed in San Angelo, Texas, in March of 1984. Prosecution evidence included a videotape showing Lucas directing police officers to the location where he had dumped the victim's body. The defence, however, tried to prove diminished responsibility by entering in evidence psychiatrist's reports labelling Lucas a schizophrenic with an IQ of

Lucas spent years on Death Row while his sentence was challenged. After a stay of execution in 1996, his sentence was commuted to life imprisonment in 1998.

'He admitted murdering Becky, who died from a single thrust in the chest with a meat-carving knife. Lucas turned tearful in the dock and told the court that he did not know how he had managed to kill her.'

only 84, and suggesting that he had a desire to feel important while also suffering feelings of inferiority and the belief that he was not in control of his actions. Lucas was so upset by these revelations that he burst into tears. He apparently wept for 15 minutes, and the court had to go into recess so that he could recover his composure.

Contradictory Evidence

The defence lost out. At the end of the trial, Lucas was declared guilty of the Orange Socks murder and was sentenced to death. But the verdict was challenged by former Attorney General investigator Michael Feary, who had witnessed Lucas's trial. Feary was convinced that Lucas had been elsewhere, in Jacksonville, Florida, when the killing took place near Georgetown, Texas. What was more, Feary had a thick file that could, he believed, prove it. Meanwhile, the death sentence stood for the next 12 years. Then, in 1996, Feary's investigation earned a stay of execution for Lucas. Two years later, the matter was considered by the then governor of Texas, George W. Bush – afterwards 43rd president of the United States. Bush judged that contradictory evidence at Lucas's trial cast doubt on whether the execution should proceed. As a result, Bush commuted the sentence to life imprisonment. The Texas Board of Pardon and Parole afterwards voted to uphold his decision.

Three years later, on 13 March 2001, Henry Lee Lucas was still in prison when he died of heart failure, aged 64.

Peter Sutcliffe

The Yorkshire Ripper

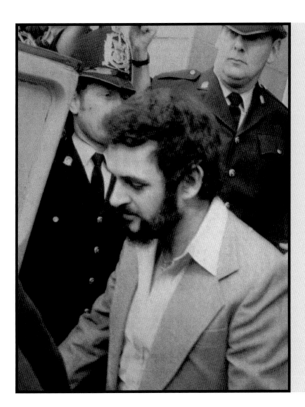

FULL NAME:
Peter William Sutcliffe

DOB:
2 June 1946

NUMBER OF VICTIMS:
13

SPAN OF KILLINGS:
October 1975–November 1980

LOCATION OF KILLINGS:
Various towns in the north of England

DATE OF ARREST:
2 January 1981

SENTENCE:
Life imprisonment on 13 counts of
murders and seven of attempted murder

Peter Sutcliffe was dubbed the Yorkshire Ripper by the British press when he terrorized eight northern English towns and cities before his arrest in Sheffield at the start of 1981. He acquired the alias from Jack the Ripper, the serial killer who slaughtered at least five prostitutes in the east end of London in 1888 and who was never caught. Sutcliffe exceeded the exploits of his 'namesake', murdering 13 women, mainly prostitutes, and attempting to kill seven more, while eluding capture for five years.

The hunt for the Yorkshire Ripper, who murdered his way around the north of England between 1975 and 1980, was one of the most intensive operations ever mounted by the police in Britain. The killings roused feverish media coverage, which fed the British public with ghoulish details and calls for extraordinary precautions to protect 'innocent' women – that is, women who were not prostitutes. Vigilante groups were formed to guard them, while prostitutes took to working the streets in groups or gave up altogether. Meanwhile, for 18 months in 1978–9, a hoaxer known as 'Wearside Jack' led the investigation from one false trail to the next with a series of cassette recordings in which he spoke with an accent common in and around Sunderland in the Wearside district of northeast England. It was not until the arrest of Peter Sutcliffe and his subsequent confession that the police at last recognized Wearside Jack for what he was.

Considering the high drama that had surrounded the Ripper murders, and the intense fear they had generated for so long, the circumstances of Sutcliffe's arrest were decidedly banal. On 2 January 1981, Sutcliffe was sitting in his brown Rover 3500, with a 24-year-old prostitute, Olivia Reivers, in a driveway in Melbourne Avenue, Sheffield. Sergeant Robert Ring and Constable Robert Hydes drove past on patrol and became suspicious of the Rover's licence plates, which were held on with black tape. A check revealed that they belonged to another car, a Skoda, and Sutcliffe was arrested for carrying false licence plates.

The arrest saved Olivia Reivers' life, for Sutcliffe had come to their meeting fully equipped with the tools to kill her. In his pocket, he had hidden a rope and a knife together with the ball-pein metalworking hammer that he used in his attacks. On the pretext of needing to use the toilet, Sutcliffe managed to get out of sight close to the entrance of a building a short way down Melbourne Avenue. He disposed of the rope, knife and hammer in a nearby tank. After he was taken to the police station, he hid a second knife in the toilet cistern.

Police supervised searches at the crime scenes left by Sutcliffe in the north of England. Despite all their careful work, officers continued to come up empty-handed.

'The killings roused feverish media coverage, which fed the British public with ghoulish details and calls to protect "innocent" women – that is, women who were not prostitutes.'

But the police had not been fooled by Sutcliffe's ruse. They found the 'weapons' in the tank and the cistern and, with their suspicions now thoroughly aroused, obtained a warrant to search Sutcliffe's home in Bradford. There, police discovered several tools, including a collection of ball-pein hammers. Sutcliffe, they were now convinced, had done much more than commit a minor motoring offence.

He was interrogated for two days before his air of imperturbable calm broke on 4 January. He confessed that he was the Yorkshire Ripper and began to describe the attacks and serial murders that he had

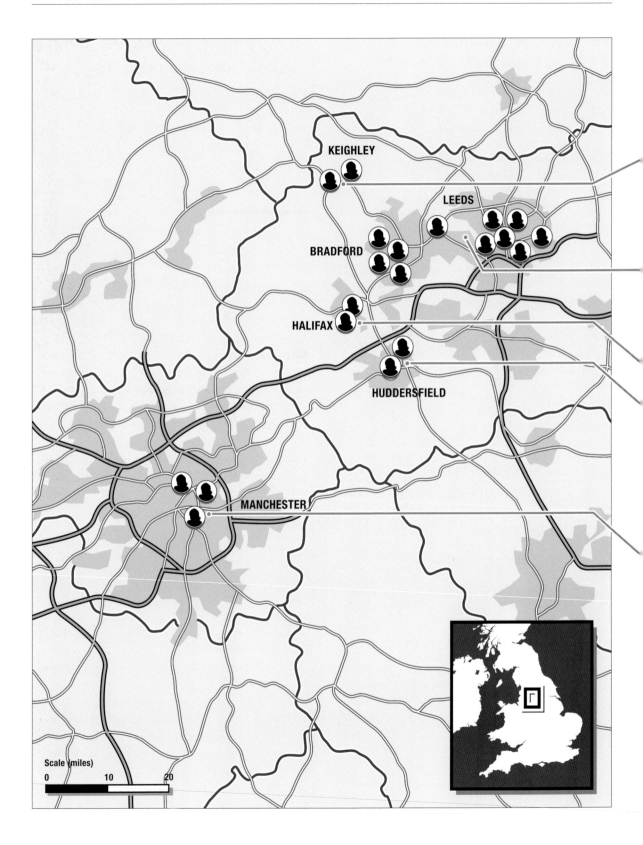

KEIGHLEY

LEEDS

BRADFORD

HALIFAX

HUDDERSFIELD

MANCHESTER

Scale (miles)

0   10   20

The Trail of Murders

Keighley, 5 July 1975:
Sutcliffe's violent path began in Keighley with an attack on a woman in her 30s. She survived when a neighbour approached and Sutcliffe retreated. Two weeks later in nearby Silsden, Sutcliffe attacked but failed to kill a 14-year-old girl in a country lane.

Leeds, 1970s–1980:
Leeds was Sutcliffe's favourite town for brutal attacks. The first three of his 13 murders were carried out here in the 1970s and his last in 1980. Three other women survived, including his first victim after the press labelled him 'The Yorkshire Ripper' in 1977.

East Yorkshire:
Besides Leeds, the Yorkshire Ripper used his lorry trips to bring death to towns just to the east. Two victims died in Bradford, one in Halifax and another in Huddersfield. Among those murdered were three prostitutes, a student and a bank clerk. Two other women survived.

Manchester, 1977:
In a change of habit, Sutcliffe moved into the large urban area of Manchester in 1977, killing two prostitutes that year. Police recovered his £5 payroll note from the pocketbook of the second, Jean Jordan. The next year Sutcliffe returned to kill another Manchester woman.

Key Peter Sutcliffe's victims

Barbara Leach, 20, was a student at Bradford University when Sutcliffe killed her on 1 September 1979. She was walking home from a pub in the early hours.

committed in widely dispersed locations thanks to his job as a lorry driver. Subsequently, Sutcliffe explained his virulent hatred of women by claiming that he was under orders from God to kill prostitutes.

Attempted Murder

Sutcliffe's first victim was 36-year-old Anna Rogulskyj, who was battered unconscious with a ball-pein hammer while walking along a street in Keighley, near Bradford, on the night of 5 July 1975. Sutcliffe then slashed her across the stomach with a knife. At that juncture, he was disturbed by a nearby householder and hurriedly left the scene. Anna Rogulskyj survived, though she needed extensive surgery and was severely traumatized. Sutcliffe's second and third victims – Olive Smelt, 46, an officer cleaner attacked in Halifax on 15 August, and 14-year-old Tracy Brown, who was hit from behind five times with a hammer in Silsden, near Keighley, on 27 August – also survived when Sutcliffe was interrupted. However, three days after Tracy's escape, he managed to kill for the first time.

PETER SUTCLIFFE TIMELINE

5 July 1975: Peter Sutcliffe attacks Anna Rogulskyj, 36, in Keighley. Though badly injured, she survives after Sutcliffe is disturbed and has to leave in a hurry.

August 1975: Office cleaner Olive Smelt, 46, attacked in Halifax on 15 August, and 14-year-old Tracy Brown, attacked in Silsden on 27 August. Both survive.

30 October 1975: Sutcliffe commits his first murder, killing Wilma McCann, 28, in Leeds. In December 2007, one of her daughters commits suicide after 32 years of grief over her mother's death. 150 police officers are assigned to the crime and 11,000 interviews are conducted, but the killer is not found.

20 January 1976: Emily Jackson, 42, killed by Peter Sutcliffe in Leeds.

9 May 1976: Marcela Claxton survives an attack by Sutcliffe in Roundhay Park, Leeds.

5 February 1977: Prostitute Irene Richardson murdered in Leeds.

23 April 1977: Prostitute Patricia Atkinson murdered in Bradford.

26 June 1977: Prostitute Jayne Macdonald murdered in Manchester.

1 October 1977: Prostitute Jean Jordan, 20, killed in Manchester.

9 October 1977: Sutcliffe returns to the murder scene to retrieve a £5 note he gave Jean Jordan but has no success.

10 October 1977: Jean Jordan's mutilated body is found by police.

15 October 1977: Jean Jordan's handbag, in which the £5 note is concealed, is found by police. An intensive search for the owner of the note is a failure. Peter Sutcliffe is among 5000 employees of T and WH Clark interviewed by police, but is not detected.

14 December 1977: Peter Sutcliffe, now known as the Yorkshire Ripper, attacks Leeds prostitute Marilyn Moore, 25, but she survives and gives police a detailed description of her assailant.

21 January 1978: Shortly after the police abandon their attempt to identify the owner of the £5 note, Sutcliffe kills 21-year-old prostitute Yvonne Pearson in Bradford.

31 January 1978: Prostitute Helen Rytka, 18, is killed in Huddersfield.

March 1978: A hoaxer, later called 'Wearside Jack' sends the first of two letters to Oldfield, claiming to be the Yorkshire Ripper. He also sends cassette recordings revealing a Sunderland, Wearside accent.

16 May 1978: Vera Millward, 40, is killed in the grounds of Manchester Royal Infirmary.

4 April 1979: Sutcliffe kills a 19-year-old bank clerk, Josephine Whitaker, in Halifax.

1 September 1979: Sutcliffe murders Bradford student Barbara Leach, 20.

18 August 1980: Marguerite Walls, 47, is murdered in Bradford.

24 September 1980: Sutcliffe attacks Dr Upadhya Bandara, 34, in Leeds, but she survives.

5 November 1980: Sutcliffe attacks 16-year-old Theresa Sykes in Huddersfield. She, too, survives.

17 November 1980: Jacqueline Hill, 20, a Leeds University student, is killed, the last victim to die at the hands of Peter Sutcliffe.

2 January 1981: Sutcliffe is arrested on the charge of using false licence plates on his vehicle. Under intensive questioning, he confesses to being the Yorkshire Ripper and gives police full details of his crimes. He is charged on 5 January.

22 May 1981: After a trial lasting 17 days, Sutcliffe is sentenced to life imprisonment on 13 counts of murder and seven of attempted murder. He is sent to Broadmoor high-security psychiatric hospital at Crowthorne, Berkshire.

20 October 2005: After 27 years, the hoaxer 'Wearside Jack' is finally identified as John Samuel Humble, an alcoholic, and is charged with attempting to pervert the course of justice.

21 March 2006: John Samuel Humble is sentenced to eight years' imprisonment.

Wilma McCann, a 28-year old-mother of four, received two hammer blows and 15 stab wounds in her neck, chest and abdomen when Sutcliffe assaulted her in Leeds on 30 October. He left her body in Prince Phillip Playing Fields. From the semen found on her clothing, it appeared that her killer had tried to rape her. Sutcliffe got clean away, for the 150 officers assigned to the crime failed to find him, and the 11,000 interviews conducted by the police revealed nothing that could help them to solve the murder.

Sutcliffe's next killing was his only murder in 1976. On 20 January, he battered Emily Jackson, 42, on the head and stabbed her in the neck, chest and abdomen with a sharpened screwdriver. Before he left her dead in Manor Street, Leeds, he stamped on her thigh, leaving behind an impression of his boot. His next victim, 20-year-old Marcela Claxton, survived Sutcliffe's hammer blows in Roundhay Park, Leeds, on 9 May. The next year, he killed three more prostitutes, one in Bradford and two in Leeds, before he made a dangerous mistake.

On 1 October, in Manchester, Sutcliffe killed his sixth murder victim, a 20-year-old prostitute and mother of two sons, Jean Jordan, after giving her a £5 note for sex. The note, serial number AW51 121565, was new and had come from a recent paypacket: that meant it could be traced back to Sutcliffe if the police ever found it. Sutcliffe became obsessed with the idea of retrieving the note from Jean's handbag before her body was located. There was still no news about the murder by 9 October, when Sutcliffe drove back to Manchester from his Bradford home. He found Jean's body where he had left it, in the allotments by the Southern Cemetery, but there was no handbag.

Frantically, Sutcliffe searched the area, but the handbag was nowhere to be found. In fear and frustration, he stabbed Jean's corpse 18 times, sinking his knife blade up to 20cm (8in) deep as he slashed at her breasts, stomach and vagina. Then, he attempted to cut off Jean's head, which was now blackened and unrecognizable, thinking to leave it elsewhere and so frustrate identification. But his knife was not up to the task. Sutcliffe abandoned the idea and returned home. Jean's much-mutilated body was found the

A crime team gathers after the discovery of another victim. Sutcliffe confused detectives by attacking victims in widely separated locations.

'He confessed that he was the Yorkshire Ripper and began to describe the attacks and serial murders committed in widely dispersed locations thanks to his job as a lorry driver.'

next day. Her handbag turned up on 15 October. Inside a hidden compartment at the front of the bag was the £5 note Sutcliffe had given her.

The Discovery of Vital Evidence

The police were sure the note would lead them to the Yorkshire Ripper – until, that is, they learned that this particular £5 was only one note in a batch of notes worth £17,500 distributed to firms in Bradford and neighbouring Shipley for paying wages. One of these firms was T and WH Clark (Holdings) Ltd, of Canal Road, Shipley, where Sutcliffe worked as a driver. A team led by Chief Superintendent Jack Ridgeway of the Manchester police began the mammoth task of interviewing every man employed by Clark's, including Peter Sutcliffe. But they failed to connect

Manpower was needed by the West Yorkshire Police to examine Sutcliffe's many crime areas. Police also recorded millions of car number plates seen at the sites.

him or anyone else with the telltale note. This was only one of nine separate occasions when Sutcliffe was questioned by the police without even coming up on a list of likely suspects.

The interviews were still going on when the Yorkshire Ripper struck again. On 14 December 1977, he attacked Leeds prostitute Marilyn Moore, 25, raining blows on her head until the blood ran. She began screaming and tried to fight him off, but was hammered to the ground and lost consciousness. But her screams had disturbed a dog, which began barking so loudly that Sutcliffe made off before anyone could come to investigate. Marilyn was badly injured but managed to give police a detailed description of her attacker – aged around 30, stockily built, 1.68m (5ft 6in) tall, with dark, wavy hair and a beard.

A Paranoid Schizophrenic

In January 1978, Ridgeway and his team abandoned their attempt to find the owner of the £5 note, believing – as was true, of course – that they had encountered the Ripper but failed to recognize him. Their suspicions that the Ripper was still at large were

brutally confirmed on 21 January, when the serial killer murdered a 21-year-old prostitute, Yvonne Pearson, on waste ground off Arthington Street in Bradford. Peter Sutcliffe killed twice more in 1978. The chance of apprehending him was diverted for several months as the police were occupied with a hopeless search of the Sunderland district for the hoaxer Wearside Jack. His identity would not be revealed for another 27 years.

An 11-month interval ensued before Sutcliffe killed a 19-year-old bank clerk, Josephine Whitaker, in Halifax on 4 April 1979. Another killing in Bradford followed on 1 September 1979, of 20-year-old Barbara Leach. It was not until 18 August 1980 that Marguerite Walls, 47, was murdered in Bradford, and Jacqueline

'In fear and frustration, he stabbed Jean's corpse 18 times, sinking his knife blade up to 20cm (8in) deep as he slashed at her breasts, stomach and vagina. Then he attempted to cut off Jean's head..."

Hill, 20, a student at Leeds University, became the 13th and last victim of the Ripper, in Leeds, on 17 November. At the time, Peter Sutcliffe, still undetected, was on remand, awaiting trial, on a charge of drunk driving. He also attacked two more women during this time. Both survived.

Sutcliffe's trial for drunk driving was due in court in January 1981. It never took place. Long before the English courts could reconvene after their Christmas recess, the truth about the Yorkshire Ripper had been revealed and Peter Sutcliffe was charged with murder at Dewsbury Court in Manchester on 5 January 1981.

At his trial, which opened at the Old Bailey in London on 5 May 1981, Sutcliffe was found guilty of 13 counts of murder and seven of attempted murder. Opinions from psychiatrists stated that he was suffering from paranoid schizophrenia, which, his defence counsel claimed, diminished his responsibility for his crimes. After a 17-day trial, Sutcliffe was sentenced to imprisonment for life. His skewed state of mind was, however, acknowledged by the venue to

'She began screaming and tried to fight him off, but she was hammered to the ground and lost consciousness. But her screams had disturbed a dog, which began barking so loudly that Sutcliffe made off...'

which he was confined and where he remains to this day: Broadmoor, the high-security psychiatric hospital at Crowthorne in Berkshire, which has often played host to Britain's crazier killers in the past.

The public's relief at the Yorkshire Ripper's capture soon turned to outrage. Enormous shock and fear had been created by the intense press coverage of his murders.

David Berkowitz
The Son of Sam Killer

FULL NAME:
Richard David Falco
(changed to Berkowitz when he
was adopted)

DOB:
1 June 1953

NUMBER OF VICTIMS:
Six killed, seven wounded

SPAN OF KILLINGS:
July 1976–July 1977

LOCATION OF KILLINGS:
New York City

DATE OF ARREST:
10 August 1977

SENTENCE:
365 years in prison

Unlike several others who enjoyed much longer careers and took a greater number of lives, David Berkowitz, the self-styled Son of Sam, was a serial killer who was at large for only a year. But during that period, 1976–7, New Yorkers lived in fear as Berkowitz conducted a reign of terror that killed six people and injured another nine.

At 1.10 a.m. on 29 July 1976, Mike and Rose Lauria returned home from a night out with their 18-year-old daughter Donna, a medical technician, and her friend Jody Valenti, 19, a student nurse. David Berkowitz was waiting for them, sitting out of sight in his car across the street. Beside him, on the passenger seat, was a paper sack. Berkowitz had spent several hours cruising around New York's Pelham Bay in the

Bronx, where the Laurias lived. He watched as Mike and Rose disappeared inside the apartment building, leaving the two girls in their car.

Donna Lauria had just opened the car door to leave in her turn when she was startled to see Berkowitz approaching. He pulled his handgun out of the paper sack, crouched down to aim and in quick succession, fired three shots. Donna died almost at once. Jody was hit in the leg, but survived. The third bullet missed. Berkowitz made a speedy getaway, but not so fast that Jody was unable to give a detailed description of him.

The killer, Jody later told police, was white, male, with a fair complexion, short, dark curly hair, around 1.75m (5ft 9in) tall and weighed some 75kg (160lb). The one thing she got wrong was his age: she said he was 'in his thirties', but Berkowitz was 23 years old when he committed his first murder.

After one of the bullets was retrieved, the New York police identified the handgun as a Charter Arms .44 calibre Bulldog, a five-shot revolver meant for shooting at close quarters. But apart from that they had no significant clues, no idea of the killer's identity and no motive for the murder. A frustrated admirer, mistaken identity and gang warfare were some of the suggestions, but none held water. Besides, this was New York, the so-called 'ungovernable city', where the early hours of the morning were a dangerous time to be out and about.

A Hatred of Women

David Berkowitz lay low for the next three months before attacking again. When he did, it was once more

Deputy Sheriff Craig Glassman shows two letters he received from Berkowitz. Glassman noticed the similarity between these and the 'Son of Sam' letters.

> '**He pulled his handgun out of the paper sack, crouched down to aim and in quick succession fired three shots. Donna died almost at once. Jody was hit in the leg, but survived. The third bullet missed.**'

in the early morning, with a .44 calibre gun, and once more his victims were sitting in a car parked by the roadside. At around 2.30 a.m. on 23 October 1976, Carl Denaro, 20, and Rosemary Keenan, 18, were on their way home after a party at Peck's Bar in the New York borough of Queens. Having reached Flushing, they were parked 800m (875yd) down the street in Rosemary's Volkswagen, when a man appeared on the sidewalk by the front passenger window. His face was hidden in the half-dark so that neither Carl nor Rosemary was able to identify him.

As this mysterious intruder began shooting, the window shattered. Rosemary suffered superficial cuts from the broken glass, but Carl was bleeding from a wound caused by a bullet that had removed part of his skull. Rosemary plunged the accelerator down and quickly drove away, out of range. She did not stop until she had reached Peck's Bar. Carl was rushed to hospital, where surgeons discovered that his injury was serious enough for him to require a steel plate to cover the gap in his skull. But though the attacks of July and October 1976 had many similarities, the police failed to spot a connection – or realize that this was the early work of a serial killer.

The one clue that seemed to fit the situation was that the killer's chief target seemed to be young women. Misogyny had long been a trigger for the depredations of male killers and David Berkowitz, who was born illegitimate and put up for adoption by his mother, had his reasons for hating women.

This theory seemed to hold good when David Berkowitz attacked again a month later, on

'Donna had been hit by a bullet that passed 6mm (¼in) from her spine before exiting her body, but Joanna's spine had shattered when the bullet struck her and she was paralyzed.'

26 November 1976. This time, the two girls who became his next victims – Donna De Masi, 16, and Joanne Lomino, 18 – had been walking home through Queens from a cinema and were standing, chatting beneath a street light when they saw a man approaching. His description closely fitted Jody Valenti's four months earlier: he was slim, around 1.75m (5ft 9in) tall and weighed about 68kg (150lb).

Suddenly producing a revolver, he shot each girl once, then turned his gun on the nearby apartment building and fired several more shots before running away. Donna had been hit by a bullet that passed 6mm (¼in) from her spine before exiting her body, but Joanna's spine had shattered when the bullet struck her and she was paralyzed.

The police were still unable to link the attacks despite several sightings of the killer, two graphic descriptions and the pattern of after-dark street crimes against young couples in cars. This situation remained essentially the same after another shooting in Queens on 30 January 1977 in which another young couple in a car were attacked: the woman, 26-year-old Christine Freund, was shot twice and later died.

Letters to the Media

Columbia University student Virginia Voskerichian, 19, was the next to be killed, in Queens on 8 March 1977. Alexander Esau, 20, and Valentina Suriani, 18, were shot in the Bronx at around 3 a.m. on 17 April. Sal Lupo and Judy Placido escaped with minor injuries when Berkowitz opened fire on them in their car in the Bayside area of Queens at 3 a.m. on 26 June.

The serial murders came to an end a year almost to the day after the first. On 31 July 1977, Stacey

The Trail of Murders

The Bronx, 29 July 1976:
The Bronx was the location of Berkowitz's first murder, Donna Lauria, on 29 July 1976. It was also here on 17 April 1977 that he killed a couple, Alexander Esau and Valentina Suriani, and left the first letter from 'Son of Sam' at the scene.

Queens, January and March 1977:
After his initial murder in the Bronx, Berkowitz moved to the largest borough of Queens for his next four attacks. After shooting and injuring two couples, he then killed Christine Freund in a car with her boyfriend and Virginia Voskerichian walking home from Columbia University.

Brooklyn, 31 July 1977:
The Son of Sam was becoming over-confident when he struck in Brooklyn on 31 July 1977, killing Stacey Moskowitz and wounding her boyfriend in view of several witnesses. A couple of days later, one woman went to the police with a description of Berkowitz.

Bayside, Queens, 26 June 1977:
Sal Lupo, 20, and Judy Placido, 17, sat in a car at 3 a.m. on 26 June 1977 in the Bayside section of Queens. Minutes after she said 'This Son of Sam is really scary', Berkowitz blasted their vehicle with bullets and ran. Both received only minor injuries.

Key David Berkowitz's victims

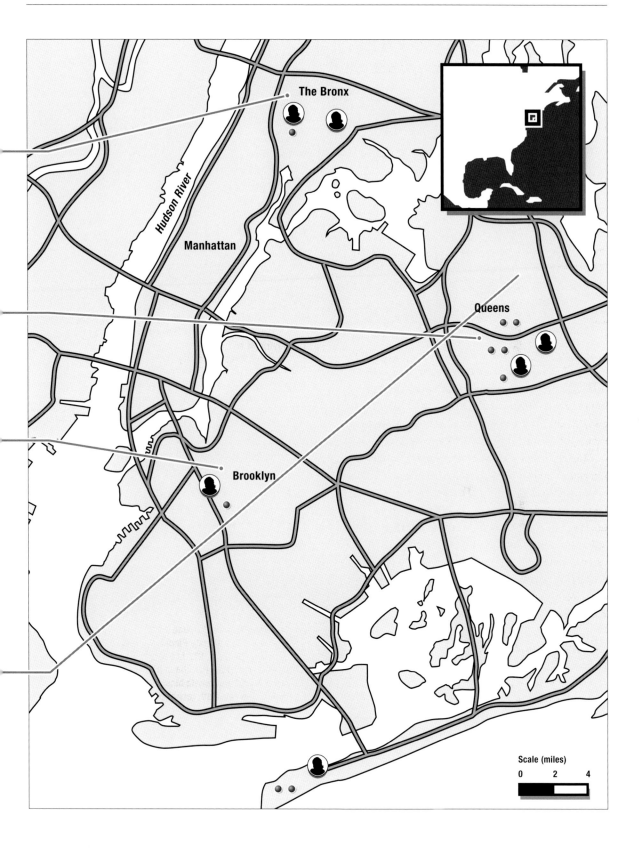

Moskowitz, 20, was killed and her friend Robert Violente, also 20, almost blinded, near a park in Brooklyn. Despite the early hour, there had been several witnesses to the Brooklyn attack, one of whom actually saw the crime being committed in the rearview mirror of his car.

Berkowitz himself was also adding to the police files with handwritten letters. In the first, left at the crime scene on 17 April 1977, Berkowitz described himself as the 'Son of Sam' and claimed that he was a thorough-going sadist and a drinker of blood. The letter was signed 'Yours in murder, Mr Monster'. On 30 May, Jimmy Breslin, a columnist on the *New York Daily News,* received the second letter. Among other

'In a psychological profile released to the media on 26 May, they diagnosed the killer as a neurotic and paranoid schizophrenic who probably thought he was possessed by the devil.'

Four young women among those killed by Berkowitz were (left to right) Valentina Suriani, Christine Freund, Virginia Voskerichian and Stacey Moskowitz.

ghoulish comments, it contained the message that 'Sam's a thirsty lad and he won't let me stop killing until he gets his fill of blood.'

A Traffic Violation

The Son of Sam killings, as the murders were soon called, received huge publicity, which escalated after the police called in psychiatrists. In a psychological profile released to the media on 26 May, they diagnosed the killer as a neurotic and paranoid schizophrenic who probably thought he was possessed by the devil. Berkowitz later claimed that he was commanded to kill by a demon who had taken up residence in his neighbour's black labrador dog.

After the murder of Virginia Voskerichian on 8 March, a 300-strong task force, *Operation Omega,* had been created to focus exclusively on the Son of Sam case. By now, the police were at last admitting that a serial killer was at large, but four months passed before they achieved a breakthrough. On 31 July, Berkowitz committed a traffic violation: he parked his Ford Galaxie where it blocked a fire hydrant. When he returned after shooting Stacey

'When he returned after shooting Stacey Moskowitz and Robert Violente, he found a ticket on his windscreen. Across the street, car driver Cecilia Davis saw him throw the ticket into the gutter.'

Moskowitz and Robert Violente, he found a ticket on his windscreen. Across the street, car driver Cecilia Davis saw him throw the ticket into the gutter. Later, she saw him again. It seemed to Mrs Davis that he was carrying a gun up his sleeve, and she informed the police.

When they checked the discarded ticket, Berkowitz came up as the owner, together with his address, 35

Pine Street, Yonkers. On 10 August, police located the Galaxie parked outside the Pine Street apartment building. Led by Detective John Falotico, they were content simply to wait. At 10 p.m., Berkowitz came out and got into his car, where he had left his .44 pistol on the seat, together with a bag full of ammunition, maps showing the crime scenes and another letter threatening more attacks. Asked to identify himself, Berkowitz told Falotico, 'I'm Sam'. He was arrested and taken to a police station, where he made a full confession.

At his trial, which began on 8 May 1978, Berkowitz was charged with two murders and five attempted murders. He pleaded guilty, even though his attorneys advised him not to do so. There was some discussion as to whether he was criminally insane and therefore not fit to face trial. Berkowitz was, however, ruled fit to plead and was eventually sentenced to a total of 365 years in prison. Two requests for parole, in 2004 and 2006, have so far been refused. Berkowitz remains behind bars to this day.

DAVID BERKOWITZ TIMELINE

29 July 1976: David Berkowitz commits his first killing: Donna Lauria is shot dead in a car outside her parents' New York apartment in the Bronx. Her friend, Jody Valenti, is injured. Fatal weapon identified as a .44 calibre Charter Arms Bulldog.

23 October 1976: David Berkowitz attacks Carl Denaro and Rosemary Keenan in Rosemary's car, parked in the New York borough of Queens. Both are injured, Carl seriously. The police fail to realize a connection between the two shootings.

26 November 1976: The next attack by Berkowitz, also in Queens, leaves Donna De Masi and Joanne Lomino injured. Although the girls' description of their attacker is very similar to Jody Valenti's back in July, the NYPD still fail to establish a link between the three incidents.

30 January 1977: Another young couple in a car is attacked in Queens. The woman, Christine Freund, is killed.

8 March 1977: In his fourth attack,

Berkowitz breaks his pattern to shoot and kill a single victim, Virginia Voskerichian, in a street in Queens. The NYPD create a special task force, *Operation Omega,* to deal exclusively with the killings.

17 April 1977: In an attack in the Bronx, another couple, Alexander Esau and Valentina Suriani, are both killed. At the crime scene, Berkowitz leaves the first of two letters identifying himself as Son of Sam and promising more deaths.

26 May 1977: The New York police issue a psychological profile of their suspect, a paranoid schizophrenic with delusions of demonic possession.

30 May 1977: Columnist Jimmy Breslin of the *New York Daily News* receives the second letter written by Berkowitz, who boasts 'Sam's a thirsty lad and he won't let me stop killing until he gets his fill of blood'.

26 June 1977: A young couple in a car suffer minor injuries in a shooting in the Bayside area of Queens.

31 July 1977: Berkowitz kills a woman, Stacey Moskowitz, and nearly blinds her friend, Robert Violente, in an attack close to a Brooklyn park. Berkowitz throws away a traffic violation ticket, which he finds on the windscreen of his Ford Galaxie after the attack. He is observed by a car driver, Cecilia Davis, who sees him again hiding up his sleeve what she suspects is a gun. Mrs Davis informs the police.

10 August 1977: Having identified the car and its owner's name and address from the ticket, Detective John Falotico arrests Berkowitz outside his Pine Street, Yonkers, apartment building. Berkowitz gives a full confession.

8 May 1978: The trial of David Berkowitz opens. He pleads guilty to two murders and five attempted murders.

12 June 1978: Berkowitz is sentenced to a total of 365 years in prison. Requests for parole in 2004 and 2006 are refused.

Andrei Chikatilo

The Butcher of Rostov

FULL NAME:
Andrei Romanovich Chikatilo

DOB:
16 October 1936

DIED:
14 February 1994

NUMBER OF VICTIMS:
52 women and children

SPAN OF KILLINGS:
22 December 1978–6 November 1990

LOCATION OF KILLINGS:
Mostly in Rostov Oblast, Russia

DATE OF ARREST:
20 November 1990

SENTENCE:
The death penalty (by shooting)

Andrei Romanovich Chikatilo, known by various grisly nicknames (the Butcher of Rostov, The Red or Rostov Ripper) was a latecomer to the annals of serial killing. The Ukrainian was 42 in 1978, when he murdered the first of his 52 victims – 9-year-old Lochkha Zakotnova – in Shakhty, a coal-mining town 64km (40 miles) from Rostov-on-Don in the southwest of what was then the Soviet Union.

It was sadly indicative of Andrei Chikatilo's physical and psychological problems that he failed in his attempt to rape his first murder victim. Instead, on 22 December 1978, he stabbed little Lochkha Zakotnova to death – and in the process achieved the sexual climax that had eluded him a few minutes earlier. From then on, orgasm for Andrei Chikatilo could usually be orchestrated by the process of killing his victims. When he had finished with her, Chikatilo threw Lochkha's body into the freezing Grushevka river. She was found floating in the water the next day.

The Rostov police found very little evidence on which to base a proper investigation. There were, though, sufficient signs of violence to show that in addition to stab wounds, an attempt had been made to gouge out the young girl's eyes. This reflected an old Russian superstition that the eyes 'photographed' the last scene a person witnessed before death.

Despite the lack of evidence, the police found a culprit: 25-year-old Alexandr Kravchenko, who had already been convicted of rape and was now out of prison on parole. Kravchenko was arrested, tortured until he confessed, and was executed in 1983.

Although Chikatilo had managed to get away with his first killing, this did not, as yet, encourage him to commit more. But considering his traumatic mindset, more violent crimes were inevitable. Chikatilo believed that, soon after his birth in 1936, he had been castrated and blinded, a conclusion he drew from his near-sightedness and a sexual dysfunction caused by brain damage at birth.

The Thrill of the Kill

Unsurprisingly, Chikatilo grew up timid and periodically impotent. He made a target for the boys he taught at a school in Novoshakhtinsk, near Rostov. He was taunted as a 'faggot' after he molested some of the boys, and a group of them beat him severely after he attempted to fellate a boy sleeping in the school dormitory. He began to carry a knife for protection. Chikatilo was removed from his post at the school for interfering with the boys, but found another job as a procurement officer for a Shakhty factory.

'In addition to stab wounds, an attempt had been made to gouge out the young girl's eyes. This reflected an old Russian superstition that the eyes "photographed" the last scene a person witnessed before death.'

His new job involved constant travel, an advantage that enabled him to resume killing. Targeting anonymous victims like runaways, he then moved on, out of the area and beyond suspicion.

On 3 March 1982, 17-year-old Larisa Tkachenko encountered Andrei Chikatilo at a bus stop outside the Rostov public library. He asked her to come into

Chikatilo's long spate of murder began with female victims, such as the four shown below. They had often run away from home and were vulnerable.

Young boys, as shown, became Chikatilo's preferred victims in 1990. He had once been beaten by his male students and sacked for molesting some of them.

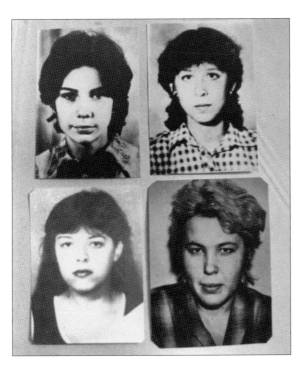

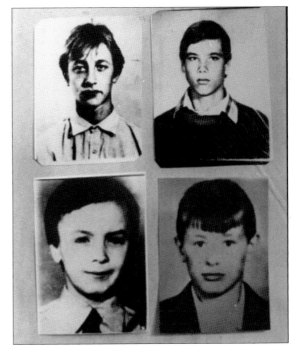

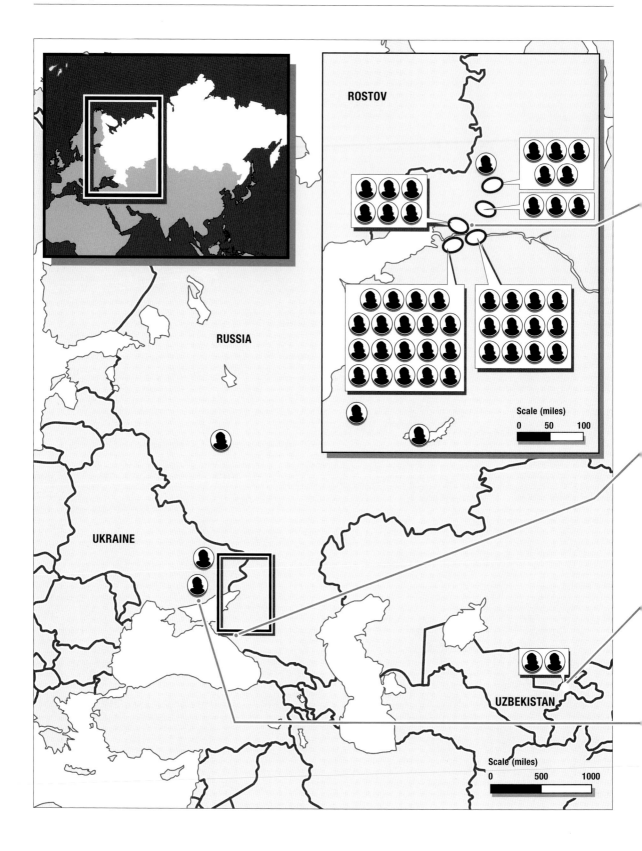

ROSTOV

RUSSIA

UKRAINE

Scale (miles)
0   50   100

UZBEKISTAN

Scale (miles)
0   500   1000

The Trail of Murders

Rostov-on-Don, 1978:
Rostov-on-Don in southern Russia gave Chikatilo two of his infamous nicknames, the Butcher of Rostov and the Rostov Ripper. He moved into the area in 1978 and that year killed his first victim. He committed only a few murders away from Rostov's environs.

Krasnodar, 25 July 1982:
In an unusual move, Chikatilo chose Krasnodar, a town distant from Rostov, for his fourth murder, that of a 14-year-old girl, Lynbna Volubeyeva. The deed was done while he was there on business, an indication of how little Chikatilo's crimes affected him.

Tashkent, August 1984:
Chikatilo visited Tashkent, the capital of Uzbekistan (then part of the Soviet Union), and killed two locals, an unknown woman and Akmaral Seydaliyeva, a 12-year-old girl. By now, police back in Rostov were patrolling train, tram and bus stations.

Eastern Ukraine, 1988:
To avoid police, Chikatilo travelled to eastern Ukraine in 1988. In April he murdered an unknown 30-year-old woman near Krashny-Sulin, leaving her body near railway tracks. A month later in Ilovaisk he killed a 9-year-old boy, Alyosha Voronka, in woods.

Key Chikatilo's victims

'It did not seem to occur to police that they were uncovering the work of a serial killer. Serial killing was thought to characterize Western decadence and did not occur in the Soviet Union. '

the woods nearby and have sex. Larisa, who was already sexually experienced, agreed. Before long, though, she discovered that Chikatilo was unable to do the deed. She started to laugh at him, driving Chikatilo into such a murderous rage that he beat her about the head with his fists. Larisa began screaming. Chikatilo stuffed earth into her mouth to smother her cries. When that failed, he grabbed her by the throat and strangled her. He sank his teeth into her throat, and gnawed her arms and breasts. Chikatilo grew so frenzied that he bit off one of Larisa's nipples and swallowed it. Finally, he raped her with a stick and, by now thoroughly aroused, ejaculated over her body.

An Inept Police Force

When Larisa's ravished remains were discovered next day, police once again found no clues that could lead them to her killer. Chikatilo remained free to move on to his third victim, 12-year-old Lyuba Biryuk, who lived in the village of Zaplavskaya near Rostov. On 12 June 1982, he spotted Lyuba at a bus stop and followed her into nearby woods. There, he grabbed her and attempted to rape her, but yet again, he failed and resorted instead to stabbing her some 40 times before gaining the sexual satisfaction he sought. Like his first victim, Lyuba was found, two weeks after her death, with her eyes gouged out.

Yet again, the Rostov police were mystified and grew even more so as the bodies of four more similarly mutilated victims were discovered during the rest of 1982. It did not seem to occur to police that they were uncovering the work of a serial killer. Serial killing was thought to characterize Western decadence and did not occur in the Soviet Union. By September

1983, when the deaths of 14 adults and children had been reported and only six bodies found, no substantial clues to the perpetrator had been discovered. The police, still flummoxed, contacted the more sophisticated force in Moscow for help.

Arrested – for Theft

Major Mikhail Fetisov of the central Moscow militia brought a team down from the Soviet capital to take over the investigation. Fetisov was horrified at the ineptitude of the Rostov police and reported back to Moscow Headquarters that, contrary to traditional belief, the murders of 1982–3 had undoubtedly been the work of a single killer. Fetisov formed a special team, ponderously named the Division of Especially Serious Crimes, to investigate the 'Forest Belt' murders, as Chikatilo's crimes became known.

The Division was headed by the forensic analyst Victor Burako, who ordered a search of the records at mental hospitals to discover whether any inmates had a history of sexual violence. Criminal records were scanned for sex offenders. A total of 150,000 suspects were interviewed. Hundreds of tests were carried out to find men whose blood was Type AB, the same type found in the semen left on the bodies of the killer's victims. Andre Chikatilo's blood was tested, yet by mistake or incompetence, the police failed to detect a match.

Despite all this activity, Chikatilo added 15 more murders to his toll between January and September 1984. A year after arriving in the Rostov region, Major Fetisov seemed to have reached a dead end. However, things seemed to improve once a psychiatrist,

'The savagery of Chikatilo's murders had escalated so far that he was routinely mutilating his victims. During the next year, when he killed eight more times, he cut off the head and legs of one woman.'

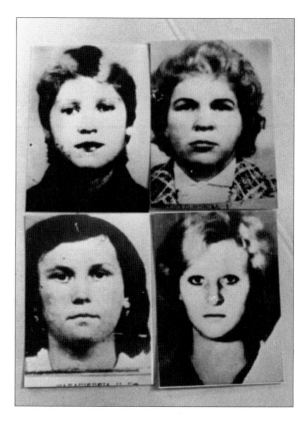

A portfolio of Chikatilo's female victims indicates he did not seek out a particular look. Instead, he waited at transport stops for encounters with lonely women.

Aleksandr Bukhanovsky, formulated a profile. The murderer, he concluded, was a sexual deviant, around 178cm (5ft 10in) tall, with size 10 feet and between 25 and 50 years of age. This described Andrei Chikatilo, who was 48 at the time and wore size 10 shoes.

Armed with this information, a watch was kept on bus, tram and railway stations in Rostov for suspicious-seeming men who paid too much attention to young women and boys. During the surveillance, Andrei Chikatilo was one of the first suspects apprehended after he put his hand inside a woman's blouse and fondled her breasts. The woman stalked off angrily, but this was hardly enough to charge Chikatilo with murder. Instead, he was sent to prison for 10 months for a previous misdemeanour – stealing from his employers a roll of linoleum and a car battery.

ANDREI CHIKATILO TIMELINE

22 December 1978: Andrei Chikatilo, 42, murders his first victim, 9-year-old Lochkha Zakotnova, after failing to rape her. He attains climax, however, as he knifes her to death. Chikatilo is not suspected, and a convicted rapist, Alexandr Kravchenko, 25, is charged with the murder and executed instead.

3 March 1982: Resuming his killings, Chikatilo murders Larisa Tkachenko, 17, after she ridicules his failure to have sex with her.

12 June 1982: Chikatilo's next victim, Lyuba Biryuk, 12, is stabbed 40 times and, like Lochkha, has her eyes gouged out. By the end of 1982, Chikatilo murders four more victims.

25 July 1982: Chikatilo murders 14-year-old Lynbna Volubeyeva. during a business trip to Krasnodar, some 258km (160 miles) from Rostov.

11 December 1982: Olya Kuprina, 16, is savagely murdered by Chikatilo near Rostov.

September 1983: By this time, 14 adult and child deaths have been reported. Six bodies are discovered. The Rostov police are baffled. More sophisticated police officers from Moscow, led by Major Mikhail Fetisov, deduce that the murders are the work of a single killer.

27 October 1983: Vera Shevkun, a 19-year-old prostitute, murdered by Chikatilo near Shakhty.

January–September 1984: Chikatilo commits 15 more murders. Intensive surveillance begins at bus and train stations. Chikatilo is arrested after fondling a woman's breasts, but though he is suspected, there is not enough information to charge him with murder. Instead, he is sent to prison on a previous indictment, for theft. The experience brings his serial killings to a temporary halt.

1 August 1985: Chikatilo kills a mentally retarded 18-year-old, Irina Gulyayeva, stabbing her 38 times. Next, he murders a woman after she laughs at his failure to have sex.

May–September 1987: Chikatilo kills three young boys, but unknown to him, the police are slowly building up evidence in the 'Forest Belt' killings, as his crimes have become known.

Spring 1988: Aware of police activity in his area of operations, Chikatilo moves out of the district to eastern Ukraine and murders a woman in April. On 14 May, he murders another, Alyosha Voronka, in Ilovaisk, in the Donets basin.

1 November 1989: Chikatilo kills Tatyana

Ryzhova, another victim who laughs at his inability to have sex. Afterwards, he cuts her to pieces with a folding knife.

1990: Chikatilo's murders become more and more ghoulish as he disfigures and mutilates his victims and eats their body parts. He kills a young boy, Vadim Tishchenko, 16, on 3 November and three days later commits his last murder, that of Svetlana Korostik. She is found stabbed and disfigured.

20 November 1990: Police trailing Chikatilo arrest him after seeing him approach two boys. Police interrogate him in a KGB isolation cell, but fail to procure a confession.

30 November 1990: Psychiatrist Aleksandr Bukhanovsky finally breaks down Chikatilo's resistance. He confesses to 36 murders and admits another 16.

14 April 1992: Trial of Andrei Chikatilo opens. The indictment takes two days to read out in court.

15 October 1992: Sentencing is postponed but he is finally found guilty on 52 counts of murder, Chikatilo is given 52 death sentences.

14 February 1994: Chikatilo is executed by a single shot in the back of his neck.

The Police Close In

After this daunting experience, Andrei Chikatilo did not resume killing until the late summer of 1985. On 1 August, he murdered a mentally retarded 18-year-old he met on a train, leaving her close by the railroad line with 38 stab wounds in her body. His next victim was a woman he picked up at Shakhty bus station: like an earlier victim, she laughed at him when he failed in his attempt to have sex with her. Chikatilo left her corpse in a field. During 1987, Chikatilo killed three young boys.

Unknown to him, however, police investigators were painstakingly gathering information piece by piece from cases and occurrences linked to sexual motivation, homosexuality, pornographic clubs and stores and the movements of railway employees and travellers. Trains were patrolled by plain-clothes police. The papers carried by anyone who aroused suspicions were checked. Red Army helicopters overflew rail lines and forests, looking for anything that seemed dubious.

Possibly realizing that gigantic efforts were being made to find him, Chikatilo called a halt to his activities in the three areas on which the police concentrated – Shakhty, Rostov and Novoshakhtinsk – and moved out of surveillance to places like Krasny-Sulin in eastern Ukraine. In April 1988, it was near Krashny-Sulin that he killed a 30-year-old woman he met on a train. Next, on 14 May, he killed Alyosha Voronka, in the city of Ilovaisk in the Donets basin.

Savage Violence

By now, the savagery of Chikatilo's murders had escalated so far that he was routinely mutilating his victims. During the next year, when he killed eight more times, he cut off the head and legs of one woman. He sliced out the womb of another, together with most of her face. The body parts missing when police discovered Chikatilo's latest victims included tongues, more wombs and nipples, and male genitals, some of which he had chewed. Young boys became

'The body parts missing when police discovered Chikatilo's latest victims included tongues, more wombs and nipples, and male genitals, some of which were chewed.'

Psychiatrist Aleksandr Bukhanovsky examining the case file on Chikatilo. His psychological and physical profile of the Butcher of Rostov tightened the police search.

Chikatilo's preferred targets during 1990, when he murdered one of his last victims, 16-year-old Vadim Tishchenko.

Vadim's body was found at Leskhoz rail station in Rostov, which had been stiff with scrutiny until 3 November, when it went unpatrolled due to a shortage of manpower. Chikatilo chose that very night to strike again and escaped unobserved. His luck was, however, running out: an attendant at Shakhty station recognized Vadim's photograph and told police that when the boy bought his ticket there, he was accompanied by a grey-haired man wearing spectacles. By a stroke of luck, the attendant's daughter knew Chikatilo by sight and was able to identify him as the man involved and give a detailed description.

The police were closing in on Andrei Chikatilo, but not before he killed his last victim. Svetlana

'Chikatilo had been such a prolific killer that after his trial opened, on 14 April 1992, the indictment took two days to read out in court.'

Korostik, 22 years old, was stabbed and mutilated in the woods near Leskhoz station on 6 November 1990. But armed with his description, the police were able to trail Chikatilo and then, on 20 November 1990, they observed him trying to strike up conversations with two young boys. Fortunately, they got away from him. Chikatilo now continued on his way, but three men in leather jackets approached him, identified themselves as police officers and arrested him on the spot.

Chikatilo was interrogated in a KGB isolation cell, where police hoped to frighten a confession out of him. Chikatilo failed to lose his nerve, however. He remained calm, although it was clear that he was rattled. Then, on 30 November, the police put him under increased pressure. The psychiatrist Aleksandr Bukhanovsky was brought in and, after patient probing, he at last managed to get Chikatilo to tell the whole story. Chikatilo finally confessed to the 36 murders with which he was charged as well as to 16 others.

Sentenced to Death

Chikatilo had been such a prolific killer that after his trial opened, on 14 April 1992, the indictment took two days to read out in court. The trial lasted three months, ending with Guilty verdicts on each of the 52 counts of murder for which he was indicted. Chikatilo received 52 death sentences and all were carried out simultaneously when he was executed by a single shot in the back of the neck on 14 February 1994.

Chikatilo was confined to an iron cage during his long trial in 1992. He appeared bored hearing the testimony but would sometimes shout angrily at the spectators.

Bittaker and Norris

Pacific Coast Highway Killers

FULL NAME:
Lawrence Sigmund Bittaker and
Roy Lewis Norris

DOB:
27 September 1940

2 February 1948

NUMBER OF VICTIMS:
Raped and murdered five young women

SPAN OF KILLINGS:
June–October 1979

LOCATION OF KILLINGS:
Los Angeles, California

DATE OF ARREST:
20 November 1979

SENTENCE:
Life imprisonment (Norris)
The death penalty (Bittaker)

After Lawrence Sigmund Bittaker met Roy Lewis Norris in prison, they became partners in depravity. Both were sociopaths addicted to rape and torture – and both were released from prison despite psychiatrists' warnings that they were extremely dangerous. This became clear in 1979, when they raped, tortured and murdered five young women in California.

Lawrence Bittaker and Roy Norris became friends in 1977 or 1978, when both of them were imprisoned in the Men's Colony at San Luis Obispo, California, Bittaker for burglary, Norris for forcible rape. Bittaker was the older of the two and assumed a leading role in their later activities after twice saving Norris's life during their time in the Colony: by the 'rules' of the

so-called Prisoner's Code, this gave Bittaker the right to expect obedience from Norris in any plan he might care to devise, however outlandish that plan might be.

Like Bittaker, Norris was imprisoned after committing a long line of offences that had marked him out as psychotic. A diagnosis of Bittaker by forensic psychiatrist Dr Robert Markman was as true for Norris: he had 'no internal controls over his impulses' and was 'a man who could kill without hesitation or remorse.'

The 'Murder Mack'

Bittaker was released from San Luis Obispo on 15 November 1978, even though psychiatrists had labelled him a 'classic sociopath'. He moved to Los Angeles, where he found work as a machinist. Norris left the Colony two months later, on 15 January 1979, and went to live with his mother in a Los Angeles trailer park. He got a job as an electrician.

In February 1979, Bittaker got in touch with Norris and renewed their friendship. He had a plan that was as bizarre as it was fiendish: to kidnap, rape and kill teenage girls. For this purpose, he purchased a silver 1977 GMS cargo van. The van had no side windows, so that anything going on inside could not be seen from the street, and featured a large sliding door on the passenger side. This door, Bittaker calculated, made it possible to snatch victims off the sidewalk without being observed by passers-by.

Bittaker christened the van the 'Murder Mack' and chose for its hunting ground the Pacific Coast Highway that ran from Los Angeles to San Francisco. The Highway, 1054km (655 miles) long, ran through Orange County, LA County and Ventura County, along the Central Coast from Emma Wood State Beach and the Mobil Pier Undercrossing to the San Francisco Bay area and the Redwood Empire. With several popular beaches along the way and major

During his trial, Bittaker remained calm and seemed to enjoy the proceedings. He had written his memoirs, titled _The Last Ride_, hoping to place the blame on Norris.

'…they cruised along the highway and stopped at various beaches along the way. They approached about 20 girls, talked to some, flirted with others … but laid not a finger on any of them.'

junctions at cities that included Santa Monica, Monterrey and Santa Cruz, Bittaker reckoned that there would be plenty of young girls on whom to prey.

First, though, Bittaker and Norris gave the 'Murder Mack' several dry runs to check out the feasibility of their plan. Between February and June 1979, they cruised along the Highway and stopped at various beaches along the way. They approached about 20 girls, talked to some, flirted with others and took their photographs, but laid not a finger on any of them. At night, they parked the Murder Mack next to the trailer where Norris lived with his mother.

But the Pacific Coast Highway was a busy route, always full of traffic: what Bittaker and Norris needed was a remote place where they could take their victims and dispatch them without being detected. They found it late in April when they discovered an isolated side road in the San Gabriel Mountains that overlooked Glendora, 37km (23 miles) east of Los Angeles. It was well away from the main road, hidden by the mountainous terrain and unlikely to be frequently used by other traffic. By 24 June 1979, Bittaker and Norris were ready to start killing.

Taking Turns

At 11 a.m., the men began prowling round the area of Redondo Beach in Los Angeles County until they noticed 16-year-old Cindy Schaeffer, who was walking back to her grandmother's house after a church meeting. Bittaker drove up in the Murder Mack and Norris offered her a lift, which she refused. Further down the road, Norris tried again. Again she refused, but Norris grabbed her, slid the passenger door aside and pushed her into the van. Cindy started to shout for help, but Bittaker blanked out her cries by turning up the van's radio while Norris taped her mouth with duct tape. He also bound her wrists and ankles.

Bittaker and Norris now drove to the remote road in the San Gabriel Mountains and parked the van. Bittaker let Norris have first 'go' and left the van to give him time to strangle Cindy. After an hour or so, Bittaker returned, only to find Norris struggling with the girl who was still alive and jerking around, probably in an effort to loosen her assailant's grip. To settle matters, Bittaker fetched a wire coat hanger, which he twisted round the girl's neck. Gradually, he tightened it and after about 15 seconds, Cindy died.

The two men wrapped Cindy's body in a plastic shower curtain, drove to the edge of a ravine and threw it over into the gorge below.

Bittaker and Norris came upon their second victim two weeks later. Andrea Hall, 18, was thumbing rides along the Pacific Coast Highway when Bittaker drove up and brought the Murder Mack to a halt. At that juncture, Norris was hiding under the bed installed in the back of the van, on the premise that one man in the vehicle might seem less threatening than two. It was a hot day and Andrea gratefully accepted the cold drink Bittaker suggested she fetch from the cooler in the back of the van. While she was by the cooler pouring herself a soda, Norris reached out from under the bed, swept her legs from under her and threw her to the floor.

Andrea fought hard for her life, but Norris managed to bind her wrists and tape her mouth before Bittaker halted the Murder Mack at the San Gabriel Mountains side road. There, Bittaker and Norris took turns to rape the girl until they were tired out. Then they dragged Andrea out of the van and onto the road, where Bittaker took pictures of her with his Polaroid camera. Norris, meanwhile, went down the mountain slope to a small store to fetch some beer. He returned to find Andrea still alive, even though Bittaker had stabbed her in each ear with an ice pick. The girl, Norris realized, was utterly terrified.

Norris later told police that Bittaker 'told me that he told her he was going to kill her. He wanted to see

The Trail of Murders

Redondo Beach, June 1979:
Bittaker and Norris's travels in the 'Murder Mack' began in June 1979 in Redondo Beach, cruising the streets for likely victims. Cindy Schaeffer was spotted walking alone from church, and she twice refused Norris's offer of a ride before they forced her into the vehicle.

San Gabriel Mountains, June–September 1979:
A road in the San Gabriel Mountains was used by the men to rape and murder Cindy Schaeffer, Andrea Hall and finally Jackie Gilliam and Leah Lamp together. The murderers threw the bodies into gorges. They abandoned the site when their next intended victim escaped.

Manhattan Beach, 30 September 1979:
Manhattan Beach was where Shirley Sanders from Oregon became the only victim to escape. She had mace sprayed in her face and was raped by both men, but when they became careless, she escaped. Sanders returned to Oregon, unable to provide police with accurate details of the attack.

Hermosa Beach, 31 October 1979:
Bittaker and Norris became more blatant after their final murder. Thinking the effect would be amusing, they dumped the body of Lynette Ledford in the front lawn of a house picked at random in Hermosa Beach. They left her corpse in a bed of ivy.

Key   Bittaker and Norris's victims

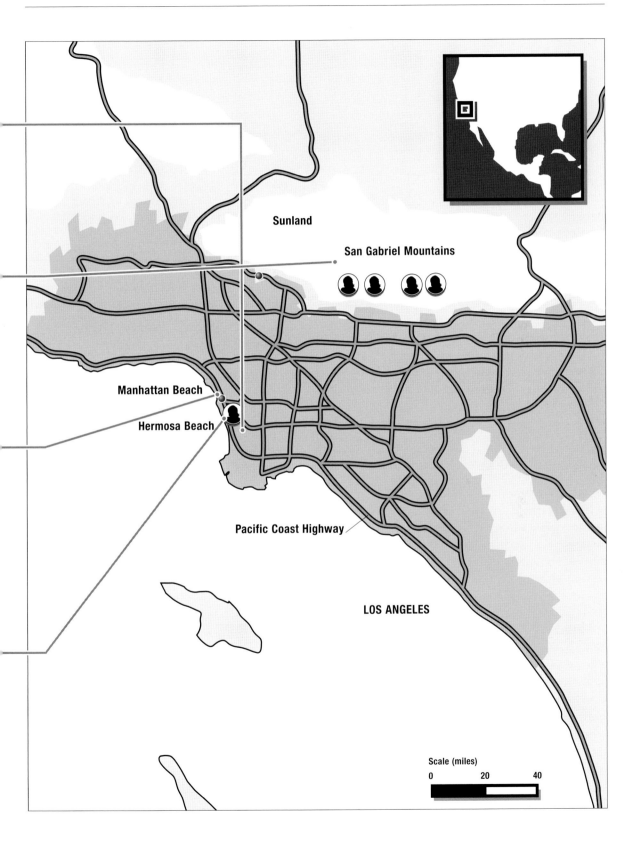

Sunland

San Gabriel Mountains

Manhattan Beach

Hermosa Beach

Pacific Coast Highway

LOS ANGELES

Scale (miles)

0   20   40

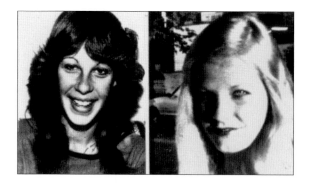

Two victims falling into the hands of Bittaker and Norris were Jackie Gilliam (left), 15, and Cindy Schaeffer, 16, their first victim as she left a church meeting.

what her argument would be for staying alive. He said she didn't put up much of an argument.'

Bittaker was getting impatient. Andrea was taking too much time to die, so he strangled her instead. Her body was thrown over a cliff into the canyon below.

Bittaker and Norris waited nearly two months before they once more ventured out in the Murder Mack. On 3 September 1979, they saw two girls, 15-year-old Jackie Gilliam and 13-year-old Leah Lamp, at a bus stop at the junction of Pier Avenue and the Pacific Coast Highway. When Bittaker offered them a ride – as well as a 'joint' – the two girls accepted.

Bittaker started the engine and told the girls that he was heading for the beach, but moments later they noticed that he was driving north instead, away from the ocean. Leah was so alarmed that when the van came to a halt near some tennis courts, she tried to open the passenger door. But Norris hit her over the head with a baseball bat. Then he trussed the girls up with duct tape as Bittaker started the engine and drove off at speed for the San Bernardino Mountains.

Once on the side road, Norris raped Jackie Gilliam while Bittaker kept a tape running to record her screams and pleas for mercy. The two girls were kept alive for two days as they were repeatedly tortured and assaulted. Finally, Bittaker decided to kill them and stabbed Jackie in both ears with an ice pick. When she failed to die, Bittaker and Norris took turns to strangle her. Leah was next: Bittaker grabbed her by the throat and started to strangle her while Norris

beat her on the head with a sledgehammer. By the seventh blow, Leah was dead. Together with Jackie, who still had the ice pick embedded in her head, Leah was thrown over the nearby cliff.

A Victim Survives

The next intended victim, Shirley Sanders, was attacked near Manhattan Beach on 30 September, when mace was sprayed in her face. She was dragged into the Murder Mack and both men raped her, but she managed to escape and report the assault. Unfortunately, her description of her attackers was vague and she was unable to remember the number on the van's licence plate.

Bittaker and Norris were now frantic with worry, expecting the police to arrive at any moment. For the next month, Bittaker remained in his new apartment in Burbank, while Norris stayed at his mother's trailer. But no police came for them. Their self-confidence restored, the pair resumed prowling on 31 October, targeting streets in the Sunland and Tujunga district in the San Fernando Valley.

There, they encountered 16-year-old Lynette Ledford. Bittaker decided to abandon his practice of driving into the San Bernardino Mountains before raping and killing the victim. Instead, he told Norris to drive round the Los Angeles suburbs while he switched on the tape recorder and went to work on Lynette. He started by slapping her, harder and harder, until she began to scream. Norris stopped the van and joined in, repeatedly hitting Lynette with a sledgehammer. Both of them raped her and tortured her with a pair of pliers. Finally, Bittaker wrapped a coat hanger round the girl's throat and twisted it with the pliers until she died.

This time, the killers left the corpse on the front lawn of a house in Hermosa Beach, where it was discovered the following morning. The event shocked Los Angeles, but the police had no evidence, no witnesses and no leads.

But then, Roy Norris revealed everything.

He had enjoyed the murder spree so much that he could not keep his mouth shut. He boasted about the murders to Jimmy Dalton, a friend from his days in prison. Dalton thought it was all hot air – until

Lynette's body was discovered. Accompanied by his lawyer, Dalton went to the Los Angeles police.

Dalton's revelations were not enough for the Hermosa Beach detective Paul Bynum to build a watertight case against Bittaker and Norris, but, he reckoned, a start could be made with Shirley Sanders, the only victim to have survived. Bynum provided an officer with photographs of both the killers and dispatched him to Oregon, where Shirley lived. She had no hesitation in identifying Bittaker and Norris as the men who had attacked and raped her.

The evidence was sufficient to arrest Bittaker, but Norris had to be trapped, too. The Hermosa police placed him under surveillance and he was seen selling marijuana on a Los Angeles street. They arrested him on the marijuana charge and jailed Bittaker for his crimes against Shirley Saunders.

Under questioning, Norris soon confessed. Both he and Bittaker were charged with five counts of murder, with extra charges for kidnapping, robbery, rape, sexual assault and conspiracy. In February 1980, realizing that he faced the death penalty, Norris made

> **"He boasted about the murders to Jimmy Dalton, a friend from his days in prison. He thought it was all hot air – until Lynette's body was discovered. Accompanied by his lawyer, Dalton went to the LA police."**

a plea bargain and showed the police the San Gabriel Mountain sites where the victims' bodies were to be found. He also gave evidence against Bittaker, and was rewarded at their trial with a life sentence in Pelican Bay prison near Crescent City, California, with the chance of parole after 30 years. Bittaker, however, was convicted on all counts and, on 24 March 1981, was sentenced to death. He remains on Death Row at San Quentin prison, near San Rafael, California.

LAWRENCE BITTAKER AND ROY NORRIS TIMELINE

27 September 1940: Lawrence Sigmund Bittaker born in Pittsburgh, Pennsylvania.

2 February 1948: Roy Lewis Norris born in Greeley, Colorado.

1977/8: Bittaker and Norris meet in prison at the Men's Colony, San Luis Obispo, California.

15 November 1978: Bittaker is released from San Luis Obispo.

15 January 1979: Norris is released from San Luis Obispo.

February 1979: Bittaker contacts Norris. Bittaker purchases the 'Murder Mack', a silver 1977 GMS cargo van, where he and Norris intend to torture and murder kidnapped girls.

February–June 1979: Bittaker and Norris 'practise' picking up girls along the Pacific Coast Highway, the venue they have chosen to locate their future murder victims.

24 June 1979: Bittaker and Norris kidnap and murder Cindy Schaeffer, 16, and throw her body into a ravine in the San Bernardino Mountains.

8 July 1979: Bittaker and Norris rape and kill 18-year-old Andrea Hall.

3 September 1979: Bittaker and Norris kidnap two girls, Jackie Gilliam, 15, and Leah Lamp, 13. They repeatedly assault them for two days, then kill them and throw their bodies over a nearby cliff.

30 September 1979: Bittaker and Norris kidnap Shirley Sanders and rape her, but she manages to get away.

31 October 1979: After lying low for a month, fearing arrest, Bittaker and Norris prowl for a victim in the Sunland and Tujunga district of the San Fernando Valley. They kidnap Lynette Ledford, 16, then torture, rape and kill her. Norris boasts about the murder spree to Jimmy Dalton, a friend

from prison. Dalton reports their conversation to the Los Angeles police. Shirley Sanders is interviewed at her Oregon home and identifies Bittaker and Norris as her attackers. Bittaker is jailed for raping and assaulting Shirley.

20 November 1979: Norris is arrested after he is seen selling marijuana in the street.

February 1980: Norris makes a plea bargain and implicates Bittaker, who is charged on five counts of murder, as well as rape, torture and kidnapping.

17 February 1981: At his trial, Bittaker is convicted on all counts. He is still on Death Row in San Quentin prison, California 28 years later.

24 March 1981: Norris is imprisoned for life with the chance of parole after 30 years, in 2010.

Gary Ridgway
The Green River Killer

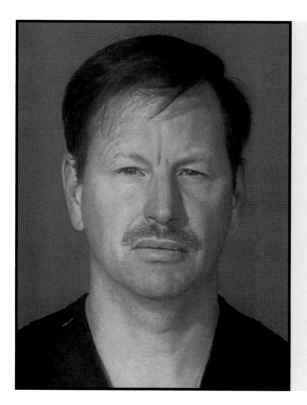

FULL NAME:
Gary Leon Ridgway

DOB:
5 February 1949

NUMBER OF VICTIMS:
Convicted of 48, suspected of
several more

SPAN OF KILLINGS:
1982–1998

LOCATION OF KILLINGS:
In and around the Green River near
Seattle, Washington

DATE OF ARREST:
30 November 2001

SENTENCE:
48 life sentences without parole

The Green River murderer who operated in the area in and around the Green River near Seattle, Washington State, challenged several records in the annals of serial killing. According to his own admission, the death count scaled extraordinary heights, with up to 90 victims. Although a special task force was created to find the killer, the case took nearly 20 years to solve despite the fact that the police got their hands on the culprit at the very start of those two decades. The investigation was the largest ever in US history and cost US$15 million, including US$200,000 for a special computer system to process more than 20,000 separate pieces of information.

Three victims of the Green River killer were found together on 15 August 1982 in and around the waterway that wound through Washington State near Seattle. Two of them – afterwards identified as Marcia Chapman, 31, and Cynthia Hinds, 17 – lay in the water, held down below the surface by rocks. Chapman had disappeared on 1 August 1982; Hinds, 10 days later. The third and youngest, Opal Mills, 16, last seen on 12 August, was discovered on the grass some 9m (30ft) away. All three had been strangled.

The First Victims

This, though, was not the beginning of the Green River killer's long career. On 15 July 1982, a month before the horrific triple discovery, the body of 16-year-old Wendy Lee Coffield was found floating in the Green River, a week after she had disappeared. Another woman, Deborah Bonner, 23, who vanished on 25 July, was found on 12 August, draped, naked, over a log in the river. Both had been strangled.

The Task Force Falters

Five dead woman, all of them murdered in the same way in and around the same place in Washington state, did not comprise a series of coincidences. The police soon geared up to hunt for a serial killer. A special Task Force was created in King County, Washington state, to solve the killings. The Force was led by high-ranking personalities – Major Richard Kraske, head of the Criminal Investigation Division, Detective Dave Reichert of the King County Major Crime Squad and John Douglas, the FBI's serial killer profiler. They were later joined by Robert Keppel, who had worked on the Ted Bundy case in 1974.

Yet, despite this range of talent, the Task Force soon faltered. This was due not to lack of expertise but to the flood of information that swamped the team from the first. The technology to deal with it was lacking at the time – the computer revolution began only in about 1981 – and existing methods were slow. All the same, they could be effective once detectives discovered that some victims were personally acquainted and had worked as prostitutes.

Police interviews were concentrated on prostitutes who 'worked' the 'strip' between South 139th Street

'Although a special task force was created to find the killer, the case took nearly 20 years to solve despite the fact that the police got their hands on the culprit at the very start of those two decades.'

and South 272nd Street in Seattle, seeking information about any suspicious characters the women may have encountered. Their work was not easy, for the prostitutes had a built-in distrust of the police, but one of them did produce a valuable clue; a man who had raped her, she told police, had talked about the Green River murders.

Two other women, who were interviewed separately, told the police that a man driving a white and blue truck had kidnapped and tried to kill them.

Ridgway was named 'the Green River Killer' because he put the first bodies of his victims in that waterway. Its name changes to Duwamish River before Seattle.

One of these women, 21-year-old Susan Widmark, described how a middle-aged man lured her into his truck, pointed a pistol at her head, then drove off fast. He stopped in a quiet road, where he raped her – violently. Afterwards, with the gun still at her head, he talked of the Green River murders. Realizing she was in danger of death, Widmark contrived to escape from the truck when it halted at the lights and memorized part of the registration number before her assailant drove the truck away. Another girl, Debra Estes, 15, recounted a similar story.

The First Arrests

The search for the murderer began in earnest soon after the interviews were completed and appeared to produce a rapid result. On 20 August 1982, only five days after the gruesome triple discovery at the River, an arrest was made. Unfortunately, there was insufficient evidence for a conviction, let alone a trial. The man in question was released, but he was soon succeeded by another suspect.

Charles Clinton Clark, a butcher who owned two handguns and a white and blue truck, was detained for assault, with the added suspicion that he was the Green River killer. Although both Widmark and Estes identified him as their assailant, other evidence failed to convince. Clark had a watertight alibi for the dates when the first few women disappeared. Secondly, murder did not appear to be part of his *modus operandi:* he was more intent on rape, and afterwards let his victims go. Debra Estes, for instance, was handcuffed and released in woodland.

Most significant, though, was the fact that another murder took place while Clark was in police custody. This sixth victim was 19-year-old Mary Bridgett Meehan, who disappeared on 15 September 1982 while walking near the Western Six Motel, which was located along the 'strip' in Seattle between South 139th Street and South 272nd Street. It was more than a year before her body was found, on 13 November 1983. Two weeks after Meehan vanished, on 29 August 1982, another girl, Terri Rene Milligan, had vanished, together with Kase Anne Lee: both were 16 years old. Lee's remains were never found. It was 20 months before Milligan's body was discovered, on 1 April

The Trail of Murders

Seattle, 1982:
Seattle was the centre for Ridgway's lethal strikes. He cruised along the city's 'strip' picking up prostitutes who frequented it. In his court statement, Ridgway said 'The plan was, I wanted to kill as many women I thought were prostitutes as I possibly could.'

Maple Valley, 3 May 1983
Maple Valley, just southeast of Seattle, was the small town where Ridgway left the body of Carol Ann Christensen, 21, in a macabre fashion. A brown paper bag was over her head, fish placed on her neck and left breast, and ground beef on one hand.

Interstate 90, 1984:
In 1984, Ridgway was leaving bodies near Interstate 90. One was found in April after a volunteer task force worker and psychic, Barbara Kubik-Pattern, had a vision of its location. When police ignored her, she and her daughter found the corpse of Amina Agisheff, 36.

Auburn, Washington, 30 November 2001:
Ridgway resided in Auburn, Washington State, with his wife of 13 years, Judith, who described him as gentle. He was a painter at the Kenworth Truck Company. The Green River runs through Auburn, and Ridgway buried many of his victims close to this residential area. He was arrested at his home in 2001.

Key   Ridgway's victims

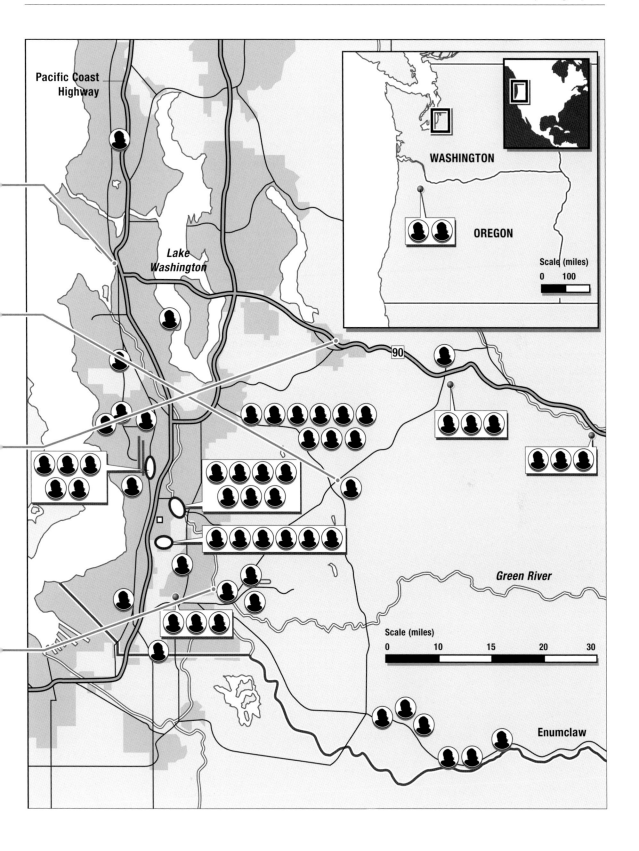

GARY RIDGWAY TIMELINE

15 July 1982: Children playing near Kent find strangled body of Wendy Coffield, 16, of Puyallup, in Green River.

13–15 August 1982: Bodies of four more young women found in or near Green River. Police suspect serial killer at work.

16 August 1982: King County police set up the biggest police task force since the Ted Bundy murders.

4 October 1982: Melvin Wayne Foster, 44, unemployed cab driver from Lacey, Thurston County, says he's a prime suspect in the Green River killings but that he's innocent.

30 April 1983: First apparent police attention to Gary Ridgway occurs when victim Marie Malvar disappears. Boyfriend follows pickup suspected in disappearance. Pickup is identified as Ridgway's. Des Moines police respond. Ridgway denies any contact with Malvar.

3 May 1983: Victim Carol Ann Christensen disappears from Pacific Highway South.

20 November 1983: Police say same man killed 11 women found in South King County since summer of 1982.

2 April 1984: Five more sets of skeletal remains found. Official number of victims attributed to the serial killer is 20, but number could be as high as 30.

20 April 1984: Two more sets of remains found near North Bend, including those of Amina Agisheff, 36, who was last seen in Seattle in 1982. Eventually listed as the killer's first victim.

May 1984: Ridgway contacts the Green River Task Force, ostensibly to offer information. Given a polygraph, he passes.

9 December 1984: Suspected toll rises to 42.

6 February 1986: Police search a home near Seattle-Tacoma International Airport. The occupant, described as a 'person of interest', is questioned by the task force.

May 1986: Officials say nothing links the man to the case.

8 April 1987: Police search home and vehicles of a man who was last seen with at least two of the victims. The victim list is now thought to number 46. Police take 'bodily samples' from the man, but there is insufficient evidence to arrest him. The man is Ridgway.

July 1991: Green River Task Force is essentially down to one investigator, Tom Jensen. The killer has not been found despite years of investigative work, the creation of the task force, the expenditure of more than $15 million, the use of a $200,000 computer, the accumulation of thousands of suspects and the filling of more than 750 three-ring binders with millions of facts.

2 November 1999: The remains of a victim found near the Green River in Kent in 1986 are identified as Tracy Winston, 19, last seen near Northgate in Seattle in 1983. Police use the new DNA process to identify her remains.

March 2001: State crime lab starts using the new DNA method to test Green River killer evidence.

30 November 2001: King County Sheriff Dave Reichert announces arrest of Ridgway, 52, of Auburn, in connection with the slayings of four of the early victims of the Green River killer. Ridgway's DNA is linked to three of them.

15 December 2001: Reichert assembles 11 investigators to work full-time on building evidence against Ridgway.

18 December 2001: Ridgway enters Not Guilty plea to four counts of aggravated murder in deaths of Marcia Chapman, 31; Cynthia Hinds, 17; and Opal Mills, 16 – whose bodies were all found in or near the Green River on 15 August 1982; and Carol Christensen, 21, whose remains were found outside Maple Valley on 8 May 1983.

27 March 2003: Ridgway is charged with aggravated first-degree murder in the slayings of three more women: Coffield, 16; Debra Bonner, 23, and Debra Estes, 15. Police and prosecutors say microscopic paint dust on the clothing of three women ties Ridgway, a truck painter, to their deaths.

3 April 2003: Ridgway pleads Not Guilty in King County Superior Court to the three most recent charges of aggravated first-degree murder.

26 July 2003: Ridgway is moved from the King County jail in Seattle to an undisclosed location amid reports he may want to co-operate with authorities in return for taking the death penalty off the table.

19 August 2003: 16-year-old Pammy Avent's remains, found east of Enumclaw, are identified, after reports that Ridgway is trading information for his life.

24 August 2003: Seven more bones are found by detectives investigating the Green River serial killings. An investigator from the King County Medical Examiner's Office says the bones appear to be human.

27 September 2003: The bones of 17-year-old April Buttram are identified. The Green River Task Force announces that two bones found on 30 August and 2 September near Snoqualmie match the DNA of Buttram, who vanished in late August 1983.

2 October 2003: Green River Task Force investigators identify remains found in a ravine outside Auburn as those of Marie Malvar, who was 18 when she disappeared on 30 April 1983.

October 2003: Ridgway provides details of at least two slayings that were not on the official list: Patricia Yellow Robe, 38, who was found dead on 6 August 1998, and Marta Reeves, 36, who was killed in 1990.

5 November 2003: Ridgway pleads guilty to 48 counts of aggravated first-degree murder, including 42 of the original 49 murders attributed to the Green River serial killer. The other counts involve Linda Rule, Roberta Hayes, Marta Reeves, Patricia Barczak, Patricia Yellow Robe and an unidentified victim.

'Marie Malvar went missing on 30 April. She was seen by her boyfriend, apparently having an argument with a truck driver before getting into his vehicle. Malvar's boyfriend gave chase, but lost the truck at stoplights.'

1984. Even so, in 1982, the suspicion was that she, too, was another victim of the Green River killer.

The suspect this time was an unemployed taxi driver who had volunteered to work on the Green River case. But the only evidence against him was that he was acquainted with five of the six victims so far found. More cogent, though, was his apparent similarity to a profile of the killer authored by FBI agent John Douglas. Douglas reckoned that he was middle-aged – the taxi driver was 44 years old – and that he made a habit of visiting the murder scenes around the Green River and was devoutly, perhaps fanatically, religious.

While the Task Force was diligently monitoring the taxi driver's movements, the body of a 17-year-old prostitute, Gisele Ann Lovvorn, was found in an advanced state of decomposition on 25 September 1982, near empty houses south of the Sea-Tac International Airport. Lovvorn had disappeared 10 weeks earlier, on 17 July. She had been strangled with a pair of men's black socks. The airport was not in the immediate vicinity of the Green River but police were convinced that she, too, had fallen victim to the same killer as the rest of the women so far found.

Insufficient Evidence

In the seven months between the discovery of Lovvorn's corpse and April 1983, a total of 14 women and girls disappeared, all of them prostitutes frequenting the Seattle 'strip'. The last of them, Marie Malvar, went missing on 30 April. She was seen by her boyfriend, apparently having an argument with a truck driver before getting into his vehicle. Malvar's boyfriend gave chase, but lost the truck at stoplights.

About a week later, Malvar's father and brother saw the truck driver again and followed him to a house in Seattle's South 348th Street. They called the police, who arrived to interview the driver, a man named Gary Ridgway. Ridgway managed to convince the police that he never even knew Marie Malvar and no arrest was made.

Ridgway stands as the judge gives him 48 life sentences. The murderer avoided the death sentence by agreeing to help police locate the remains of his victims.

Carol Estes holds up a picture of her murdered daughter, Deborah, during a press conference. Deborah had disappeared on 20 September 1982.

Already, though, the investigation into the Green River killings seemed to be running into the ground. The police had no credible suspects and by now some 39 women had disappeared, with the bodies of 18 found in and around the Green River area. The 44-year-old taxi driver had been taken off the list of suspects, for the chance of convicting him of murder now appeared low. There were no other leads, only the continued disappearance of young Seattle prostitutes and a mountain of tips and information, which the police were struggling — and failing – to sort out.

At this juncture, one of the Task Force detectives, Mark Haney, decided on a different tack. He remained deeply suspicious of Gary Ridgway, even though Ridgway had taken and passed a lie detector test in 1984. Haney decided to dig deeper into the existing information about Ridgway, and came up with a revelation. The detective discovered that, in 1982, Ridgway had been questioned by police while in his truck with a prostitute. The prostitute, it turned out, was Keli McGinness, 18, who later appeared on a list of possible Green River victims after she disappeared

on 28 June 1983. McGinness' body was never found and no charges had ever been filed.

Nevertheless, Haney still suspected that Ridgway was the Green River killer. Many of the bodies already found had been left on dumpsites that, according to Ridgway's ex-wife, her former husband visited frequently. In addition, when Ridgway's description was circulated among prostitutes on the Seattle 'strip', many of them recognized him as a man who passed by regularly on his way to work and could often be seen at other times, cruising the area. Ridgway, it transpired, was employed as a truck painter at the Kenworth Truck Company in Seattle. When Haney consulted his work record, it transpired that every time Ridgway was absent from the factory, another Green River victim disappeared.

Although all this provided grounds for suspicion, it was only circumstantial evidence, not the sort on which to build a solid case for multiple Murder One.

Haney's task was made more difficult by the fact that in 1984 there were only two Green River-style disappearances, none in 1985 and one in 1986, and only one body – 16-year old Mary Exzetta West's – was found over that three-year period. Fresh evidence that might have supported Haney's theory about Gary Ridgway seemed to be fading fast. Growing desperate, the police placed Ridgway in custody and obtained a warrant to search his house. The search took place on 8 April 1987, but nothing incriminating was found. The police also took hair and saliva samples from Ridgway, hoping to find a match with material left on the bodies of some of the Green River killer's victims. But to their great disappointment, there was insufficient evidence and Ridgway had to be released.

Subsequently, and before the whole ghastly sequence was over, there were two more murders that could be ascribed to the Green River killer, bringing the total of known killings to 48. Marta Reeves, 36, disappeared some time in the spring of 1990; her body was discovered several months later, on 20 September. Patricia Yellow robe, 38, disappeared in 1998 and was discovered on 6 August the same year. At that stage, it seemed that the Green River killings might join the history of other unsolved murders, but a revolution in crime detection would eventually reveal the truth in the Green River and many other criminal cases.

Caught by DNA

In the United States, the first state appellate court decision to admit DNA evidence was made in Florida in 1988, and in subsequent years DNA evidence gradually became a regular feature of criminal cases. DNA examinations were applied to the hair and saliva samples taken in 1987 and with that the case of the Green River killings opened up at last.

'What cracked this case,' one police official remarked, 'was science.'

On 30 November 2001, Ridgway was at the Kenworth factory, hurrying to finish work early in order to attend a party. But there would be no party for him. Instead, police arrived to arrest him on suspicion of murder. Their evidence comprised semen the DNA of which matched that found in four of the

'When Ridgway's description was circulated among prostitutes on the Seattle "strip", many of them recognized him as a man who passed by regularly on his way to work and could often be seen at other times.'

Green River victims who had been raped before being killed. Subsequently, three more victims were added to the roster when forensics laboratories found tiny particles that matched the paint used at Ridgway's place of work.

Five days later, on 5 December, Gary Ridgway was formally charged with murdering four women: Marcia Chapman, Opal Mills, Cynthia Hinds and Carol Ann Christensen, 21, who disappeared on 3 May 1983 and was found dead in a wood near Maple Valley, in King County, Washington, five days later.

On 5 November 2003, almost 20 years after his killing spree began. Gary Ridgway pleaded guilty to 48 charges of 'aggravated first degree murder'. It was part of a plea bargain that ensured that the death sentence would not apply as long as he aided the police in locating the as yet undiscovered remains of his victims. He was sentenced instead to serve 48 life sentences without hope of parole.

This apparent act of clemency towards a killer who claimed to have committed 90 murders, and who looked on his serial killings as his 'career', caused a good deal of controversy in the United States. But Norman Maleng, the King County prosecuting attorney who authored the plea bargain deal, explained the value of Ridgway's information on the whereabouts of his undiscovered victims:

'This deal was an avenue to the truth.... Gary Ridgway does not deserve our mercy. He does not deserve to live. (But) the mercy provided by today's resolution is directed ... towards the families who have suffered so much.'

Richard Ramirez

The Night Stalker

FULL NAME:
Ricardo Levya Muñoz Ramirez

DOB:
29 February 1960

NUMBER OF VICTIMS:
13

SPAN OF KILLINGS:
June 1984–August 1985

LOCATION OF KILLINGS:
Los Angeles, California, USA

DATE OF ARREST:
31 August 1985

SENTENCE:
The death penalty (gas chamber);
he remains on Death Row

Richard Ramirez, born in El Paso, Texas, on 29 February 1960, was a Devil worshipper who punctuated the courtroom at his trial in 1989 with regular cries of of 'Hail, Satan!'. Popularly known as the Night Stalker for using the hours of darkness for his serial killings, Ramirez caused a wave of panic in and around Los Angeles in 1984 and 1985, committing murders that for sheer horror have rarely, if ever, been equalled.

Richard Ramirez, real name Ricardo Levya Muñoz Ramirez, was the youngest, epileptic, child of a Mexican family of five sons. An incident when he was barely in his teens presaged a gruesome future. In 1973, aged 13, he saw his cousin Michael murder his wife by shooting her in the face. Ramirez was spattered with the woman's blood. Michael was a Vietnam War veteran and was so acutely brutalized by the experience that he boasted of torturing and mutilating enemy combatants: what was more, he had the Polaroid pictures to prove it.

Making Fantasies Real

The young Ramirez, who kept company with Michael for long periods of time, was fascinated by these ghastly pictures, and it may be no coincidence that shortly after the murder he began to smoke marijuana. Before long, the youngster was thieving to buy supplies of the drug. That led to more elaborate thefts, with Ramirez regularly breaking and entering houses to steal whatever valuables he could find. Somewhere along the line, he started to indulge in fantasies, horrible fantasies involving violence, brutality and bloodshed. For a while, just thinking about them satisfied him. But the day came when that was no longer good enough, and Ramirez began to turn fantasy into reality.

The evening of 28 June 1984 was very hot in Los Angeles and 79-year-old Jennie Vincow decided to leave a window open to make her apartment in Glassel Park a bit cooler. It was a fatal mistake. That night, Ramirez climbed in through the window. Next day, Jennie was discovered by her son sprawled out on her bed, smothered in blood from several stab wounds and a cut throat. She had been sexually assaulted, and her throat had been slashed so deeply that she was almost decapitated. The killer had ransacked the apartment and several valuables were missing. The only clues to the murderer's identity was a fingerprint found on the windowsill.

A Lucky Escape

Eight months later, Ramirez struck again. This time, his victim, was much younger, 20-year-old Angela Barrios, who lived in a condominium in Rosemead, a town northeast of Los Angeles. On 17 March 1985,

'Somewhere along the line, he started to indulge in fantasies involving violence, brutality and bloodshed. For a while, just thinking about them satisfied him. But the day came when that was no longer enough ...'

Angela Barrios came home late from work at around 11.30 p.m. She had just used the remote control to open her garage and was getting out of her car when Ramirez rushed up, dressed from head to foot in black and brandishing a gun. The gun was pointed at her face. Angela begged for her life, but Ramirez ignored her pleas. He fired and she collapsed onto

A police drawing of the murder suspect issued in 1985 bears a striking likeness to Ramirez. A surviving victim, Lilian Doi, gave police a description in April.

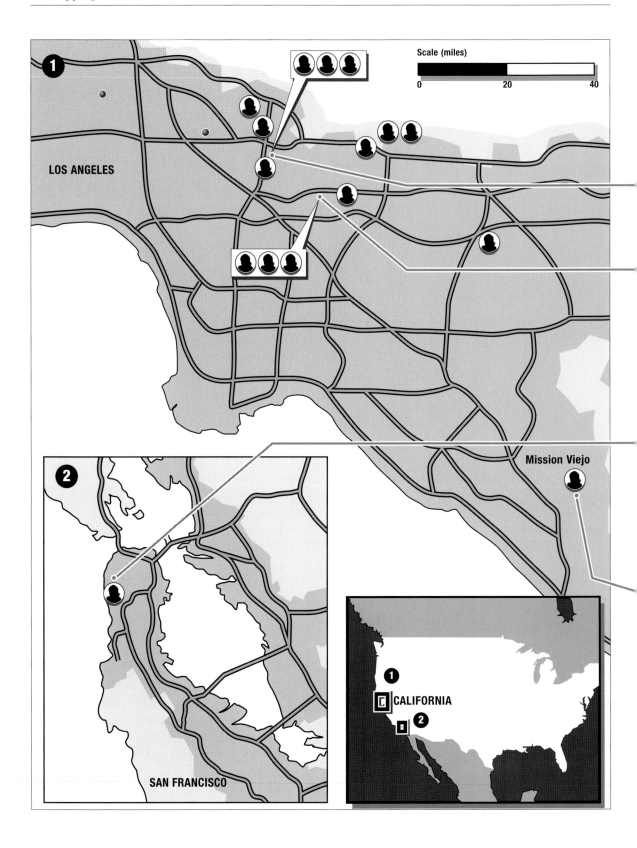

The Trail of Murders

Eagle Rock, March 1985:
Three early murders happened in Eagle Rock, a community in the mountains of northeast Los Angeles. On 20 March 1985, Ramirez killed an 8-year-old girl and a week later shot dead Vincent Zazzara, 64, and his wife Maxine, 44, gouging out her eyes.

Monterey Park, March, April and July 1985:
Monterey Park, whose boundary touches Los Angeles, saw three of Ramirez's attacks in 1985. In the first, on 17 March, Tsia-Lian Yu was beaten to death in her car. Then, on 15 April, William Doi was murdered in his home. On 7 July, Sophie Dickman survived an attack.

Lake Merced, 18 August 1985:
Taking an unusual trip out of Los Angeles for victims, Ramirez travelled to San Francisco's suburb Lake Merced, where he killed Peter Pan, 66, and his wife Barbara, 64. Afterwards he used lipstick to write 'Jack the Knife' on the wall and added an inverted pentagram.

Mission Viejo, 25 August 1985:
Ramirez made a fatal mistake by visiting Mission Viejo, 80km (50 miles) south of Los Angeles. A teenager became suspicious of his car in the neighbourhood and passed the number plate along to police. Indeed, Ramirez had attacked and seriously injured a couple there.

Key
Ramirez's victims

'Angela started to scramble away, ran into her attacker as he came out of the front door of the condominium, but managed to reach the garage. All the while, she was sure he would fire again and kill her ...'

the concrete floor of the garage. But she was not dead. In fact, she was not even seriously injured. Angela had tried to shield her face with her hand. The shot had ricocheted off the car keys she was still holding and did not more than graze her hand, which was bleeding. Ramirez, meanwhile, had gone inside the condominium.

Angela started to scramble away, ran into her attacker as he came out of the front door of the condominium, but managed to reach the garage. All the while, she was sure he would fire again and kill her, but suddenly he pushed the gun into his belt and made off.

Ramirez had already found his victim. Angela found her roommate, 34-year-old Dayle Okazaki, lying in a spreading pool of blood on the kitchen floor. There was a bullet wound in her forehead and her blood was everywhere – on the furniture, the kitchen appliance and the walls. When the police arrived, Ramirez was long gone, but they did find his baseball cap lying on the garage floor.

Savage Violence

Meanwhile, Richard Ramirez had already sought out his next victim. In nearby Monterey Park, a woman was found unconscious on the ground close to a yellow Chevrolet, which was parked with its motor still running. She had been shot several times and was still alive, though barely. She was a 30-year-old Taiwanese woman named Tsia-Lian Yu and though the police officer who discovered her did his best to save her, she died before the ambulance could arrive.

From this point onwards, the serial killings escalated. On 20 March 1985, Ramirez killed a girl of 8 at Eagle Rock, California and followed this up on 27 March by murdering two people, Vincent Zazzara, 64, a retired investment counsellor, and his 44-year-old wife Maxine. Vincent had been killed relatively cleanly, by a shot in the head, but Maxine was in a fearful state. She, too, had been shot, but in addition, her eyes had been gouged out and there were several stab wounds in her face and neck, her abdomen and groin. There was a large wound in the shape of a T on her left breast. Mercifully, it seemed that these frightful injuries had been inflicted after she died. The Zazzara home had been ransacked and valuables were stolen.

The next killing was equally horrific, though this time, there was a survivor. On 15 April 1985, Ramirez broke into the home in Monterey Park of William and

RICHARD RAMIREZ TIMELINE

29 February 1960: Richard Ramirez (Ricardo Levya Muñoz Ramirez) is born, the youngest, epileptic, child in a Mexican family of five sons.

1973: Ramirez, aged 13, witnesses his cousin Michael, a deeply disturbed Vietnam War veteran, murder his wife. Shortly afterwards, the teenager becomes a marijuana addict and indulges in bloodthirsty fantasies.

28 June 1984: Ramirez, now a Satanist, kills his first victim, Jennie Vincow, 79, in her Los Angeles apartment. He leaves a fingerprint on a windowsill.

17 March 1985: Ramirez attacks Angela Barrios, 20. She survives, but her roommate, Dayle Okazaki, 34, is killed.

20 March 1985: Ramirez kills a girl of 8 at Eagle Rock, California.

27 March: Vincent Zazzara, 64, is shot dead by Ramirez at Eagle Rock, California. His 44-year-old wife Maxine is also shot dead, and is stabbed and mutilated after death.

15 April 1985: Ramirez murders William Doi, 66, at his home in Monterey Park and ties up and rapes his wife Lilian, 63, who survives the attack.

29 May 1985: Two sisters, Malvia Keller, 83, and the disabled Blanche Wolfe, 80, are attacked with a hammer at their home in Monrovia, Los Angeles County. Malvia is raped and murdered. Blanche is assailed with the hammer, but survives.

30 May 1985: Ruth Wilson, 41, is raped by Ramirez at her home in Burbank, California, and her 12-year-old son is attacked. Both of them survive.

2 July 1985: Mary Louise Cannon, 75, is murdered by Ramirez at her home in Arcadia. She is beaten, her throat is cut and her house is ransacked.

5 July 1985: Ramirez beats Whitney Bennett, 16, with a tyre iron. She needs 478 stitches but survives her injuries.

7 July 1985: The corpse of Joyce Lucille Nelson is found at her Monterey Park home.

7 July 1985: Ramirez tries but fails to rape and sodomize Sophie Dickman, a 63-year-old registered nurse in Monterey Park. He ransacks her home, but then leaves.

20 July 1985: Lela and Max Kneiding, both 66, are attacked by Ramirez in Glendale, Los Angeles. He is wielding a machete but finds it inefficient. Instead, he shoots the couple dead. Then, he uses the machete to mutilate both of them, and ransacks the house.

6 August 1985: Ramirez breaks into the Northridge, Los Angeles, home of Christopher Petersen, 38, and his wife Virginia, 27. Ramirez shoots both of them. Both survive.

8 August 1985: In Diamond Bar in Los Angeles County, Ramirez shoots and kills Elyas Abowath, 35, and rapes and sodomizes his wife Sakina, 27.

18 August 1985: Peter Pan, 66, an accountant and his wife Barbara, 64, are shot by Ramirez at their home in Lake Merced in San Francisco. Peter is killed and though Barbara survives, she becomes an invalid for life.

24 August 1985: William Carns and his 29-year-old fiancée are attacked by Ramirez in

Mission Viejo, south of Los Angeles. Carns is seriously injured, his fiancée is tied up, raped twice and forced to declare her 'love' for Satan. But she survives.

25 August 1985: A teenage biker sees an orange-coloured Toyota car arriving and leaving Mission Viejo on the previous night and gives its licence plate number to the police.

27 August 1985: The Toyota is located in the Rampart district of Los Angeles and is found to be stolen. A fingerprint is found inside the Toyota and identified as belonging to Richard Ramirez. It matches the print discovered on Jennie Vincow's windowsill in June 1984.

31 August 1985: Ramirez arrives back in Los Angeles after visiting his brother in Tucson, Arizona. His picture is displayed on a magazine cover and he is recognized. After a long chase, he is apprehended by three passers-by, who hold him down until the police arrive.

22 July 1988: Jury selection begins for the trial of Ramirez.

20 September 1989: Ramirez is found guilty of 13 killings, 5 attempted murders, 11 sexual assaults and 14 burglaries. He is sentenced to death.

6 August 2006: The last appeal by Ramirez, one of many, fails.

7 September 2006: The California Supreme Court rejects an application by Ramirez for a new hearing.

'She, too, had been shot, but in addition, her eyes had been gouged out and there were stab wounds to her face and neck, her abdomen and groin. There was a large wound in the shape of a T on her left breast.'

Lilian Doi. William Doi, 66, was shot in the head and lived long enough to phone for an ambulance. He died while being rushed to hospital. His wife, Lilian 63, was tied up and raped, but was otherwise uninjured and was subsequently able to give the police a description of the assailant.

The police released a mugshot of Ramirez; when members of the public recognized him, they helped to restrain him.

A Killer Boasts

Two elderly sisters, Malvia Keller, 83, and Blanche Wolfe, 80, were both attacked with a hammer at their home at Monrovia in Los Angeles County on 29 May 1985. Two pentagrams – a magic symbol in the form of a five-pointed star – were found, one on a bedroom wall, the other drawn in lipstick on Malvia's inner thigh. Malvia, who had been raped as well as severely battered, died of her injuries, but doctors managed to save Blanche.

In the next three months, Ramirez mounted 11 more attacks, causing a wave of panic in Los Angeles and the surrounding parts of California. Six of his victims died, but another 16 survived. One of the most bizarre assaults was the last, the attack on William Carns and his fiancée at their home in Mission Viejo, 80km (50 miles) south of Los Angeles, on 24 August 1985. Ramirez shot William Carns, seriously wounding him, but grabbed his 29-year-old fiancée by the hair and lugged her into another bedroom. There, he took several neckties out of the wardrobe and tied her up. Next, he raped her twice.

The Night Stalker, as Ramirez was being described by then, had been sensational fare for the newspapers and television for several weeks, and he now freely boasted to his terrified captive that he was the killer who had attracted all this coverage. Certain now that he was going to add her to his list of victims, she told Ramirez about a drawer where there was money. Ramirez took it, but then told her to swear her love for Satan. She did so, and Ramirez then made her repeat 'I love Satan' over and over again. Next,

'Ramirez shot William Carns, seriously wounding him, but grabbed his 29-year-old fiancée by the hair and lugged her into another bedroom. There he took several neckties out of the wardrobe and tied her up.'

Ramirez demanded that she perform oral sex on him. But when it was finished, instead of killing her as she still expected, Ramirez just laughed at her and left.

Unknown to Ramirez, something had happened earlier that same night that was going to bring his reign of terror to an abrupt end. An orange-coloured Toyota had caught the attention of a teenager who was working on his motorcycle as it drove into Mission Viejo. A short while later, the car drove out again. The boy became suspicious and took a note of the car's licence plate number. On the morning of 25 August, he informed the police, who discovered that the plate belonged to a 1976 model stolen in Chinatown, Los Angeles. With its distinctive colour, the Toyota was soon located, on 27 August, in the Rampart district of Los Angeles.

The police kept the Toyota under surveillance for the next 24 hours, hoping that the driver would return, but he never did. The car had another purpose, though. A forensic team thoroughly worked over the vehicle and came up with a clear fingerprint; within hours, the Sacramento laboratory had identified it as belonging to Ricardo Levya Muñoz Ramirez, the petty thief who had been so frequently in trouble with the police in the 1970s. What was more, it matched the fingerprint left on Jennie Vincow's windowsill in June 1984.

Actually detaining Richard Ramirez was not quite so straightforward. On 31 August 1985, he was at the Greyhound bus station in downtown Los Angeles after arriving from a visit to his brother's home in Tucson, Arizona. But until he stopped off at a corner store, he did not know that he had walked into a veritable

'rogues' gallery' featuring a single wanted criminal: himself. His face was plastered all over the cover of *LA Opinion*, which filled the magazine rack, and he was recognized immediately. Ramirez ran off and covered 3km (2 miles) in the next 12 minutes, heading east. He tried to steal a red Ford Mustang for a quicker getaway, but was spotted by the owner, Faustino Pinon, who lugged him out of the driving seat and threw him to the ground.

Ramirez managed to get away, but he was closely pursued by three passers-by, Manuel de la Torres and two young brothers, Jaime and Julio Burgoin. During the pursuit, all three kept on hitting Ramirez until, at last, he collapsed to the ground and they were able to hold him down until the police arrived.

Sentenced to Death

At his trial, which began on 22 July 1988 with jury selection, Ramirez was charged with 13 killings, 5 attempted murders, 11 sexual assaults and 14 burglaries. On 20 September 1989, he was found

The wedding photo of Ramirez and Doreen Lioy, 41, was taken in the visiting room of San Quentin prison. They married while Ramirez was on Death Row there.

'Ramirez was charged with 13 killings, five attempted murders, 11 sexual assaults and 14 burglaries. On 20 September, he was found guilty on all these counts and was sentenced to die in the gas chamber.'

guilty on all these counts and was sentenced to die in the gas chamber at San Quentin prison near San Rafael, California.

'I will be in Hell with Satan!' Ramirez is said to have remarked when told he faced execution.

Even so, the usual protracted round of appeals began soon after sentencing. It took 17 years, until 7 August 2006, for all these avenues to be exhausted. A month later, on 7 September 2006, the California

During his trial, Ramirez seemed unwilling to defend himself. When the judge said the trial must continue, Ramirez shouted and had to be restrained.

Supreme Court disallowed an application from Ramirez for another hearing. All the same, after 20 years, he remains on Death Row at San Quentin prison. Satan, it seems, will have to wait some time longer.

Tommy Lynn Sells

Serial Killer and Predator

FULL NAME:
Tommy Lynn Sells

DOB:
28 June 1964

NUMBER OF VICTIMS:
6–70

SPAN OF KILLINGS:
1985–31 December 1999

LOCATION OF KILLINGS:
Missouri, New York, Illinois and Texas, USA

DATE OF ARREST:
2 January 2000

SENTENCE:
The death penalty (lethal injection); he remains on Death Row

Tommy Lynn Sells began killing young. He claims that he was 16 years old when he committed his first murder. Five years passed before he killed again, and by the time he was apprehended, in 2000, at least another 22 people in 13 US states were dead, including two entire families. That may not have been the end of it. Sells has boasted that his real total exceeds the number of killings to which he confessed: moving from 'coast to coast', a phrase he used to denote the spread of his killings, he says he took 70 lives in all.

Tommy Lee Sells was a daunting illustration of the theory that a damaged boyhood breeds a dangerous man. At age 2, in 1966, Sells' neglectful mother sent him to live with his aunt, Bonnie Walpole, then took

him back three years later to prevent Walpole from adopting him. When he was 7 years old, Sells was already a truant from school, and the following year he was allowed to spend time with a man who molested him. By that time, Sells was already a regular drinker and, at age 10, he moved on to marijuana. When he was about 13 years old, Sells slept with his grandmother and tried to rape his mother. Finally, at 14, he was off on his own, travelling the United States by freight train, stealing whatever he needed, including cars, begging on the streets or working short-term in a variety of menial jobs.

In July 1985, when he was 21 years old, Sells was working at a carnival in Forsyth, Missouri. There, he met Ena Cordt, 35, who had brought her 4-year-old son to the carnival as a treat. Cordt found Sells

'Tommy Lynn Sells was a daunting illustration of the theory that a damaged boyhood breeds a dangerous man.'

attractive and invited him back to her home that same evening. According to Sells, he had sex with Cordt, but awoke during the night to find her stealing from his backpack. Seizing her son's baseball bat, he beat her to death. He also murdered her son in case he could be used as a witness. The two badly bludgeoned bodies were found three days later, by which time, of course, Tommy Lynn Sells had moved on. This, in fact, became part of his technique – to make sure he was somewhere else when his killings were discovered.

A Savage Killer

Two years later, in May 1987, Sells was apparently in a bar in Lockport in Niagara County, New York, when a quarrel broke out between 28-year-old Suzanne Korcz and her boyfriend. Korcz stalked out in a fury – and disappeared. Her skeleton was found in 1995 at the bottom of a long, steep slope on the American side of Niagara Falls. Seven years later, in 2002, Sells confessed to investigators that he had killed Korcz. His description of the victim and the circumstances of her disappearance convinced them that, this time at least, he was telling the truth.

It was much more usual, though, for Sells's accounts of his exploits to prove unreliable. What is beyond doubt is the savagery of the Sells style of killing. This was revealed once again in 1987, when he murdered a family of four, the Dardeens, at Ina, Illinois, 129km (80 miles) from St Louis in Missouri.

According to Sells, he was at a truck stop when he met Keith Dardeen, who invited him to his trailer home. Relatives, and others who knew Dardeen, find his account hard to believe. Dardeen was mortally afraid of crime and criminals, and was unlikely to ask a stranger to his home, particularly as his pregnant wife and 3-year-old son were there. At this time, Sells was a heavy drinker and a drug addict: his preference

was for heroin, but he would take, or snort, any other drug that was to hand. Between the drink and the drugs, Sells was often in a dazed state, a circumstance unlikely to be lost on Keith Dardeen.

However that may have been, something sparked off a ferocious rage and, once inside the trailer, Sells began to kill. He may have murdered Keith Dardeen in the field near Ina, where his body was found by hunters shortly before Thanksgiving. Dardeen was shot in the head and, hopefully, was already dead when his killer mutilated his genitals. Sells went on to rape his wife Elaine and afterwards bludgeon her to death. He also murdered young Pete. During the frenzied attack, Elaine went into premature labour and gave birth to a daughter: the infant lived only a few minutes before Sells battered her to death.

Personality Disorders

After this, it appears that Tommy Lynn Sells got into his stride and more killings followed in 1988 and

Sells arrives in Little Rock, Arkansas, to talk about two murders he claims to have committed. He has delayed his execution by slowly releasing details of his killings.

1989. As he told investigators, he went on a veritable binge while moving from place to place around the United States. Sells professes to have killed a teenage girl in New Hampshire and a woman and her 3-year-old son on a bridge near Twin Falls, Idaho. Moving on to Arizona, he became involved in a fight over marijuana in a hobo camp at Tucson, and knifed to death a man named Kent Lauten, aged 51. This was followed by the killings of a prostitute in Truckee, California, and a female hitchhiker in Oregon.

On 12 January 1990, Tommy Sells was in the town of Rawlings, Wyoming, where he stole a truck, sold the tyres to a young couple and used the money to buy drugs. Taking other items from the theft, he then hid out near the railway track. There, he waited for a freight train, meaning to jump on board and so travel to his next destination. By this time, Sells was high on narcotics and when the freight train arrived, he staggered when trying to get on board. Unfortunately for him, his wobbly performance was witnessed by a police officer, and Sells was arrested for being drunk in public and also for possession of stolen goods. The result was a sentence of 16 months' imprisonment.

In fact, he spent only 12 months in prison, but they were nightmare months. The drugs he had been taking induced anxiety attacks and hallucinations, which were diagnosed as personality disorders, psychoses and addictions. The medications prescribed for him by psychiatrists managed to sort out his addled brain, but did nothing for his continuing urge to kill. Once released, Sells returned to murder, killing Margaret McClain and her daughter in Charleston, West Virginia, in September 1991.

In May 1992, Sells was still in Charleston, begging for food on a street corner and holding up a notice that read: 'Hungry. Will work for food.' A young woman, 20 years old, took pity on him. Taking him home, she gave him food and clothing, only to be attacked. Sells raped her and stabbed her repeatedly, but she fought back, managed to get hold of the knife and slashed him 23 times. Grabbing a piano stool, Sells beat her with it and then left, believing that she was dead. But she survived and later identified Sells as her assailant. Charged with malicious wounding, he pleaded guilty and was sentenced to a prison term of

The Trail of Murders

Lockport, New York, May 1987:
Sells criss-crossed America for 20 years searching for victims. This led him once to Lockport, New York, where he murdered Suzanne Korcz, 28. She had had an argument with her boyfriend in a bar and Sells took advantage. He left her body at Niagara Falls.

Charleston, West Virginia, 1991 and 1992:
Released from jail in 1991, Sells returned to murder in Charleston, West Virginia. He killed Margaret McClain and her daughter, Pamela, in September, and the next May raped and stabbed a 20-year-old woman who survived and identified him, putting him back in prison.

Ina, Illinois, 1987:
One of Sells's most savage killings occurred in Ina, Illinois, in 1987 when he murdered an entire family. He shot Keith Dardeen dead, raped and bludgeoned his pregnant wife Elaine, who gave birth during the attack, killed the infant, and also their 3-year-old son.

Del Rio, Texas, 1998:
Sells seemed to settle with his new wife, Jessica Levrie, in Del Rio, Texas, in 1998, but more murder followed. In nearby Guajia Bay, he killed 12-year-old Katy Harris in December 1999 and seriously wounded her friend Krystal Surles, who testified against him.

Key Sells's victims

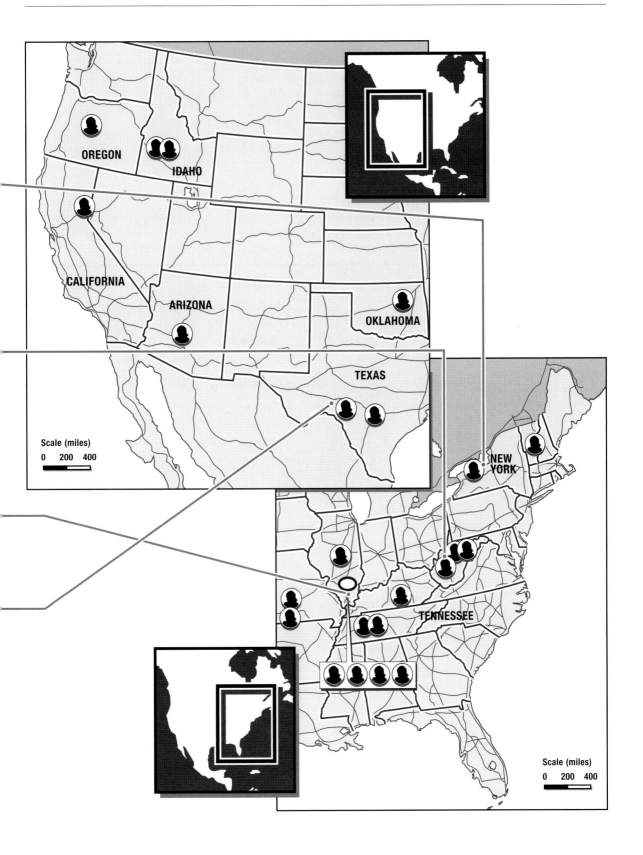

OREGON

IDAHO

CALIFORNIA

ARIZONA

OKLAHOMA

TEXAS

Scale (miles)
0   200   400

NEW
YORK

TENNESSEE

Scale (miles)
0   200   400

Sells takes a break outside the courtroom in Del Rio, Texas, in 2000. His conservative dress, including a suit covering his tattoos, could not overcome the evidence.

up to 10 years in West Virginia state prison. He served less than four, but before his release in May 1997, he was diagnosed as suffering from bipolar disorder, formerly known as manic depression. Sells also got married, to a woman called Nora Price. Once he was out of prison, the couple moved to Tennessee. Although she soon fell pregnant, Price found herself deserted by her husband, who resumed his cross-country travels together with his murderous habits. He later claimed that, in October 1997, he strangled a 13-year-old girl, Stephanie Mahaney, near Springfield, Missouri, and left her corpse in a pond.

Full Confession

In the winter of 1997, Sells joined the Heart of America carnival, which advertised itself as 'the best in family entertainment.' He operated the Ferris wheel and drove one of the the trucks that took the carnival between towns. Late in February 1998, the carnival reached Del Rio, Texas, a town bordering Mexico, on

the Rio Grande below the Amistad Reservoir dam. During the carnival's eight-day stay, one of the visitors was Jessica Levrie, a 28-year-old mother of four small children. She became besotted with Sells and it seems that the attraction was mutual: after leaving the carnival at the end of its stay, he returned to Del Rio. On 31 March 1998, he joined Levrie and her children in their trailer home. A few days later, in Tennessee, Nora Price gave birth to his son.

Deciding to settle down, Sells found a job selling used cars at Amigo Auto Sales in Del Rio and married Levrie in October 1998. As a born-again Christian, she was the last woman able to handle him. Indeed, unknown to her, he continued to drink, take drugs, lie about his whereabouts – and murder at will.

One of his victims was a 32-year-old woman living in Gibson County, Tennessee, 121km (75 miles) northeast of Memphis. On 4 April 1999, Sells broke into her trailer home, where he raped her and knifed her to death: he also killed her 8-year-old daughter. Two weeks later, Sells returned to Texas, but not to Jessica Levrie. Instead, he joined another carnival that had just arrived in San Antonio for the city's fiesta. In San Antonio, Sells lost little time before returning to murder. On 18 April, he abducted and later murdered 9-year-old Mary Bea Perez, whose ravaged body turned up 10 days later in a San Antonio creek.

Heading east for Lexington, Kentucky, he worked for a while as a day labourer before raping and strangling Haley McHone, 13, in woods close by Lexington Park. By the time the body of his latest victim was found, Sells was heading back to Del Rio. But before rejoining Jessica Levrie, he stopped off in Kingfisher, Oklahoma, where he raped and murdered another young girl, Bobby Lynn Wofford, 14.

When, finally, he returned to Del Rio and Jessica Levrie, Tommy Lynn Sells, a thoroughgoing atheist, appeared to 'get' religion; he started attending Grace Community Church on a regular basis. At the same time, he encountered Terry Harris, his wife Crystal and their 12-year-old daughter, Katy. Then, at 4 a.m. on 31 December 1999, when he knew that Harris was away, he drove to the the family's trailer home in Guajia Bay, west of Del Rio and parked outside. He was armed with a 30cm (12in) boning knife. He entered the trailer through an open window at the front and searched through the rooms until he found Katy, who was sleeping in the lower of two bunk beds.

Katy was shocked awake when Sells used his knife to cut off her shorts and underwear and began to fondle her. She yelled out to her friend, 10-year-old Krystal Surles, who lay in the top bunk: 'Go get Mama!' Until then, Krystal's presence was unknown to Sells. The girl watched in horror as Sells twice drew his knife across Katy's throat. Katy collapsed, blood spurting from her throat, but Sells kept on cutting until he had caused 16 wounds, three of them so deep that they penetrated her body, front and back.

Next, Sells advanced on Krystal and cut her throat, severing her windpipe and nicking the vital carotid artery. Krystal had the presence of mind to pretend that she was dead, and Sells left. She then managed to stagger 400km (437yd) to the next house and alert the neighbours, who called the Guajia Bay police.

She required several hours of surgery to repair the damage done by a 13cm (5in) cut across her throat. Although unable to speak, she used pen and paper to give police a comprehensive description of the man who had killed Katy Harris. She also identified Tommy Lynn Sells from a series of six photographs.

On 2 January 2000, Sells was arrested at the trailer he shared with Jessica Levrie and her four children. He went quietly. Afterwards, he did not stop talking, giving police a copious account of his 20-year criminal career. Or as Victor Garcia, the attorney appointed to represent Sells, put it: 'Well, I understand you've already confessed to everything but the kitchen sink!'

Consequently, there was no shortage of evidence for Sells's three-day trial, which took place in Del Rio in September 2000. At the end, the jury took no more than an hour to pronounced a verdict of Guilty and recommend that Sells be executed by lethal injection. Afterwards, Sells was sent to the prison at Livingston, Texas, where, since 1982, more criminals have been executed than anywhere else in the United States. He remains there, on Death Row, to this day, having discovered how to postpone a death sentence: by producing a long drawn-out series of detailed confessions.

TOMMY LYNN SELLS TIMELINE

28 June 1964: Tommy Lynn Sells born in Oakland, California.

1980: According to his own confession, Sells commits his first murder at age 16.

July 1985: Sells murders Ena Cordt, 35, and her 4-year-old son in Missouri.

May 1987: Sells kills Suzanne Korcz, 28, in Niagara Falls, New York.

1987: Sells murders Keith Dardeen, his wife Elaine, his son Pete, 3, and newborn daughter in Illinois.

1988–1989: Sells confesses to killing a teenage girl in New Hampshire, a woman and her 3-year-old son in Idaho, Kent Lauten at a hobo camp in Arizona, a prostitute in Truckee, California, and a female hitchhiker in Oregon.

12 January 1990: Sells arrested for being drunk in public and for possessing stolen goods – items taken from a truck that he stole. Sells is sent to prison for 16 months, but spends only 12 months behind bars.

September 1991: Nine months after being released from prison, Sells murders Margaret McClain and her daughter in West Virginia.

May 1992: Sells rapes and stabs a 20-year-old girl in West Virginia, she survives and later identifies him. He pleads guilty to malicious wounding, is jailed for four years and released in 1997. Sells marries while in prison. After moving to Tennessee, Sells deserts his wife and resumes his travels.

October 1997: Sells strangles Stephanie Mahaney, 13, in Illinois and afterwards joins the Heart of America carnival.

February 1998: The carnival reaches Del Rio, Texas, where Sells meets Jessica Levrie, 28, and her four small children. Sells marries Levrie in October 1998.

4 April 1999: Sells rapes and kills a 32-year-old woman in Tennessee and also kills her 8-year-old daughter.

18 April 1999: Back now in Texas, Sells abducts and murders Mary Bea Perez, 9, later followed by Haley McHone, 13, in Kentucky and Bobby Lynn Wofford, 14, in Oklahoma.

31 December 1999: Sells murders Katy Harris, 12, in Texas and badly injures Krystal Surles, 10. But Krystal survives and later identifies Sells from a photograph.

2 January 2000: Sells is arrested and begins a long series of detailed confessions.

September 2000: After a three-day trial, Sells is found guilty of murder and is sentenced to execution by lethal injection. He is currently on Death Row in Livingston, Texas.

Kenneth Erskine

The Stockwell Strangler

FULL NAME:
Kenneth Erskine

DOB:
1962

NUMBER OF VICTIMS:
Killed seven elderly people and attempted to kill one other

SPAN OF KILLINGS:
April 1986–July 1986

LOCATION OF KILLINGS:
Mainly South London, sometimes North London

DATE OF ARREST:
28 July 1986

SENTENCE:
Seven life sentences

L ike several other serial killers, Kenneth Erskine was a 'loner' who lived in a reclusive world of his own, mixing fantasy and reality. He was also retarded, for at the age of 24 his mental age was established by psychiatrists at 11 or 12. Erskine began his life of crime as a burglar, but he was essentially a sexual psychopath. Eventually, perhaps inevitably, he drifted into more serious offences, murdering at least seven victims in various parts of London. Afterwards, he ransacked their homes for money, valuables and anything else he could sell for cash.

Kenneth Erskine, who was born in 1962, was a 'difficult' child, hard to control and at times dangerously unpredictable. He proved too much for his English mother and Antiguan father, who had three other sons. Ultimately, they abandoned him and rarely contacted him again. Having been forced out of the family home in affluent Putney, in southwest London, Erskine ended up in a variety of care homes and was sent to special schools for the maladjusted. There, his fantasies and tendency to violence were all too evident. He frequently attacked teachers and fellow pupils and once tried to drown several children while on an outing to a swimming pool.

At some time after he left school, Erskine became a Rastafarian, but other members of the sect spurned him when he embarked on his first career in crime, as a burglar. Although he was successful enough to amass sufficient loot to open 10 bank and building society accounts, Erskine was often caught and served several sentences in jail. Subsequently, after he turned to murder, he was more elusive, managing to kill seven elderly pensioners within four months in 1986.

Murder Goes Undetected

Kenneth Erskine committed his first murder in Stockwell, an inner city district of London, 3.9km (2.4 miles) southeast of Charing Cross. Newspapers were quick to dub him the 'Stockwell Strangler', but he did not confine his activities to this one area. In Wandsworth, in the southwest of London, he gained entry to the home of 78-year-old Mrs Eileen Emms on 9 April 1986. She was, in many ways, typical of his preferred victims. An elderly pensioner, she lived alone and was not especially alert to the danger posed by open or poorly fastened windows or unlocked doors and therefore very vulnerable. Erskine probably got into her home through an open window. He then strangled the old lady and sexually assaulted her.

When her body was found, murder was not at first suspected: there were no obvious marks of violence, and the death of an old lady living alone is, sadly, not all that unusual. In fact, the doctor called to examine her body decided that she had been dead for about three days, and signed a death certificate citing death by natural causes. Later, though, Mrs Emms' home help noticed that a portable TV was missing, and the police were called. A post mortem examination revealed foul play, demonstrating that she had been raped as well as strangled.

Erskine now lay low for two months before he targeted his second victim, Mrs Janet Cockett, 67, the chairwoman of the tenants' association on the

The faces of Erskine's victims reveal his preference for the elderly. Some were weak in nursing homes and others were casual about security in their homes.

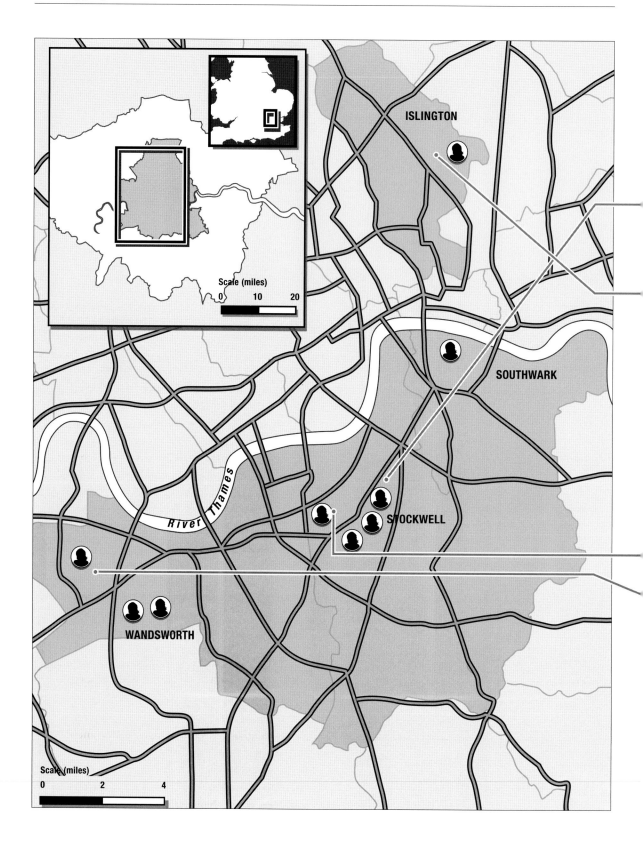

The Trail of Murders

Stockwell, June and July 1986:
Erskine became known as 'The Stockwell Strangler' after he had killed three people in that south London area in June and July 1986. The first two were Polish pensioners in an old people's home and the other victim lived alone in a one-room flat.

Islington, 8 July 1986:
Islington was where Erskine made one of his most profitable killings. After murdering 84-year-old William Carmen in his flat, he took £600 in cash. This was Erskine's only murder north of the River Thames as he tried to elude the tightening police dragnet.

Clapham, 27 June 1986:
The only person to survive Erskine's deadly visits was Frederick Prentice in an old peoples' home in Clapham. While Erskine's hands were on the man's throat, he noticed his victim pressing an alarm button. Although it was silent, this was enough to make him flee.

Putney, 24 July 1986:
Erskine committed one murder in Putney, where years before his parents had forced him to leave the family home. This victim was to be his last. She was 80-year-old Florence Tisdall, a widow who lived in a retirement complex near Putney Bridge.

Key Erskine's victims

Wandsworth housing estate where she lived. Erskine strangled her on 9 June 1986, after entering her flat through a window, where his palm print was later found on the glass.

Caught in the Act

Some three weeks later, in the early hours of 27 June, Erskine entered an old people's home in Cedars Road, Clapham, in south London and made his way to the room where Frederick Prentice, a retired engineer, was asleep. Mr Prentice was suddenly woken by a noise in the corridor outside and saw Erskine enter his room. He managed to switch on his bedside light, but the intruder jumped on him as he lay in bed. Erskine knelt on the old man's chest, gripped his windpipe and started to squeeze. Then, he relaxed his grip and squeezed again, all the while muttering, 'Kill, kill, kill!' There was an alarm button by the bed and Mr Prentice managed to stretch out an arm and strike it. The alarm made no sound, but Erskine took fright, and ran out of the room.

Next day, 28 June, Erskine not only succeeded where he had failed with Mr Prentice, but killed twice, murdering pensioners in adjoining rooms at Somerville Hastings House, an old peoples' home in Stockwell Park Crescent, Stockwell. This time, Erskine was spotted by night duty staff. The police were called, but the intruder had vanished before they arrived. Both victims – Valentine Gleim, 84, and Zbigniew Strabawa, 94 – had been strangled and sexually assaulted. It seems that Erskine used the same technique as he had tried to employ on Mr Prentice. He knelt on the pensioners' chests as they lay in bed, placed his left hand over their mouths and with his right hand gripped their windpipes. They lost consciousness after about 30 seconds and died within two to three minutes. That done, it seems that their killer washed and shaved, using a flannel and an electric shaver before leaving.

With four victims now dead, the case of the Stockwell Strangler received high-ranking attention from Scotland Yard, the headquarters of the Metropolitan Police in London. Detective Chief Superintendent Kenneth Thompson of the murder squad was put in charge of the case, with more than

200 detectives at his disposal. Thompson's first move was to order plain clothes officers to place a close watch on dozens of old peoples' homes in London throughout the night.

Thus far, Erskine's serial killings had all taken place south of the River Thames, which runs through London. Now, Erskine eluded the police by moving north of the river and selecting Islington as his next venue for murder. Islington, an inner city area of London, was a well-to-do, fashionable district in the 1980s. This was where Mr William Carmen, 84, lived in a flat on the Marques estate. Erskine gained entry, on 8 July 1986, and, like the other victims, Mr Carmen was both strangled and sexually abused. Afterwards, Erskine ransacked the old gentleman's flat for cash and by the time the police arrived, around £600 – and the killer – were missing.

Erskine's sixth victim was another old man, 74-year-old Mr William Downes, who was killed in his one-room 'bedsit' on the Overton estate, Stockwell, on 20 July 1986. Perhaps becoming careless after getting away with so many killings, Erskine left his palm prints on a garden gate and the kitchen wall of Mr Downes' home. But in 1986, high-tech methods of crime detection had not yet caught up with the science of transferring palm prints onto computer disc, although it was possible to do so with fingerprints. This imposed on Scotland Yard detectives the immensely tedious task of manually searching through some four million files, trying to match the palm prints to those already on record.

'He knelt on the pensioners' chests as they lay in bed, placed his left hand over their mouths and with his right hand gripped their windpipes. They lost consciousness after about 30 seconds and died within two to three minutes.'

Erskine gave no resistance when arrested in Southwark claiming unemployment benefits. In custody, he refused to answer any police questions, giggling at the situation.

The search took all of three months, even though it was narrowed down by concentrating solely on burglars and petty criminals based in London. At last, the prints were matched to those of Kenneth Erskine, who, until then, had been known to the police only as a small-time criminal with an extensive record of theft and minor offences. Knowing that they were looking for Erskine was one thing; knowing where to find him was, however, quite another. He had become a drifter with no known address and London was full of hundreds of hostels, as well as 'squats', where vagrants like him parked themselves illegally in uninhabited buildings. Tragically, it was while police were hunting for him that Erskine committed his last murder.

Limited Co-operation

Mrs Florence Tisdall, an 80-year-old widow, lived in an apartment on a retirement complex in Ranelagh Gardens, an upmarket address near Putney Bridge in southwest London. On 24 July 1986, she was found dead by the caretaker of the property. As before, the old lady had been strangled and sexually assaulted. She had also suffered two broken ribs where her killer had knelt on her chest.

Only four days later, Scotland Yard achieved the breakthrough they had been so desperately seeking. Police discovered that Kenneth Erskine had been claiming unemployment benefit at a Department of Social Security office in Southwark near central London. Payments were made weekly, and Erskine was due to collect his next cheque on 28 July. A team of detectives was sent to watch the office. All they had to do was wait for Erskine to appear, join the queue of claimants and arrest him. Erskine neither protested nor struggled but stood calmly as a detective clicked the handcuffs onto his wrists.

But where detaining Erskine had been simple, interrogating him proved both tedious and intensely frustrating. He simply failed to respond to any questions, preferring to stare out of the window or giggle or even masturbate. In this situation, it was fortunate that the police had independent evidence against him. When arrested, Erskine was carrying details of his 10 bank and building society accounts, which contained not only the proceeds of his

burglaries but some £2000 he had gained from his serial killings. The police also had the damning palm prints and, most importantly, a witness in Frederick Prentice, the only survivor of Erskine's murder spree: he picked out the killer from a police line-up without any hesitation.

Kenneth Erskine went on trial at the Old Bailey in London on 12 January 1988, charged with seven murders and the attempted killing of Frederick Prentice. Erskine was willing to admit to stealing from his victims, but maintained that someone else must have come in afterwards and killed them.

'I don't remember killing anyone,' Erskine maintained. 'I could have done it without knowing it. I am not sure if I did it.'

The jury refused to believe him. After proceedings that lasted for 18 days, he was found guilty of all the charges and received seven life sentences. Erskine was sentenced to serve a minimum term of 40 years, but psychiatrists who examined him on behalf of the court found him so confused and disturbed that it seemed likely even then that he would never be released. Indeed, Erskine's mental condition steadily worsened over time, and it eventually became necessary to confine him in Broadmoor Psychiatric Hospital at Crowthorne, Berkshire.

KENNETH ERSKINE TIMELINE

1962: Kenneth Erskine is born in Putney, southwest London, the fourth and youngest son of an English mother and an Antiguan father. After being abandoned by his parents, he is later brought up in care homes and is sent to schools for maladjusted children.

About 1978: After leaving school, Erskine embarks on a career as a burglar.

9 April 1986: Erskine commits his first murder, killing Mrs Eileen Emms, 78, in Wandsworth, London. Like all Erskine's subsequent victims, she is strangled and sexually assaulted.

9 June 1986: Erskine murders Mrs Janet Cockett, 67, in Wandsworth.

27 June 1986: Erskine attempts to murder Frederick Prentice in Clapham, but he survives after he tries to raise the alarm, frightening his would-be killer into running away.

28 June 1986: A double murder – two Polish pensioners are murdered by Erskine in a Stockwell old people's home. After four killings, Scotland Yard, the headquarters of the Metropolitan Police in London, forms a special squad to handle the case.

8 July 1986: The murder of Mr William Carmen, 84, in Islington. Erskine escapes after stealing £600 in cash.

20 July 1986: Erskine kills Mr William Downes, 74, in Stockwell.

24 July 1986: Erskine's last murder: he kills Mrs Florence Tisdall, 80, in Putney.

28 July 1986: Erskine is arrested while waiting to collect his unemployment benefit cheque in Southwark.

12 January 1988: Erskine's trial opens at the Old Bailey in London. He denies committing the seven murders with which he is charged, although he confesses to burglary.

30 January 1988: Erskine is found guilty and is given seven life sentences. Later, he is placed in Broadmoor Psychiatric Hospital, Crowthorne, Berkshire, where he remains today.

Charles Cullen

Healthcare Serial Killer

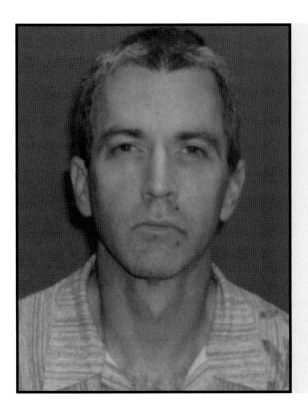

FULL NAME:
Charles Williams Dublin Cullen

DOB:
22 February 1960

NUMBER OF VICTIMS:
35–45

SPAN OF KILLINGS:
1988–2003

LOCATION OF KILLINGS:
Various locations in New Jersey
and Pennsylvania, USA

DATE OF ARREST:
12 December 2003

SENTENCE:
397 years in prison without parole

The trail of a serial killer takes a particularly terrifying turn where the victims are the most vulnerable people possible: hospital patients. It was this terror that Charles Cullen brought to a series of hospitals in New Jersey and Pennsylvania, where he worked as a nurse between 1988 and 2003. He seems to have had few, if any, problems finding work, for he moved with comparative ease from one hospital to the next. Somehow, successive employers missed or ignored Cullen's history of mental instability and his 20 bids to commit suicide – until, that is, his twisted mind turned to multiple murder.

On 11 June 1988, a retired Jersey City judge, 72-year-old John W. Yengo Sr was admitted to the burns unit at St Barnabas Medical Center in Livingston, New Jersey. The judge, who suffered from heart problems, was taken into hospital with severe sunburn. But shortly after arriving, he was dead. The cause was an intravenous injection of lidocaine, an anaesthetic that, in overdose proportions, was lethal. And the old judge had been given quite a hefty overdose.

Working to Kill

Sixteen years passed before Charles Cullen, who worked as a nurse at St Barnabas in 1988, appeared before the Superior Court in Essex County, New Jersey, and confessed to killing Judge Yengo. This was a shocking admission in itself, but, as Cullen had already revealed, Yengo's murder was only one of around 40 hospital killings he had perpetrated before he was finally brought to court in 2004.

Killer nurses were not unknown in the United States, where an investigation by *Forensic Nurse* magazine in 2004 revealed that 146,000 male registered nurses had resorted to murdering their patients. Even so, the toll exacted by Charles Cullen was of unprecedented proportions, exceeding the official record of 37 healthcare killings perpetrated by Donald Harvey between 1970 and 1987. Cullen's confessions sparked off media coverage across the country. The consensus that emerged pinpointed some likely causes: the atmosphere of trust engendered by the medical profession and hospital conditions, the ready availability of drugs, and the fact that patient death is such a regular occurrence that it is easy to conceal a killing and even several killings.

Cullen, though, had a further advantage: until his case prompted a radical rethink, there was a lack of

Cullen's hospital employment began as an orderly at St Barnabas Medical Center in Livingston, New Jersey, in 1988. His first 11 murders occurred there.

'**Somehow, successive employers missed or ignored Cullen's history of mental instability and his 20 bids to commit suicide – until, that is, his twisted mind turned to multiple murder.**'

sufficient vigilance in the US healthcare system. Employers had no legal right to investigate a prospective worker's previous employment record. They were also reluctant – for fear of being sued – to investigate suspicious incidents or to give an employee a negative work record. It was no wonder, then, that 'angels of death' such as Cullen managed to go undetected for many years.

As Kelly Pyrek of *Forensic Nurse* magazine put it: 'Many experts speculate that healthcare has contributed more serial killers than all other professions combined and that the field attracts a disproportionately high number of people with a pathological interest in life and death.'

This was a fair description of Charles Cullen, who was born on 22 February 1960 in West Orange, New Jersey, the youngest in a family of nine children. Cullen's early years were, by his own admission, miserable – so miserable, in fact, that he first tried to kill himself when he was 9 years old, by drinking the chemicals from a chemistry set. Early on, too, Cullen was intrigued by drugs and often fantasized about stealing a supply of them in order to commit suicide. Instead, Cullen contented himself on one occasion with purloining a green surgical gown, mask and latex gloves from the medical cabinet on the USS *Woodrow Wilson*, a ballistic missile submarine on which he was assigned after joining the navy in 1977.

Suspicions Ignored

In March 1984, he was discharged from the navy after showing signs of mental instability: not only did he wear the stolen surgeon's get-up to serve a shift on the submarine, but he tried to kill himself on several occasions. It was the last of these attempts that led to his discharge. Yet despite this fraught history, Cullen was accepted at the Mountainside School of Nursing in Montclair, New Jersey, and qualified in 1987. He soon found a placement as a medical orderly at St Barnabas Medical Center.

Judge Yengo died a few months later. He was the first of 11 patients murdered by Cullen at St Barnabas, one of them an AIDS patient who died after being injected with an overdose of insulin. Cullen later maintained, like many other 'angels of death', that he had killed his victims to put an end to their suffering. He remained at St Barnabas for nearly four years before the hospital staff discovered, at the end of 1991, that someone had been interfering with bags of intravenous fluid. The culprit may or may not have been Charles Cullen, but he resigned anyway, in January 1992. He moved in February to his next job, at Warren Hospital in Phillipsburg, New Jersey.

The Trail of Murders

Livingston, New Jersey, 1988:
This was the first town to suffer hospital homicides by Cullen. His first victim was a retired judge in 1988, and 10 more deaths would follow. It took four years for suspicions to be aroused, and Cullen moved away to his next hospital.

Phillipsburg, New Jersey, 1992 and 1993:
Cullen's second nursing job was at Warren Hospital in Phillipsburg, New Jersey, in 1992 and 1993. He killed three elderly women patients, stalked a female hospital worker and attempted suicide. During Cullen's time there, his wife Adrienne sued for divorce, citing his violence.

Bethlehem, Pennsylvania, 1999–2002:
Cullen moved into the cardiac care unit while employed at St Luke's Hospital in Bethlehem, Pennsylvania, from 1999 to 2002. The staff were alert to abuses, and he was suspected of using drugs to kill patients. No action was taken and he left the area.

Somerset, New Jersey, 2003:
Somerset Medical Center in Somerset, New Jersey, was the end of the road for Cullen's years of killing. His careless intrusion into patients' cases caught the attention of officials. He was dismissed and arrested, confessing to murdering 13 patients there in 2003.

Key   Cullen's victims

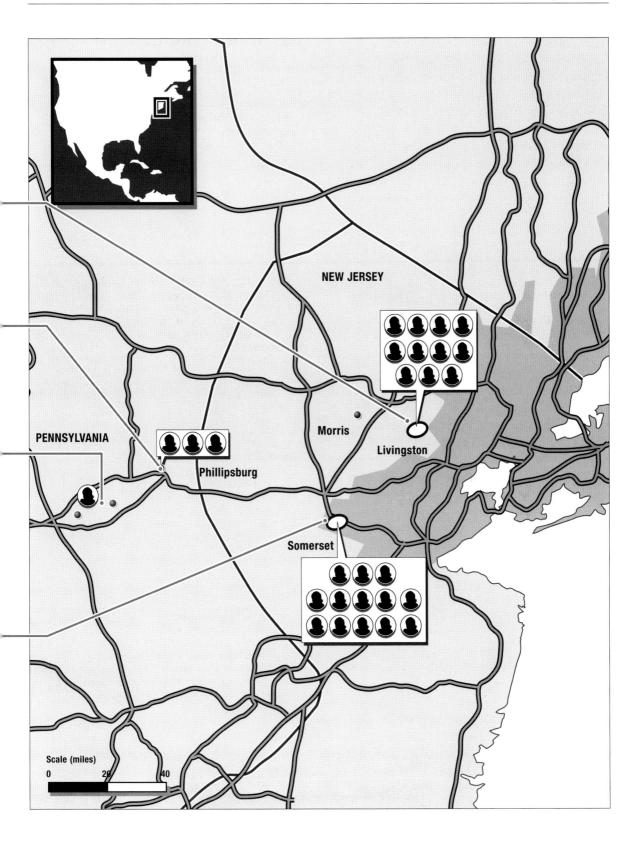

NEW JERSEY

PENNSYLVANIA

Morris

Phillipsburg

Livingston

Somerset

Scale (miles)

0   20   40

CHARLES CULLEN TIMELINE

22 February 1960: Charles Cullen born in West Orange, New Jersey.

1969: Cullen's first attempt to commit suicide, aged 9.

1977: Cullen joins the US Navy and is assigned to the ballistic missile submarine USS *Woodrow Wilson*.

March 1984: Cullen is discharged from the navy for mental instability and suicide attempts.

11 June 1988: Cullen murders retired Jersey City judge John W. Yengo, 72, at St Barnabas Medical Center in Livingston, New Jersey. The judge was the first of 11 patients murdered by Cullen at St Barnabas.

January 1992: Charles Cullen resigned from St Barnabas.

February 1992: Cullen begins a job at Warren Hospital, Phillipsburg, New Jersey, where he murders three elderly patients. His wife Adrienne sues him for divorce.

March 1993: Cullen is charged with stalking a colleague and pleads guilty.

August 1993: Cullen is implicated in the death of Helen Dean, a 91-year-old cancer patient. Despite the efforts of Dean's son, Larry, neither an investigation nor an autopsy on the dead woman proved anything incriminating. At the end of 1993, Cullen resigns from Warren Hospital and moves on to the Hunter Memorial Hospital, Rarity Township, New Jersey.

1994: Cullen is granted a nursing licence in Pennsylvania.

1996: After an interval of three years, Cullen murders five Hunter Memorial patients between January and September.

1997: Cullen finds a new post at Morris Memorial Hospital, Morris, New Jersey, but is dismissed for incompetence in August.

February 1998: Cullen begins work at the Liberty Nursing and Rehabilitation Center, Allentown, Pennsylvania. He is fired for wrongful practices in September.

November 1998: Another new post for Charles Cullen, this time at Elston Hospital in Elston, Pennsylvania.

30 December 1998: A patient at Elston Hospital dies from an overdose of digoxin.

March 1999: After leaving Elston Hospital, Cullen moves to Lehigh Valley Hospital in Allentown, Pennsylvania. He murders one patient and attempts to kill another before changing jobs again.

April 1999: Cullen begins work at St Luke's Hospital, Bethlehem, Pennsylvania, in the cardiac care unit. Cullen was dismissed for leaving a number of vials of unused medications in a waste bin. Although he was suspected of administering drugs to kill patients, there was a lack of evidence to charge him.

June 2002: Cullen is dismissed from St Luke's and frogmarched out of the hospital.

September 2002: Cullen returns to New Jersey for a post at the critical care center at Somerset Medical Center.

15 June 2003: Cullen orders digoxin for Jin Kyushu Han, 40, a cancer patient. She goes

into cardiac arrest but is saved when given an antidote.

29 June 2003: Reverend Florian Gall, 68, dies at the Somerset Medical Center with a high level of digoxin in his blood. By this time, six other patients in the Center have also died.

July 2003: The New Jersey Poison Information and Education System becomes suspicious of Cullen, but nothing is done about him for three months. By that time, Cullen has murdered five patients and tried to kill a sixth.

October 2003: After the death of Cullen's last victim, the New Jersey center contacts the police, who begin to scrutinize his employment history.

31 October 2003: Cullen is dismissed from the Somerset Center for giving false details on his work application.

12 December 2003: Cullen is arrested leaving a restaurant in Somerset and confesses to murdering Reverend Florian Gall and trying to kill Jin Kyushu Han.

April 2004: Cullen pleads guilty to killing 13 patients at Somerset Center, and trying to murder two more. He avoids the death penalty by promising to co-operate with the authorities over his other murders. Ultimately, sentences passed on him in New Jersey and Pennsylvania amount to imprisonment for 397 years without parole.

2004–2005: Radical changes are introduced in the laws concerning healthcare to prevent killer nurses from getting jobs in hospitals.

At Phillipsburg, Cullen murdered three elderly women patients with overdoses of digoxin, one of a group of medicines for heart patients known as cardiac glycosides. Before she died, the last of them complained that a 'sneaky male nurse' had given her the injection while she was asleep. Unfortunately, no one believed her.

While Cullen was still at Warren Hospital, his wife Adrienne filed for divorce, painting a fearful picture of a violent, sadistic husband who delighted in

torturing animals and poisoning drinks with lighter fluid. Despite these allegations, Cullen was given joint custody of their two daughters.

He was nonetheless unsettled by the divorce, and took to some strange behaviour. Around March 1993, he broke into the home of a fellow hospital worker and began stalking her through Phillipsburg. He was charged with trespassing and pleaded guilty, after which he made another bid to kill himself. Yet, amazingly enough, he was able to continue working at Warren Hospital. Then, in August 1993, the son of one of his patients became suspicious.

Larry Dean, the son of cancer patient Helen Dean, 91, found himself ordered out of his mother's room by a male nurse. He complied, but afterwards returned to find his mother in a distressed state. 'He stuck me!' she complained to her son and showed him an injection mark on her inner thigh. Both mother and son complained about the incident, but none of the other nurses appeared interested. The following day, Helen Dean became seriously ill, and in the afternoon she suffered heart failure and died. Larry Dean became convinced that his mother had been murdered, and he thought that he knew who had done the deed. But he failed to convince the hospital authorities, and although there was an investigation, it found no evidence of foul play. An autopsy was performed, but nothing incriminating was found.

At the end of 1993, Charles Cullen resigned from Warren Hospital and moved on to the Hunter Memorial Hospital in Rarity Township, New Jersey. There, he worked in the intensive care and cardiac

Mary Strenko displays a photograph of her son, Michael, who was killed by Cullen. She was among 20 family members allowed to address Cullen during his trial.

'Larry Dean became convinced that his mother had been murdered, and he thought that he knew who had done the deed. But he failed to convince the hospital authorities.'

care unit. In his later confessions, Cullen maintained that he did not resume his murders until 1996, when he killed five patients by giving them digoxin injections during the first nine months of that year.

Erratic Behaviour

Subsequently, Cullen moved on to another post, at Morris Memorial Hospital in Morris, New Jersey, but was dismissed in August 1997 for incompetence. Two months later, he reappeared at the Warren Hospital, not as a medical worker but as a patient. He began treatment for depression at a psychiatric facility, but soon stopped attending sessions there. He was now behaving very oddly, demonstrating a hatred of cats by chasing them down the street, shouting, talking to himself or making faces at passers-by.

Evidence that Cullen was unhinged and dangerous seemed to be piling up, yet it seems to have gone largely unnoticed. In February 1998, he found work again at the Liberty Nursing and Rehabilitation Center in Allentown, Pennsylvania. Four years earlier, Cullen had obtained a nursing licence in the Quaker State, which meant that he was able to work in a ward where patients needed ventilators to breathe. But he lasted only eight months before he was spotted going into a patient's room carrying several syringes. There seems to have been some sort of struggle in which the patient's arm was broken, but at least there were no injections. Cullen was accused of administering drugs at the wrong times and was dismissed.

Cullen had escaped detection once again and in November 1998 he began work at Elston Hospital in Elston, Pennsylvania. Soon afterwards, on 30 December, another patient died from a lethal amount of digoxin. This time, though, there was a coroner's investigation and a test revealed the digoxin overdose in the dead patient's blood. Yet once again, the investigation was inconclusive and nothing was uncovered that could have pointed the finger at Charles Cullen.

The shortage of nurses that then existed in the United States was making it hard for hospitals to recruit staff. This may explain why, in March 1999, the authorities at Lehigh Valley Hospital in Allentown, Pennsylvania, asked no questions when Cullen applied for work in the burns unit. There was, in any case, no official way he could have been identified as a risk to patients or have his employment record and state of mind and health checked. As a result, Cullen was able to murder one patient at Lehigh Valley and attempt the murder of another before he moved on again, in April 1999, this time to St Luke's Hospital in Bethlehem, Pennsylvania, where he worked in the cardiac care unit.

The staff at St Luke's were more alert to malpractice than those in Cullen's previous places of work. It was when one of them noticed vials of unused medications lying in a waste bin that alarm bells began to ring. An enquiry into the affair soon picked out Cullen as the culprit. He was dismissed, and in June 2002 he was frogmarched out of the hospital.

The incident encouraged seven of St Luke's nurses to report longstanding suspicions about Charles Cullen. They were certain that he was administering drugs to kill patients. They offered as evidence to the Lehigh County District Attorney the fact that in the six months up to June 2002 Cullen

'It was when one of them noticed vials of unused medications lying in a waste bin that alarm bells began to ring. An enquiry into the affair soon picked out Cullen as the culprit. He was dismissed.'

had worked only one-fifth of the hours in the cardiac care unit, yet had been present when almost two-thirds of the patients had died. Yet once again, Cullen managed to escape: investigators failed to examine his past history, and the case was abandoned for lack of evidence.

A Thorough Investigation

In September 2002, Cullen returned to New Jersey and took up yet another post at the critical care centre in the Somerset Medical Center. On 15 June 2003, he accessed the Medical Center's records of Jin Kyushu Han, 40, and ordered digoxin for her: yet Jin was a cancer patient, with no need of heart medication. Cullen later cancelled the order for digoxin, but nevertheless the drug disappeared from stock. Not only that, it had obviously been administered to Jin, for the next day she went into cardiac arrest. A blood test showed an unusually high level of digoxin in Jin's system and she was given an antidote. Fortunately, this stabilized her.

The digoxin mystery was repeated with another patient two weeks later, but this time the outcome was fatal. After the Reverend Florian Gall, a 68-year-old Roman Catholic priest, died at the Somerset Medical Center at the end of June, a high level of digoxin was found in his blood. The presence of digoxin was not, in itself, particularly suspicious: the Reverend Gall was, after all, a heart patient. What *was* dubious was the unusually large amount he had received. By the time of his death, six other patients had expired at Somerset Medical Center, all from injections of digoxin or insulin. In one other case, Cullen tried to kill Philip Gregor on 18 June, but Gregor managed to survive.

Perhaps boosted by the number of times he had escaped detection, Charles Cullen was growing careless. He left entries on the Somerset Center's computer that showed he had accessed the records of patients unconnected to his work. He was observed in the rooms of patients where he had no right to be. He requested medications for patients that had not been prescribed. In July 2003, the New Jersey Poison Information and Education System alerted the Somerset Center to the possibility that one of its employees was killing patients. Even now, nothing was done for another three months, until October. By then, Cullen had claimed another five victims and attempted to kill a sixth. The police were contacted only after his last victim died of low blood sugar.

Now, at long last, the employment history of Charles Cullen was scrutinized and it revealed strong indications about his participation in the deaths of patients. The police took time to complete their investigations. Meanwhile, on 31 October 2003, Somerset Medical Center dismissed Cullen in a way that avoided rousing his suspicions; he was fired for including false details on his work application.

By the end of the year, the police were equipped with enough evidence to detain Cullen. He was

Police escort Cullen into court in 2006 in Allentown, Pennsylvania, where he received six life sentences. He yelled at the judge, 'Your honour, you need to step down.'

'He was arrested on 12 December 2003. Shortly afterwards, he confessed to the murder of the Reverend Gall and the attempted killing of Jin Kyushu Han. But there was much more to come.'

arrested on 12 December 2003 as he was leaving a Somerset restaurant. Shortly afterwards, he confessed to the murder of the Reverend Gall and the attempted killing of Jin Kyushu Han. But there was much more to come.

In April 2004, in a Somerville, New Jersey, court, Cullen pleaded guilty to murdering 13 patients at Somerset Medical Center and attempting to kill two more by lethal injection. He was able to avoid the death penalty, which he had expected to receive, by agreeing to give the authorities information about his other murders. As a result, he later received additional prison sentences in Pennsylvania and more in New Jersey. Several were to be served consecutively, so that in total Cullen was imprisoned for 397 years without parole.

The legal significance of Cullen's 15 years of serial killing meant that a long, hard think was required about the standard of protection offered to both patients and healthcare employers. The law was patently lax, with no proper provision for reporting and recording possible breaches of procedure and no legal protection for employers against the depredations of dangerous workers.

As a result of Charles Cullen's activities, 37 US states, including New Jersey and Pennsylvania, passed new laws in 2004 and 2005, which allowed employers to investigate and appraise the work of applicants, permitted healthcare facilities to disclose poor or illegal patient care, and required healthcare workers to provide fingerprints and have their backgrounds checked for criminal records.

Aileen Wuornos

America's First Female Serial Killer

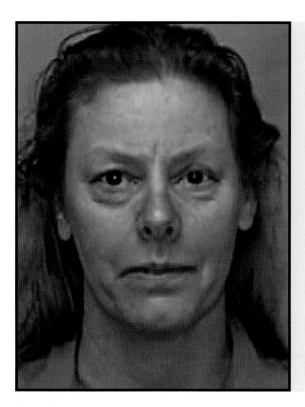

FULL NAME:
Aileen Carol Wuornos (née Pittman)

DOB:
29 February 1956

DIED:
9 October 2002

NUMBER OF VICTIMS:
7

SPAN OF KILLINGS:
30 November 1989–19 November 1990

LOCATION OF KILLINGS:
Florida, USA

DATE OF ARREST:
9 January 1991

SENTENCE:
The death penalty (lethal injection)

The life of Aileen Carol Wuornos, often claimed as America's first female serial killer, was a story of serial trauma. Deserted by her mother at age 4, a prostitute and an unwed mother at 15, she graduated to theft, fraud, armed robbery, violent assault and, ultimately, to multiple murder. The driving force behind Wuornos's life of crime was her hatred of humanity. 'I seriously hate human life. I have hate crawling through my system,' she said after her conviction for killing six men.

Aileen Wuornos, sometimes known as Lee, was only 18 years old when she was arrested for the first time, on 27 May 1974. The charges brought against her in Jefferson County, Colorado, typified the violence that would become the constant theme of

her existence – disorderly conduct and firing a 22-calibre pistol from a moving vehicle. From there, Lee Wuornos moved on to a range of felonies, including assault, violent confrontations in bars, demanding money with menaces and battery with a beer bottle.

In 1976, aged 20, she married Lewis Gratz Fell, a wealthy yacht club president 50 years her senior. Fell soon realized he had made a mistake when his young wife began beating him with his own walking stick. He obtained a restraining order against her and annulled the ill-considered marriage after only nine weeks.

For the next 10 years, Aileen Wuornos continued to add to her reputation as a dangerous woman beyond control. She drank heavily and took drugs. Once, she tried to kill herself. She committed a series of offences, many of them featuring the use or possession of guns and ammunition, and spent time in prison. In attempts to cover her tracks, she frequently used aliases, including Lori Grody and Cammie Marsh Greene.

A Stable Relationship

A woman as self-destructive as Aileen Wuornos was bound to fail in her personal relationships, and her elderly husband was only the first of many people who were unable to live with her. Then, in around 1986, Wuornos met Tyria Moore, a 24-year-old motel maid, in a gay bar in Daytona Beach, Florida.

The two of them set up home together and, for once, a pleasant relationship developed. Wuornos supported herself and Moore with her earnings as a prostitute, but before long, things began to go wrong. She once boasted that she had serviced 250,000 men, but she was now in her thirties and her attractions, such as they were, had begun to fade. Clients were harder to find and eventually, money became so short that Wuornos had to consider some other form of income. With her extensive criminal background, and especially her experience with firearms, the alternative – murder and robbery – was not hard to find.

'Wuornos had to consider some other form of income. With her extensive criminal background, and especially her experience with firearms, the alternative – murder and robbery – was not hard to find.'

All of Aileen Wuornos's victims were shot dead in Florida. The first was Richard Mallory, 51, the owner of an electronics store in Clearwater, Florida. Mallory had a habit of disappearing from time to time to indulge in drinking and sex binges that normally lasted a few days. But by early December 1989, two weeks had passed since he had last been seen, and his

Wuornos was caught after registering as Cammie Marsh Greene at a motel in Harbor Oaks, Florida. Police found she used that name pawning a victim's items.

1977 Cadillac was found abandoned in a wooded area outside Daytona.

Then, on 13 December, two youngsters out looking for scrap metal along a road near Interstate 95 in Volusia County, Florida, found a man's body wrapped up in a carpet runner. The corpse was seriously decomposed, but the police managed to take fingerprints and later identified the dead man as Richard Mallory: he had been shot with three bullets fired from a .22 calibre rifle. The police followed several apparently promising leads, but before long, the trail went cold.

A Car Crash

A few months later, on 19 May 1990, a 43-year-old heavy-equipment operator named David Spears set out for Orlando, Florida. He never reached his destination. Soon after that, the truck he was driving was found on Interstate 75 in Florida: the doors were unlocked and the licence plate was gone. On 1 June, Spears' naked corpse was found in another wooded area in Citrus County, Florida, with a used condom nearby. Like Mallory, he had been shot several times with a .22 rifle.

Aileen Wuornos's third victim was discovered 6 days later, 48km (30 miles) to the south, in Pasco County, Florida. The body was so badly decomposed that it yielded no usable fingerprints, but the nine bullets found in the remains had come from a .22 rifle. Later, it was established that this third corpse was the body of Charles Carskaddon, aged 40, who worked part-time at a rodeo. But at the time it was found the detective assigned to the case, Tom Muck, had no means of identifying him.

Detective Muck was acquainted with the Spears case in Citrus County. Noting the similarities – middle-aged men, abandoned vehicles, .22 rifle bullets – he soon began to suspect that he was looking at a pattern of serial killings. Muck contacted Marvin Padgett, the Sheriff's investigator in Citrus County, and advised him of his suspicions.

Padgett promised to keep in touch, but no real progress was made until a fortuitous accident occurred on 4 July 1990. That day, a 1988 Pontiac Sunbird swerved off State Road 315 near Orange

The Trail of Murders

Volusia County, 13 December 1989:
The body of Wuornos's first victim, Richard Mallory, was found in Volusia County on 13 December 1989. He had been shot with three bullets. His Cadillac was also found earlier in Volusia outside Daytona. Wuornos would be arrested in the county on 9 January 1991.

Marion County, August and September 1990:
Marion County was the dumping ground used by Wuornos for her fifth and sixth victims. Troy Burress, a salesman from Ocala, was found in woods there on 4 August 1990, and Dick Humphreys, a former police chief in Alabama, was discovered on 12 September.

South Florida, 7 June 1990:
The only victim from south Florida was Peter Siems who disappeared after leaving Jupiter on 7 June 1990. It was his Pontiac that Wuornos and her companion Tyria Moore were driving when they crashed near Orange Springs in Marion County. Its interior contained bloodstains and a bloody palm print.

West Florida, May and June 1990:
Three bodies were discovered in 1990 in counties along the Gulf Coast of west Florida. David Spears's naked body was found in Citrus County in May, Charles Carskaddon in Pasco County in June and the final victim, Walter Jeno Antonio, in Dixie County in November.

Key
Wournos's victims

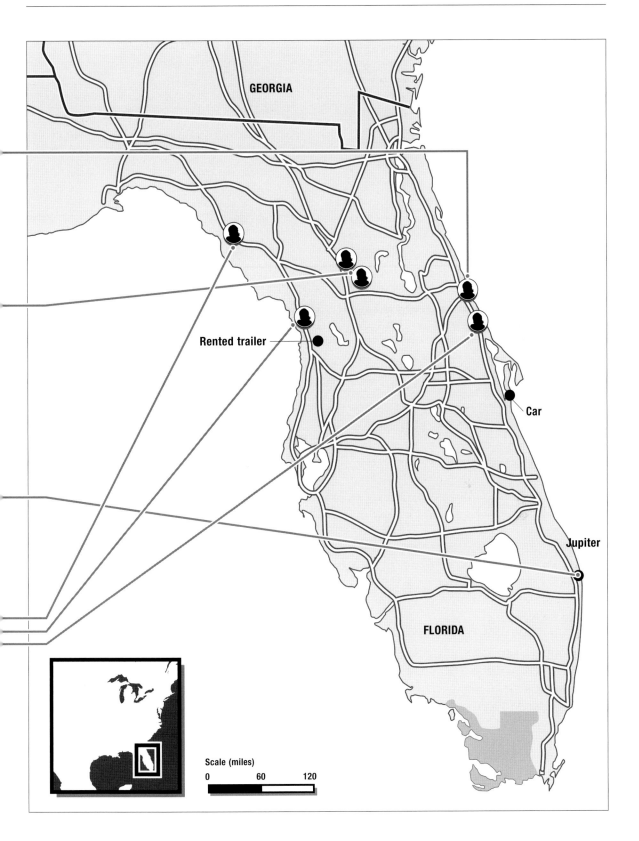

GEORGIA

Rented trailer

Car

Jupiter

FLORIDA

Scale (miles)

0   60   120

Springs in Florida's Marion County and crashed into a patch of brushwood. A householder named Rhonda Bailey was a witness to the incident. As Mrs Bailey watched from her porch, two women emerged from the crashed vehicle and threw a number of beer cans into the nearby woods. One of the women had brown hair, the other was a blonde whose arm was cut and bleeding. Mrs Bailey offered to call the police but the blonde said that was not necessary, claiming that her father lived a short way up the road.

The two women got back in the car, which had a smashed windshield but was otherwise driveable, and managed to get it out of the brushwood and onto the road. Then, they drove off, but failed to get far. The automobile broke down and the two women abandoned it and started walking. When Hubert Hewett of the Orange Springs volunteer Fire Department arrived on the scene, he asked the women if they had been in the car, but they denied it. They also denied needing any help and kept on walking down the road.

Up to this point, it appears that no one on the scene had looked inside the Pontiac, until sheriff's deputies from Marion County turned up and saw that the interior was virtually awash with bloodstains. There was also a bloody palm print on an interior door handle. The licence plate could not be found, but the deputies located the vehicle identification number and from that, a computer search revealed that the Pontiac belonged to Peter Siems, 65, a retired merchant seaman and Christian outreach worker.

Siems had left his home in Jupiter, Florida, on 7 June, bound for Arkansas, where he planned to visit

'The public response was immediate and prolific. By mid-December, data was flooding in and one item, provided by a man in Homosassa Springs, Florida, even put names to the two women.'

The women killed Peter Siems from Jupiter, Florida, in 1990 and accidentally wrecked his car. Since his body was never found, Wuornos was not tried for his murder.

relatives. When Siems was reported missing, John Wisnieski of the Jupiter police was assigned the case. Wisnieski dispatched a nationwide teletype, giving descriptions of the two women together with sketches of them to the Florida Criminal Activity Bulletin. But any hopes Wisnieski might have entertained about finding Peter Siems were not fulfilled. Siems had completely disappeared.

Searching for a Lead
Meanwhile, the murders continued. Troy Burress, a sausage salesman from Ocala, Florida, was reported missing on 31 July 1990 and was found shot dead on 4 August in woods close to State Road 19 in Marion County. Just a few weeks later, the body of Dick Humphreys, 56, an investigator into child injury and abuse, and a former police chief in Alabama, was discovered in Marion County on the evening of 12 September 1990: he had been shot with seven bullets fired from a .22 rifle. The car belonging to

AILEEN WUORNOS TIMELINE

29 February 1956: Aileen Carol Wuornos (née Pittman) born in Rochester, Michigan.

January 1960: Aileen's mother deserts her and her elder brother Keith. Aileen and Keith go to live with their grandparents, Lauri and Britta Wuornos.

18 March 1960: Aileen and Keith are legally adopted by their grandparents and take their surname as their own.

23 March 1971: Aileen Wuornos, aged 15, gives birth to a son at a Detroit home for unwed mothers. Aileen is thrown out by her grandfather. Now destitute and homeless, she becomes a prostitute.

27 March 1974: Wuornos begins a career in crime that includes disorderly conduct, firing a .22 calibre pistol from a moving vehicle, assault, armed robbery and several other acts of violence.

1976: Wuornos, 20, marries wealthy yacht club president Lewis Graz Fell, 70, but makes a habit of assaulting him. Fell gets the marriage annulled after nine weeks.

1986: Wuornos meets motel maid Tyria Moore, 24, and sets up home with her. They live off Wuornos's earnings as a prostitute, but after a while, the money runs out.

30 November 1989: Wuornos kills her first murder victim, Clearwater electronics store owner Richard Mallory, 51, with a .22 calibre rifle. His abandoned car, a 1977 Cadillac, is found on 1 December and his dead body is discovered near Interstate 95, Volusia County, on 13 December.

19 May 1990: Heavy-equipment operator David Spears, 43, disappears on his way to Orlando, Florida. His abandoned truck is found on Interstate 75 soon afterwards and his naked body on 1 June.

7 June 1990: A victim later identified as Charles Carskaddon, 40, a part-time rodeo worker, is discovered in Pasco County. Detective Tom Muck is assigned to the case and suspects a serial killer is at work.

4 July 1990: A 1988 Pontiac Sunbird swerves off State Road 315 near Orange Springs, Marion County, and crashes into a patch of brushwood. Two women emerge from the vehicle, observed by a local householder, Rhonda Bailey. The women attempt to drive on in the Pontiac, but walk off after it breaks down. Later examination shows extensive bloodstains in the interior of the Pontiac and a bloody palm print on the interior door handle. The Pontiac turns out to belong to Peter Siems, 65, who disappeared from Jupiter, Florida, on 7 June and is not seen again.

31 July 1990: Troy Burress, an Ocala sausage salesman, is reported missing. He is found shot dead on 4 August.

12 September 1990: Dick Humphreys, 56, is found murdered in Marion County.

19 November 1990: Walter Jeno Antonio, 62, is discovered dead in Dixie County.

9 January 1991: After following up leads and information from the automobile crash of the previous 4 July, Aileen Wuornos is arrested in Volusia County. Tyria Moore helps the police in persuading Wuornos to confess to the serial killings..

14 January 1992: Aileen Wuornos goes on trial for the murder of Richard Mallory. Other trials follow for five of the other six murders, except for the killing of Peter Siems, whose body is never found. Wuornos is found guilty and is given six life sentences. The last of the trials ends in February 1993.

9 October 2002: After a protracted series of appeals, Wuornos, aged 46, is executed by lethal injection.

Humphreys was found later the same month in Suwanee County, Florida.

Two months later, on 19 November, Walter Jeno Antonio, 62, was discovered close to a logging road in Dixie County, Florida, with four .22 rifle bullets in his body, two in the chest and two in the back. His vehicle was found on 24 November in Brevard County.

At this stage, after seven murders that bore several similarities to each other, the Florida police had no clues, no leads and no viable suspects – except, that is, for the circumstantial evidence provided by the crash of Peter Siems's Pontiac on 4 July 1990. The two women had denied being in the car, a lie that was easy to refute considering the number of witnesses who were able to provide descriptions of them and the evidence of Rhonda Bailey.

Together with graphic details of the murders, which clearly indicated a serial killer at work, this information was used by Captain Steven Binegar, commander of the Marion County Sheriff's Criminal Investigation Division, to mount a press campaign designed to track the women down. Reuters, the worldwide news service, ran the story in late November 1990, and from that point newspapers in Florida made it a prominent feature in their own editions. The public response was immediate and prolific. By mid-December, data was flooding in and one item, provided by a man in Homosassa Springs, Florida, even provided names for the two women: about a year earlier, he told police, Tyria Moore and a woman who went by the name of Lee had rented a trailer from him.

'Wuornos confessed to the seven murders but added a defence that she had killed to protect herself, for the men had all tried to rape her.'

Other details, from Daytona, revealed that Tyria and Lee had moved from one motel to another and that at one of them, the Fairview Motel in Harbor Oaks, Lee had registered as Cammie Marsh Greene. Detectives in Volusia County who set about checking Daytona pawnshops found that 'Greene' had pawned a camera and a radar detector in one of them and that she had marked her thumbprint on the receipt. The camera and detector were traced back to Richard Mallory, and at Ormond Beach a set of tools also pawned by 'Greene' proved to be the same as that taken from David Spears's truck.

The thumbprint was the key that unlocked the truth about the serial killings. Wuornos's early adventures in crime came back to haunt her, for the thumbprint was found on a weapons charge made many years before in Volusia County. Wuornos's frequent use of aliases counted against her, too, for an unanswered warrant for the arrest of Lori Grody also turned up. So did data from Michigan and Colorado as well as Florida, proving that Grody and Cammie Marsh Greene were all, in reality, Aileen Carol Wuornos. In addition, the bloody palm print found on the door handle of Peter Siems's car matched an earlier sample taken from 'Lori Grody'.

On 9 January 1991, Aileen Wuornos was arrested in a biker bar in Volusia County after a brief, four-day search. To detain her, police used the unanswered warrant originally issued against Lori Grody. Next day, Tyria Moore was located in Scranton, Pennsylvania,

Investigators hold up a mugshot of Aileen Wuornos and her first victim, Richard Mallory, of Clearwater, Florida. His body was found wrapped up in a carpet runner.

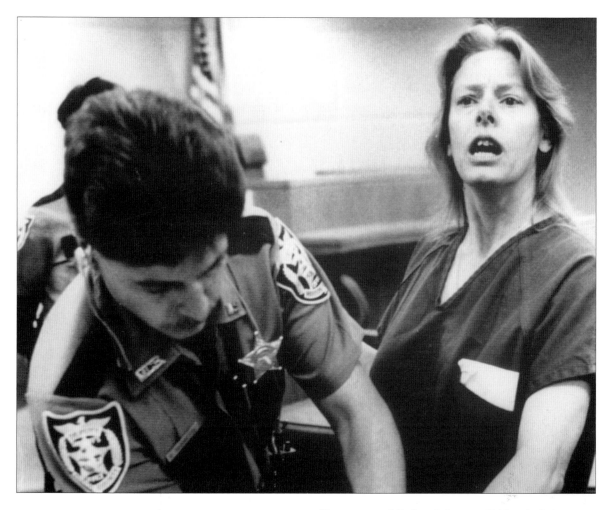

Wuornos was jailed on 9 January 1991 and tried a year later. After the jury had convicted her, she raged against them, calling them 'scumbags of America'.

and was persuaded by police to obtain a confession from Wuornos in exchange for immunity from prosecution. Under police supervision, Moore made several telephone calls to Wuornos, pleading for aid in clearing her name. The ruse worked, and on 16 January, Wuornos confessed to the seven murders but added a defence that she had killed to protect herself, for the men had all tried to rape her. Psychiatrists had their own explanation for Wuornos's behaviour – mental instability and a borderline personality disorder.

Wuornos was tried separately for six of the seven murders, the exception being the case of Peter Siems, whose body was never found. The series of trials began on 14 January 1992, the first being for the murder of Richard Mallory. She received a death sentence. The trials ended in February 1993, when Wuornos pleaded guilty to killing Walter Jeno Antonio: for this, she received the last of six death sentences.

The protracted US appeals process lasted for nearly 10 years until Wuornos grew tired of it and petitioned the Florida Supreme Court for a halt to the process.

'I killed those men,' she declared, 'robbed them as cold as ice. And I'd do it again, too.'

Aileen Wuornos was executed by lethal injection at 9.47 a.m. on Wednesday, 9 October 2002. She was 46 years old.

Anatoly Onoprienko

The Terminator

FULL NAME:
Anatoly Onoprienko

DOB:
25 July 1959

NUMBER OF VICTIMS:
53

SPAN OF KILLINGS:
1989–1996

LOCATION OF KILLINGS:
In and around villages close to Lvov, Ukraine

DATE OF ARREST:
16 April 1996

SENTENCE:
Sentenced to death by shooting, which was commuted to life imprisonment

Anatoly Onoprienko is a serial killer considered by some to be more than half mad. He roamed from place to place across the Ukraine, killing entire families and stealing their money, jewellery and other belongings. One of Europe's most savage murderers, Onoprienko believed that he was carrying out commands from God. His 53 killings took place in 1989, 1995 and 1996, in and around villages close to Lvov, a major cultural centre in the Ukraine. In one place, he murdered 10 people within just a few minutes.

Onoprienko was a Ukrainian born in Zhytomyr, 145km (90 miles) west of Kiev, on 25 July 1959. For his killings, his pattern of behaviour was simple: he picked out isolated houses in remote villages near the Lvov region of the Ukraine, close to the Polish frontier. Then, he entered a house and murdered everyone inside, including the children, and set the building on fire. Any witnesses were also shot dead. Once he had finished, Onoprienko moved on to the next village, continuing his murderous work there.

Going it Alone

The prelude to Onoprienko's massacres took place in 1989, when he teamed up with Sergei Rogozin, whom he had met at a gym where they both worked out. Before long, their friendship became a partnership in crime. Robbing a secluded house in the village of Bratkovichi in western Ukraine, they were discovered by the family who lived there. The two men had come armed with weapons for defence, but they now slaughtered the whole family – two adults and eight children – in order to escape. A few months later, Onoprienko broke with Rogozin. But he seems to have developed a taste for mass murder because his next killing, this time as a lone operator, involved shooting dead five people sleeping in a car, including a boy of 11. Onoprienko's original intention had been to rob the car, but five people were too many witnesses to leave alive.

Six years passed before Onoprienko chose to kill again. On 24 December 1995, he went to live with a distant cousin, Pyotr Onoprienko, in the west Ukrainian town of Yavoriv. Once there, he lost no time in getting down to his brutal business: that same night, he broke into a house in Armarnia, central Ukraine, which was owned by a forestry teacher named Zaichenko and his family. Onoprienko used a sawn-off double-barrelled shotgun to kill the entire family, including two young boys. He also stole gold wedding rings belonging to the teacher and his wife, a small gold cross on a chain, a set of earrings and a bundle of old clothes. Before he left, Onoprienko set the house on fire.

'I just shot them,' he explained to police after his eventual capture. 'It's not that it gave me pleasure, but

Onoprienko's behaviour and irrational comments while in custody led his interrogator to believe he was insane. Psychiatrists, however, said he was fit to stand trial.

> **'He drove to the remote village of Bratkovichi and broke into the Pilat family's house. He shot all six people inside the house … and then set it on fire before escaping just before dawn the following morning.'**

I felt this urge. From then on, it was almost like some game from outer space.'

Onoprienko's motive was not just a space game. It was something far more sinister. Later, he confessed that he had experienced a vision from God, ordering him to commit murder. On 2 January 1996, he apparently followed orders and shot dead a family of four, then torched their house. While leaving the scene, a man on a nearby road saw him: he became Onoprienko's fifth victim that night.

Killing Sprees

Four days later, on 6 January 1996, Onoprienko was near the highway that ran between Beryansk and Dnieprovskaya when he decided to halt passing cars and murder their drivers. He killed a Russian Navy ensign named Kasai, a taxi driver called Savitsky and a cook named Kocheregina.

'To me, it was like hunting. Hunting people down,' Onoprienko remarked. 'I would be sitting, bored, with nothing to do, and then suddenly this idea would get into my head. I would do everything to get it out of my mind, but I couldn't. It was stronger than me. So, I would get in the car or catch a train and go out to kill.'

Onoprienko got into his car with similar intent on 17 January 1996, and drove to the remote village of Bratkovichi. Breaking into the Pilat family's house, he shot all six people inside the house, including a boy of 6, and then set it on fire before escaping just before dawn the following morning. He was observed by a

27-year-old female railway worker, named Kondzela, and Zakharko, a 56-year-old man. He shot both of these witnesses dead.

By this time, according to Onoprienko himself, he was obsessed with the idea of killing, and apparently unable to stop himself. His next stop, on 30 January 1996, was in the Oblast (zone or province) of Fastova-Kievskaya. His next victims were a 28-year-old nurse named Marusina, her two young sons and a 32-year-old man called Zagranichniy, who was visiting. This was followed on 19 February 1996 at Olevsk, in the Zhitomirskaya Oblast, where he drove his car to the house of the Dubchak family. He shot the father and son, then went to work on the mother and daughter with a hammer. He demanded that the daughter tell him where the family kept their money. She refused. Later, Onoprienko admitted that he thought her strength of character 'incredible', but he smashed her head in just the same.

A Distant Cousin

Onoprienko's next stop was Malina in the Lvovskaya Oblast. On 27 February 1996, he broke into a house where the Bodnarchuk family lived. He used his gun on the husband and wife, but murdered their two daughters, aged 7 and 8, with an axe. Once again, though, there was a witness, a neighbour named Tsalk. Onoprienko saw him moving about outside the house and shot him dead. Then, he hacked his corpse to pieces with the axe.

'I had to kill them,' he confessed later. 'The inner voice spoke inside my mind and heart and pushed me so hard!'

Onoprienko committed his last murder on 22 March 1996 after driving to Busk, a small village outside Bratkovichi. There he shot dead the four members of the Novosad family, and afterwards torched their home.

Onoprienko, who said later that he wanted to be studied as 'a phenomenon of Nature', insisted, 'I am a not a maniac. I have been taken over by a higher force, something telepathic or cosmic, which drove me.'

By this time, 38 people had been brutally killed within three months, and villagers in the Ukraine

The Trail of Murder

Lvov, Ukraine, 1989–1996:
The vast majority of Onoprienko's 53 victims lived around the Lvov region in the Ukraine near Poland. From 1989 to 1996, he roamed from one remote village to another, selecting isolated houses where he killed entire families, burned the buildings and shot dead any witnesses.

Armarnia, Ukraine, 1995:
After moving in with his cousin in 1995 in the western Ukraine town of Yavoriv, Onoprienko travelled to the country's central area to murder a family of four. He entered a home in Armarnia, killing a forestry teacher, his wife and their two young sons.

Highway killing, 6 January 1996:
Days after Onoprienko believed God told him to kill, he shifted attacks to the road, murdering three motorists on 6 January 1996. He halted the cars on the highway between Beryansk and Dnieprovskaya. The victims were a Russian sailor, a taxi driver and a cook.

Malina, Lvovskaya Oblast, 27 February 1996:
In a gruesome attack, Onoprienko broke into a family's home in Malina in Lvovskaya Oblast, shooting the parents and killing their two young daughters with an axe. When a neighbour approached, Onoprienko shot him and hacked his body to pieces.

Key   Onoprienko's victims

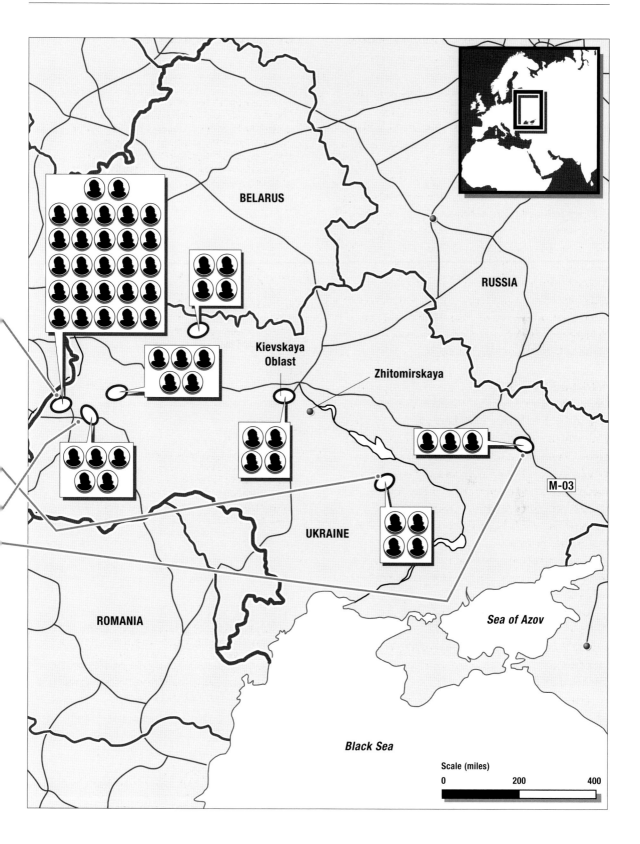

'The Terminator' faced being terminated by the state, as the furious Ukrainian public called for his execution. European law, however, prevented the death sentence.

were living in terror. The fear was so pervasive that, in several places, the army sent troops to patrol the streets. But the police had not even the faintest of leads until 7 April 1996, when Police Officer Igor Khuney received a curious call at his office in Yavoriv. The caller was Pyotr Onoprienko, who had discovered, to his great alarm, that his distant cousin Anatoly had hidden a number of weapons in his home. Pyotr ordered Anatoly to leave forthwith. His cousin was enraged and responded by threatening his family, promising that they would be 'taken care of' the following Easter. With that, he left the house and moved in with a woman and her family in the nearby town of Zhitomirskaya.

On hearing this startling news, Khuney's superior, Deputy Police Chief Sergei Kryukov, consulted General Bogdan Romanyuk, the police chief of Lvov. He received instructions to form a task force at once and search the Onoprienko apartment on Ivana Khristitelya Street, Zhitomirskaya. Twenty police officers and detectives were quick to converge on the

apartment. They seized and handcuffed Anatoly Onoprienko as soon as he opened the door, then combed the rooms for evidence. They soon found it. For one thing, there was an Akai stereo in the living room, which had been reported missing from the Novosad family home in Busk. Kryukov had brought along a list of items missing from houses where families had been killed, together with their makes and serial numbers. Several of the items were now found in the apartment.

Onoprienko quickly gave himself away after he was asked for his identification. He went to a closet where he kept it, but once the door was opened, he made a grab for a pistol hidden inside. He was soon subdued and was taken off to the police station. Meanwhile, the search continued. Eventually, 122 items connected with unsolved killings were found. They included a sawn-off Tos-34 rifle.

A Killer's Pride

Despite this copious evidence, a confession was still required of Onoprienko. At first, he refused to co-operate, so the experienced interrogator Bogdan Teslya was called in for the task. Onoprienko had already stated that he would not talk to underlings like Kryukov, only to a high-ranking general. But Teslya broke Onoprienko by suggesting that there was nothing for him to tell, so why should a general bother with him? Onoprienko's warped pride was pricked by this and he assured Teslya: 'Don't worry! There's definitely something to tell.'

There certainly was. Once General Romanyuk entered the room, Onoprienko told him everything – not just the details of the murders but also the fantasies, the divine 'commands', the urgings of 'inner voices', and the games from outer space, as well as extraordinary claims that he could exercise hypnotic powers to control animals through telepathy

'By this time, 38 people had been brutally killed within three months, and villagers in the Ukraine were living in terror.'

ANATOLY ONOPRIENKO TIMELINE

25 July 1959: Anatoly Onoprienko born in Zhytomyr, Ukraine.

1989: Onoprienko and his accomplice Sergei Rogozin kill a family of 10 during a robbery. A few months later, after breaking with Rogozin, Onoprienko shoots five people sleeping in a car.

24 December 1995: Onoprienko moves in with his distant cousin Pyotr in Yavoriv, western Ukraine, and the same night kills a family of four in Armarnia, central Ukraine.

2 January 1996: Believing he has received orders from God telling him to kill, Onoprienko murders another family of four.

6 January 1996: In separate incidents, Onoprienko kills three car drivers on the highway between Beryansk and Dnieprovskaya.

17 January 1996: Onoprienko breaks into the house of the Pilat family in Bratkovichi and shoots six people. Two witnesses passing by are also killed.

30 January 1996: In the Fastova-Kievskaya Oblast, Onoprienko murders two adults and two children.

19 February 1996: At Olevsk, in the Zhitomirskaya Oblast, the parents and two children of the Dubchak family are murdered by Onoprienko: the mother and daughter are killed with a hammer; the father and son are shot.

27 February 1996: Onoprienko breaks into a house at Malina in the Lvovskaya Oblast owned by the Bodnarchuk family. He shoots the parents and murders their two daughters with an axe. A neighbour is also shot dead, then hacked to pieces with the axe.

22 March 1996: At Busk, outside Bratkovichi, Onoprienko shoots dead the four members of the Novosad family, then sets fire to their house.

7 April 1996: Onoprienko's cousin, Pyotr Onoprienko, telephones Police Officer Igor Khuney in Yavoriv to report that Anatoly has

amassed a collection of weapons in his home. Pyotr has demanded that he leave, and an enraged Anatoly departs and goes to live with a woman and her family in nearby Zhitomirskaya. A search of the Zhitomirskaya apartment reveals a number of items missing from homes where Onoprienko has killed families. Onoprienko is arrested and interrogated.

19 April 1996: During 12 days of interrogation, Onoprienko confesses to a number of killings. His interrogator, Bogdan Teslya, is convinced that he is insane.

23 November 1996: Psychiatrists declare Onoprienko fit to stand trial.

12 February 1999: Onoprienko's trial commences in his birthplace, Zhytomyr.

31 March 1999: Onoprienko is found guilty of multiple murder and is sentenced to death. The sentence is commuted to imprisonment for life.

and use the power of his mind to stop his own heart from beating. 'I am a beast of Satan!' he declared. He also revealed that he had once been in a Kiev hospital suffering from schizophrenia, where therapists attending him were well aware that he was a killer.

Sentence Commuted

After 12 days of interrogation and confession, Teslya was convinced that Onoprienko was insane. However, on 23 November 1998, psychiatrists contradicted him and gave as their opinion that Onoprienko was mentally fit to stand trial. At the trial, 99 volumes of photographs were placed into evidence, showing dismembered bodies, houses, cars and miscellaneous objects stolen by the accused. The proceedings began on 12 February 1999, at the regional court in Zhytomyr, Onoprienko's birthplace. Onoprienko sat in an iron cage for his own protection, but this did not prevent members of the public spitting at him or raging in fury against him.

'Let us tear him apart!' one woman shouted from the back of the court. 'He does not deserve to be shot. He needs to die a slow, agonizing death!'

At the end of the trial, Anatoly Onoprienko was found guilty and was sentenced to death by shooting. But – and to the fury of Ukrainian public – the sentence was not carried out. Ukraine was a member of the Council of Europe, which meant that the country was committed to the abolition of the death penalty. Despite arguments from press, public and politicians that the Onoprienko case was exceptional, the sentence was commuted to imprisonment for life.

Onoprienko himself was disappointed. In an interview with the *Times* of London, he told a reporter: 'Death for me is nothing. Naturally, I would prefer the death penalty. I have absolutely no interest in relations with people. I have betrayed them.... If I am ever let out, I will start killing again, but this time, it will be worse, ten times worse. Seize this chance, because I am being groomed to serve Satan.... I have no competitors in my field.'

Ivan Milat

The Backpacker Murderer

FULL NAME:
Ivan Robert Marko Milat

DOB:
27 December 1944

NUMBER OF VICTIMS:
Seven

SPAN OF KILLINGS:
1989–1994

LOCATION OF KILLINGS:
New South Wales, Australia

DATE OF ARREST:
22 May 1994

SENTENCE:
Seven life sentences

On 19 September 1992, a decaying corpse was discovered by two orienteers some 244m (800ft) southwest of the Long Acre Fire trail in the Belanglo State Forest of New South Wales in Australia. The body belonged to the first of seven backpackers found dead in the forest in a period of just over a year, up to 3 November 1993. They had either been shot, strangled, beaten or stabbed to death. But another six months passed before Ivan Milat was arrested, on 22 May 1994, after Paul Onions, a victim who managed to get away, identified him as his assailant.

Ivan Milat, one of 14 children, belonged to a Yugoslav immigrant family that had settled in Australia some time before World War II. Born on 27 December 1944, Ivan exhibited psychotic tendencies early on in life, according to his brother Boris, and shared a reputation for lawlessness with the rest of the family. The problem that was Ivan Milat became truly serious after 1961, when he was regularly in trouble with the police for housebreaking, stealing cars and armed robbery. In 1971, he was put on trial for raping two hitchhikers at knifepoint. Although he was acquitted after the prosecution failed to make a sufficiently convincing case, the fact that Ivan Milat meant trouble had been firmly established.

A Lucky Escape
In 1992, when the Belanglo State Forest started to reveal its grisly secrets, the series of killings was dubbed the Backpacker Murders by the Australian

press. Two years earlier, Milat had graduated from petty offences to violent crime – or, at least, the threat of violent crime – after he picked up British backpacker Paul Onions in his car on 25 January 1990. Milat, who called himself Bill, was friendly at first, but Onions soon became alarmed when he started ranting and raving and shouting racist and xenophobic abuse. When Milat pulled the car to the roadside, Onions took the chance to escape, or so he thought. Before he could get out onto the road, Milat pulled a revolver on him and threatened to shoot him if he tried to get away. At that, Onions took a chance and ran for his life, leaving behind his backpack and passport. Before Milat could catch up with him, Onions had flagged down the driver of a passing car. She took him to the nearest police station so that he could report the incident.

Paul Onions rapidly acquired a replacement passport and returned home to Britain. He did not realize how lucky his escape had been for more than two years. But by the time he did, the story of the Belanglo Forest murders had become big news, not only in Australia, but in other parts of the world where the victims had originated. The first corpse discovered was quickly followed by a second, found on 20 September 1992 buried some 30m (98ft) away. They were identified as the remains of two British backpackers, Caroline Clarke and Joanne Walters, who had disappeared five months earlier, after leaving the King's Cross hostel in Sydney and heading south.

The bodies of the two girls showed massive damage, which pointed to a frenzied assault. Joanne Walters had been stabbed nine times in the heart and lungs by a Bowie-type knife that had penetrated all the way through her body to her spine. Two of Joanne's ribs were completely severed. Caroline Clarke had been stabbed and shot in the head 10 times. Numerous cartridge cases were unearthed in the vicinity of Caroline's body, but a five-day search revealed no more victims, nor any personal items or camping equipment belonging to the two girls. This led the New South Wales police to presume that there were no further corpses to be found in the forest. As they were to discover, though not particularly soon, they were wrong.

'Joanna Walters had been stabbed nine times in the heart and lungs by a Bowie-type knife that had penetrated all the way through her body to her spine.'

Although the investigation that followed was intensive, and the police formulated a profile of the killer, the year 1992 came to an end without any real progress being made. As the trail grew cold, the New South Wales police began to turn their attention to

Anja Habschied and her boyfriend Gabor Neugebauer disappeared at the end of 1991. their brutally stabbed bodies were not discovered until November 1993.

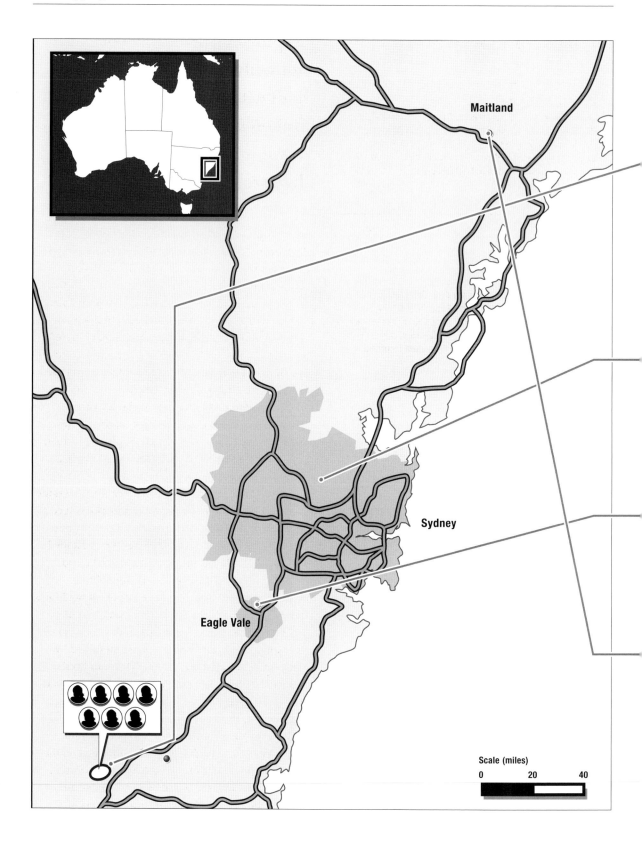

Maitland

Sydney

Eagle Vale

Scale (miles)

0   20   40

The Trail of Murders

Belanglo State Forest:
All of Milat's victims ended up in Belanglo State Forest. The area is popular with backpackers who often take isolated paths. Police brought in trained dogs to help locate remains that had been buried in shallow graves. The forest covers about 4100 hectares (10,130 acres).

Sydney, 5 October 1993:
Sydney was the headquarters for Task Force Air that investigated the murders. Led by Superintendent Clive Small, the officers would receive hundreds of telephone tips on the task force hotline in one day. Paul Onions telephoned about his escape from Milat and returned to identify him.

Eagle Vale, Campbelltown, 22 May 1994:
Milat was arrested on 22 May 1994 at his home in the Eagle Vale suburb of Campbelltown, New South Wales. After 50 police officers surrounded the house, Milat and his girlfriend, Chalinder, came outside and were taken into custody. Officers found weapons and ammunition inside their home.

Maitland, 27 July 1996:
After Milat's sentencing, he was taken in July 1996 to the maximum security prison in Maitland, New South Wales, 163km (109 miles) north of Sydney. When he attempted to escape in 1997, officials transferred him to Goulburn prison, a few miles from Belanglo State Forest.

Key Milat's victims

'Exploring further, Pryor suddenly came upon a human skull with part of the lower jaw broken away and a thin cut, possibly made by a knife, on the forehead.'

other crimes. But then, around 5 October 1993, the Backpacker Murder case was suddenly revived when Bruce Pryor, a local who knew the Belanglo Forest well, went to the area to investigate. Pryor knew that several young backpackers who had visited the forest had been reported missing. The thought that they were lying there, concealed and unfound, bothered him. Pryor knew the forest trails and concentrated on the Morice Fire Trail. This led to another track called Clearly's Exit Fire Trail, which opened out onto an area covered in rocks. Beyond that lay a clearing.

It was in the clearing that Pryor found a large bone that appeared to be human. Exploring further, Pryor suddenly came upon a human skull with part of the lower jaw broken away and a thin cut, possibly made by a knife, on the forehead. Wrapping the skull in a cloth, Pryor drove to a small hut that belonged to an orienteering club and there, he called the police. The police arrived within 30 minutes. Pryor handed over the skull. He led the police to where he had found it and while they were there, one of the detectives, Steven Murphy, noticed a pair of sandshoes sticking out of a pile of brush. As a result, two more bodies were discovered. Although both corpses were incomplete skeletons, they were later identified by means of dental charts as those of Deborah Everist and James Gibson, both of them from the Australian state of Victoria.

The news that the hunt was once again on for the Backpacker killer spread quickly. Reporters, film crews, TV cameras and helicopters converged on the forest and public interest – and fear – soon revived. The investigation now became official, under the name of Task Force Air, with its headquarters in

Sydney. Superintendent Clive Small was in control, with Detective Inspector Rod Lynch as his deputy. Small's team of detectives set to work sifting the information already obtained and finding more in systematic sweeps of the main forest area, with the help of specially trained dogs.

Two Important Leads

This effort did not bear fruit for almost four weeks, until 1 November 1993, when a skull was found in a forest clearing. The skull belonged to Simone Schmidl from Regensburg in Germany, who had last been seen hitchhiking on 20 January 1991. A pair of pink jeans found nearby were not Simone's, but belonged to another German woman, Anja Habschied. Anja and her boyfriend Gabor Neugebauer had been missing since the end of 1991. Their whereabouts were soon discovered close to Simone Schmidl's skull, on

> **'The New South Wales police now announced that they were looking for a serial killer, something the media had been touting ever since the first of the murders was discovered.'**

3 November. They lay in shallow graves 55m (180ft) apart; like other Backpacker victims, they had been brutally stabbed. Again like most others, they had been sexually molested, and where the victims had been shot, forensic examination proved that the same firearm had been used to kill them. The New South Wales police now announced that they were looking

IVAN MILAT TIMELINE

27 December 1944: Ivan Milat born into a Yugoslav immigrant family of 14 children.

1961: Ivan Milat is consistently in trouble with the police for housebreaking, stealing cars and armed robbery.

1971: Milat is put on trial for raping two female backpackers, but is acquitted after the prosecution fails to prove its case.

20 January 1991: Simone Schmidl from Regensburg, Germany, is last seen hitchhiking in Australia.

25 January 1990: Milat picks up British backpacker Paul Onions and threatens him with a gun. Onions escapes and reports the incident to the New South Wales police.

19 September 1992: The body of British backpacker Caroline Clarke is discovered in the Belanglo Forest, New South Wales.

20 September 1992: A second body, that of Joanne Walters, is found nearby. The subsequent investigation makes little progress as the trail grows cold.

5 October 1993: A skull is found in the Belanglo Forest, reviving the investigation.

Two incomplete skeletons are found and are later identified from dental records as those of Deborah Everist and James Gibson. Task Force Air is formed to handle the Backpacker Murders.

1 November 1993: Another skull, belonging to Simone Schmidl, is found in the Forest.

3 November 1993: Another German woman, Anja Habschied, and her boyfriend Gabor Neugebauer are found dead nearby.

13 November 1993: Paul Onions telephones the Task Force hotline telling them of his experience with Ivan Milat in 1990.

17 November 1993: The police search of the Belanglo Forest is called off. Among the hundreds of telephone calls received by the Task Force two are of particular importance; information given by Joanne Berry, the car driver who helped Paul Onions escape from Ivan Milat in 1990; and by a woman whose boyfriend works with Milat and knows about Milat's large collection of guns.

5 May 1994: Paul Onions identifies Milat as the man who threatened him in 1990.

22 May 1994: Milat and his girlfriend Chalinder Hughes are arrested at Milat's home in Campbelltown.

23 May 1994: Milat is charged with robbery and the attempted murder of Paul Onions.

30 May 1994: Milat is charged with the seven Backpacker Murders.

Mid-April, 1996: Milat's trial for murder begins, and lasts 15 weeks.

27 July 1996: Milat is pronounced guilty of murder and receives seven life sentences. He is also given six years' jail for his offences against Paul Onions. He is taken to the maximum security prison in Maitland, New South Wales.

17 July 1997: After a failed attempt to escape, Milat is transferred to the maximum security unit at Goulburn prison, New South Wales.

26 January 2009: In the latest of a series of self-harm incidents, Milat cuts off his little finger with a plastic knife.

for a serial killer, something the media had been touting ever since the first of the murders was discovered. The forest was systematically searched again, but nothing further was found, and the operation was called off on 17 November.

Hundreds of telephone calls were now coming in every day at the Task Force headquarters. Many, inevitably, came from cranks and people who believed, wrongly, that they had seen the Backpacker killer. But of the rest, two were of particular interest. One came from a woman whose boyfriend worked with a man who owned a property near the Belanglo Forest and had a large collection of guns: the man's name was Ivan Milat. The other call was made by Joanne Berry, the driver who had picked up Paul Onions when he was trying to escape Milat back in 1990.

Telephone Call from England
Onions himself came back into the picture round about this time. Thousands of miles away in Britain, he had been following the news of the Backpacker Murders and was horrified to realize the fate he had managed to escape back in 1990. On 13 November, he telephoned the Task Force hotline and told them of his experience. Onions' account was backed up by the statement from Joanne Berry and also tied in with the information from the woman whose boyfriend worked with Ivan Milat. Task Force detectives asked Onions to fly to Australia to help the investigation and he arrived at the beginning of May 1994. On 5 May, Onions positively identified Ivan Milat as the man who had threatened him four years earlier.

'After a few minutes, the front door opened and Milat and Hughes stepped out. Two members of the State of Victoria protection group arrested them, and handcuffed Milat.'

At 6.30 a.m. on 22 May, 50 police officers surrounded Milat's home in Cinnabar Street, Eagle Vale, a northern suburb of Campbelltown, New South Wales. The police, who knew about Milat's gun collection, played cautious and advised Milat, who was in the house with his girlfriend Chalinder Hughes, to come out onto the front lawn. After a few minutes, the

Milat is led from court during his trial in 1996. A year later he attempted an elaborate escape from prison with three other inmates, but their plan was foiled.

front door opened and Milat and Hughes stepped out. Two members of the State of Victoria protection group arrested them, and handcuffed Milat. Meanwhile, Milat's four-bedroom house was secured and thoroughly searched.

When told that he was going to be questioned about seven dead bodies found in the Belanglo Forest, Milat replied: 'I don't know what you're talking about!' Throughout the questioning that followed, Milan lied persistently. He denied having any guns,

'He denied having any guns and denied that he had ever used the name Bill. The search of his house refuted these denials: in the bedroom, a box of ammunition was found that was suitable for a Colt .45 handgun.'

Court officials visit the Belanglo State Forest to view the crime area. It is located in New South Wales in the Southern Highlands between Sydney and Canberra.

and denied that he had ever used the name Bill. The search of his house refuted these denials: in the bedroom, a box of ammunition was found that was suitable for a Colt .45 handgun, the same gun Milat had used to threaten Paul Onions. Another discovery was a Bowie-style knife 30cm (12in) long and various camping items, including two sleeping bags later identified as the property of Simone Schmidl and Deborah Everist.

At Campbelltown police station, Milat refused to co-operate, but his evasions did not help him. On 23 May, he was charged with the robbery and attempted murder of Paul Onions. A week later, on 30 May, he was also charged with killing the seven backpackers. Milat's trial opened almost two years later, in mid-April 1996, and lasted 15 weeks. His defence argued that there was no real proof that Milat was guilty of serial murder, despite the enormous amount of evidence that had been amassed to prove it. It was a futile strategy. On 27 July 1996, the jury pronounced Milat guilty of murder. He received seven life sentences for the seven killings. He was also convicted of crimes against Paul Onions – attempted murder, false imprisonment and robbery – and for these received a total of six years in jail. He was taken to the maximum security prison in Maitland, New South Wales, southwest of Sydney. After a failed escape attempt on 17 July 1997, Milat was transferred to the jail in Goulburn, New South Wales, where he was kept in solitary confinement after a hacksaw was found concealed inside a packet of biscuits in his cell.

Persistent Denial

Throughout his arrest and trial, and to this day, Ivan Milat proclaimed himself innocent of murder, even though his brother Richard Milat told reporters that he believed he was responsible for at least 28 killings. Possibly in an effort to prompt his release on compassionate grounds, Milat has inflicted several injuries on himself, including swallowing razor blades,

'Throughout his arrest and trial, and to this day, Ivan Milat proclaimed himself innocent of murder, even though his brother Richard Milat told reporters that he believed he was responsible for at least 28 killings.'

staples and other metal objects. On 26 January 2009, he cut off his little finger with a plastic knife. But neither self-harm nor the long series of appeals Milat has filed against his convictions have been – or are likely to be – successful.

Milat is transported to court in a prison van. His trial began in 1996 nearly two years after his arrest. It lasted 15 weeks, with 145 witnesses testifying.

Derrick Todd Lee

The Baton Rouge Serial Killer

FULL NAME
Derrick Todd Lee

DOB:
5 November 1968

NUMBER OF VICTIMS:
Indicted for seven but tried for only two killings

SPAN OF KILLINGS:
1992–2003

LOCATION OF KILLINGS:
The Baton Rouge and Lafayette areas of Louisiana, USA

DATE OF ARREST:
27 May 2003

SENTENCE:
The death penalty, he remains on Death Row

A frican-American Derrick Todd Lee served a long apprenticeship before he graduated to the ultimate crime and murdered at least seven women, possibly more. At 9 years of age, in 1977, he was already a 'Peeping Tom', an activity that he carried into later life. He also took up stalking, breaking and entering, burglary and assault, and in January 2000 he attempted murder. His girlfriend, Consandra Green, was lucky to survive the kicking Lee gave her after an argument in a bar.

On his next attempt, Gina Wilson Green, a 41-year old divorcée, was not so lucky. Lee broke into her home in Baton Rouge, Louisiana on the evening of Sunday, 23 September 2001. A nurse who specialized in infusion therapy, Green was alone in her apartment on Stanford Avenue near the Louisiana State University campus when Derrick Todd Lee gained entry to her home. He had several objectives in mind. He sexually molested Green and after strangling her at around 9 p.m., according to the subsequent autopsy, he stole a purse and a mobile phone. This was later recovered abandoned in an alley in Baton Rouge. Green's body was found next day. At that early stage, there were few clues to the identity of her killer. For a time, she appeared to be one more to add to the several dozen unsolved killings that had taken place in the Baton Rouge area over the previous 10 years. Four months passed before the killer struck again.

Sometime before midday on 13 January 2002, there was a break in at the home of Geralyn de Soto,

21, who lived in a mobile home across the Mississippi River from downtown Baton Rouge. The intruder hit de Soto over the head with a telephone and stabbed her three times. Though stunned and bleeding heavily, de Soto fought back. She managed to get into her bedroom, where she grabbed a shotgun. But before she was able to deploy it, the intruder knocked it out of her hand. He grabbed her, drew his knife hard across her throat and, after she collapsed to the floor, stamped on her.

Savage Violence

The following spring, on 31 May 2002, Charlotte Murray Pace, 21, was found dead in her home in the south of Baton Rouge. When found, her body was in a fearful state with over 80 stab wounds and deep injuries sustained from a beating with a clothes iron. Like Geralyn de Soto, Pace had had her throat cut. It was such a ghastly spectacle that even the hardened, experience investigator who later examined her corpse was sickened by it. The killer had stolen several items, including an expensive wallet containing keys to de Soto's BMW automobile, a mobile phone and a silver ring. He had also left behind a footprint from a

'The murder of Gina Green appeared to be just one more to add to the several dozen unsolved killings that had taken place in the Baton Rouge area over the previous 10 years.'

Rawlings brand athletic shoe, man's size 10 or 11, a style that was commonly sold at discount stores in the Baton Rouge area.

Less than two months later, on the evening of Friday, 12 July 2002, Pam Kinamore, 44, an interior decorator and antiques dealer, left her office and headed for her home in Denham Springs, Louisiana, a part of Baton Rouge. She was never seen alive again. When her husband arrived home later the same

A forensic analyst prepares DNA samples in the Baton Rouge case. After a sample was taken of his saliva, Lee was quickly identified as the serial killer.

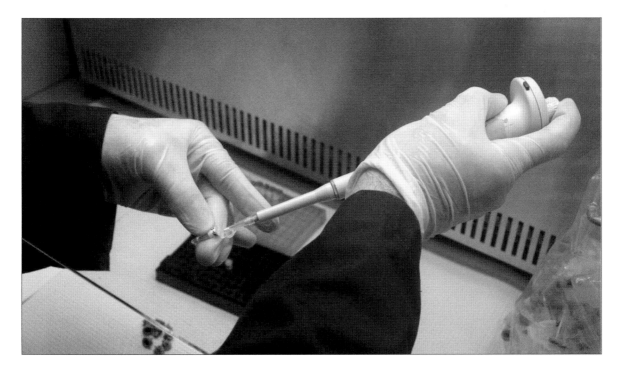

evening, he found her car in the drive, but Pam was nowhere to be seen. Mr Kinamore waited some hours for her to return, but eventually called the police and reported her missing.

After a few days had passed, the police, who had at first believed that there might be an innocent explanation for Pam's disappearance, began to suspect foul play. Pam Kinamore's family, thinking perhaps that she had been kidnapped, put up posters offering a reward of $75,000 for her safe return. No one took up the offer, and after five days all hope faded that she was still alive. On 17 July, a state survey crew were at work near Whiskey Bay Bridge, on the boundary line between Baton Rouge and Lafayette, Louisiana, when they discovered the naked body of a woman in a marshy area of the woods beneath the bridge. Her neck was deeply gashed and she had been sexually assaulted. The body was identified, and police realized they might have a lead: the silver ring that Pam wore on one toe was missing. Her death also bore similarities to the murders of Gina Wilson Green and Geralyn de Soto.

It was also evident that after arriving home on the Friday evening, Pam Kinamore had been abducted, possibly by someone she already knew. There was no sign of forced entry, although the intruder could have got in through an unlocked window and may have been waiting for her before she arrived home. This time, though, there seems to have been a witness. On 24 July, a woman went to the police and told them that she had seen Pam Kinamore's corpse slumped in the passenger seat of a white pickup truck at 3 a.m. the morning after she had originally disappeared. The driver, glimpsed by the witness, appeared to be a white man and the truck, she informed police, got off at the Whiskey Bay exit. It was close by this spot that Pam Kinamore's remains were found.

Public Fears

With four murders committed in less than a year, the time was overdue for a combined operation to track down the serial killer who was at large in the Baton Rouge area. Forty investigators came together in the Multi-Agency Homicide Task Force from the FBI, the Baton Rouge Police Department, the Louisiana State

The Trail of Murders

Zachary, 1998:
Lee began his known murders in 1998 in Zachary in the northern greater Baton Rouge area. He stabbed Randi Mebruer as her 3-year-old son slept. Her body was never found. In 2003 police matched Lee's DNA to that found at the crime scene.

Denham Springs, 12 July 2002:
Lee killed Pam Kinamore in her home in Denham Springs, part of the greater Baton Rouge area. A witness said she had seen Kinamore's corpse in a truck with a white man. This description sent the investigation off on a wrong track.

Iberville, 17 July 2002:
Five days after she was killed, Pam Kinamore's body was discovered in the neighbouring parish of Iberville. Lee had driven along Interstate 10 and thrown her from the 27km-long (17-mile) Whiskey Bay Bridge crossing the Atchafalaya Swamp in bayou country.

Lafayette, 21 November 2002:
Lee travelled 97km (60 miles) away to Lafayette, Louisiana, to murder his first black victim. He abducted a female Marine, Treneisha Dene Colomb, 23, raped her and clubbed her to death. Three days later her naked body was found in woods.

Key Todd Lee's victims

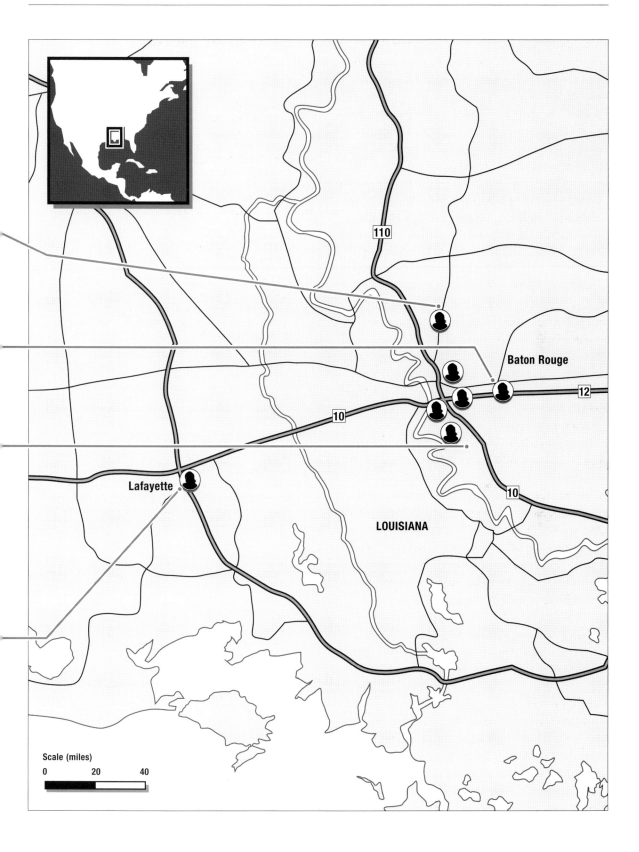

Police and the Parish Sheriff's Offices of East Baton Rouge, Lafayette and Iberville.

Among the first discoveries made by the Task Force was the fact that DNA samples from the Charlotte Murray Pace crime scene matched those taken from the other three victims. Their suspicions that a serial killer was responsible for all four murders were confirmed. When the news spread, women, understandably enough, took fright en masse. Sales of guns, pepper sprays and alarm systems soared. Women started to attend self-defence classes in greater numbers than ever before, even though

> **'Their suspicions that a serial killer was responsible for all four murders were confirmed. When the news spread, women … took fright en masse. Sales of guns, pepper sprays and alarm systems soared.'**

A hoarding displays a large photograph of one of Lee's victims, Pam Kinamore, as the frightened city searched for the killer after her murder in July 2002.

police presence on the streets of Baton Rouge and surrounding areas was everywhere visible, checks were being made on known sex offenders and the Task Force embarked on a programme of taking DNA samples from what eventually amounted to thousands of men. At this stage, all the men were white, for the FBI agents who profiled the killer believed him to be Caucasian.

The Search for Earlier Victims

The police understood that the killer was likely to strike again. After the Kinamore killing, the Baton Rouge Police Department held a 'council of war', to which they invited local law enforcement agencies. The idea was to pool information and ideas in an effort to discover how many as yet unsolved cases could be linked to the Baton Rouge serial killer. One of the investigators who attended was Detective Lieutenant David McDavid of the Police Department in Zachary, some 24km (15 miles) from Baton Rouge.

DERRICK TODD LEE TIMELINE

Killings marked ** indicate the seven for which Derrick Todd Lee was indicted, though he was tried for only two of them (marked ***).

5 November 1968: Derrick Todd Lee born in St Francisville, Louisiana.

8 November 1981: Arrested for burglary and vandalizing a candy store.

8 August 1985: Arrested for second degree murder, but later released.

2 July 1988: Arrested for attempted burglary.

29 October 1989: Arrested after a fight in a bar in St Francisville.

23 August 1992: Derrick Todd Lee suspected of murdering Connie Warner, whose body is found on 2 September, though DNA tests show no sure connection.

1 January 1993: Lee commits robbery and assault while awaiting trial for burglary.

3 April 1993: Lee is suspected of attacking a couple in a cemetery with a cane knife 1.8m (6ft) long.

5 November 1993: Lee is sentenced to four years' imprisonment for burglary, but serves two.

31 July 1997: Lee is arrested on six counts of peeping, trespass and burglary.

18 April 1998: ** The start of Lee's serial killings; he rapes, beats and stabs Randi Mebruer in Zachary, Louisiana.

20 August 1999: After stalking and peeping earlier in 1999, Lee is arrested for more stalking and unlawful entry.

17 December 1999: Lee's girlfriend Consandra Green reports Lee to the police for threats to kill her.

22 January 2000: Lee beats Consandra Green and is arrested by West Feliciana Parish Sheriff's deputies. Lee is afterwards sentenced to one year's imprisonment.

1 January 2001: Lee is released from prison.

23 September 2001: ** Lee kills Gina Wilson Green at her Stanford Avenue home close by the Louisiana State University campus.

13 January 2002: *** Lee murders Geralyn de Soto in her mobile home in Baton Rouge.

31 May 2002: *** Lee kills Charlotte Murray Pace at her home in the south of Baton Rouge.

12 July 2002: ** Lee murders Pam Kinamore at her home in Denham Springs, Louisiana

21 November 2002: ** Lee rapes Treneisha Dene Colomb and beats her to death with the branch of a tree after abducting her in Lafayette, Louisiana.

3 March 2003: ** Lee murders Carrie Lynn Yoder in Baton Rouge.

21 March 2003: After long considering that the Baton Rouge serial killer was a white man, the Multi Agency Task Force announces that he could be black.

5 May 2003: Mixon obtains a court order allowing police to take a DNA sample from Lee in connection with the murder of Randi Mebruer. A match is found after tests three weeks later.

5 August 2004: Lee goes on trial for the second degree murder of Geralyn de Soto. He is found guilty and sentenced to life imprisonment.

12 October 2004: Lee is tried for the first degree murder of Charlotte Murray Pace.

12 October 2004: Lee is found guilty of first degree murder and is sentenced to death by lethal injection, despite pleas from his attorneys that he is mentally deficient and therefore exempt from execution. Today, Lee is still on Death Row at Louisiana State Prison.

McDavid believed that the investigation had to look back, beyond the four killings of 2001/2, to the 1990s, to three, possibly four, crimes involving a local offender named Derrick Todd Lee. Since he was black, Lee had naturally been overlooked in the extensive hunt for a white-skinned killer that had followed several sightings. McDavid began with the death of Connie Warner, 41, who disappeared from her home in the Oak Shadows subdivision of Zachary on 23 August 1992. Some two weeks afterwards, Warner's body was found, severely decomposed, in a ditch near Capitol Lake. Although Lee was suspected, the murder is still unsolved.

Next, McDavid told the Baton Rouge meeting of three offences that were more definitely linked to Derrick Todd Lee. In November 1992, Lee was arrested by Zachary police after a man had come home to find him inside his house. Lee was detained again in January 1993 after he broke into a house owned by a man of 74, whom he beat and robbed of cash. Later, in 1994, Lee spent a year in prison for burglary. Finally, McDavid told how Zachary Police Officer Troy Eubanks found a badly injured couple in a cemetery close by Oak Shadows on 3 April 1993. Both of them had been stabbed with a cane knife some 1.8m (6ft) long, but fortunately they were still alive. Afterwards, the girl, Michelle Chapman, was able to describe the attacker and a police artist produced a sketch of a black suspect who closely resembled Derrick Lee: this was confirmed when the woman picked out a photograph of Lee from a subsequent line-up.

Several more cases involving Lee followed on from the examples McDavid laid before the Baton Rouge meeting. In September 1995, Lee was arrested on Peeping Tom charges, and again in July 1997, when he was also detained for trespassing. Lee was at it again in August 1999, when he was detained on peeping and stalking charges. He was twice sentenced to probation and went to prison for nine months in April 2000 for assaulting his girlfriend Consandra Green and attempting to run down a police officer who was trying to arrest him.

Surveillance Pays Off

Meanwhile, on 18 April 1998, Randi Mebruer, 28, had vanished from her home in Zachary. Neighbours, called in by Mebruer's young son, found blood on the floor and clear signs of a struggle, but no body was ever found. The death of Randi Mebruer remained an unsolved mystery for the next five years.

Despite McDavid's evidence, his police department in Zachary was not invited to join the Multi-Agency Homicide Task Force when it formed in 2002. McDavid later admitted that the Zachary police were 'bothered' by the omission, but they did not let this deter them. Indeed, he and his colleagues, Dannie Mixon and Ray Day, continued their surveillance of Derrick Todd Lee. This seemed to them all the more urgent because the Baton Rouge meeting failed to find a solution to the serial killings, which continued after the murder of Pam Kinamore with the

'Both victims had been raped and both had been severely beaten. Yoder's ribs were broken and her liver was torn. She had also been strangled.'

disappearances of Treneisha Dene Colomb, 23, from a cemetery in St Landry parish, Lafayette, on 21 November 2002 and of Carrie Lynn Yoder, 26, on 3 March 2003. Colomb's corpse was discovered some 32km (20 miles) away after two days; Yoder's was found floating in Whiskey Bay, after 10 days. Both victims had been raped and both had been severely

Lee appears in Fulton County Superior Court in Atlanta, Georgia, for an extradition hearing. He was caught in Atlanta and returned to Baton Rouge on 28 May 2003.

'This simple performance, which required a single swab of Lee's saliva to be taken from his mouth, was the breakthrough that finally cracked the case of the Baton Rouge killer.'

beaten. Yoder's ribs were broken and her liver was torn. She had also been strangled.

It was not long after the murder of Carrie Yoder that the Multi-Agency Task Force at last conceded that they could have been wrong to identify the serial killer as a white man and admitted that, instead, he could be black. This may have had something to do with new investigations being carried out by David McDavid's colleague, Dannie Mixon. Mixon began to delve more deeply into Derrick Todd Lee's criminal record after the Zachary police received fresh complaints about a stalker, from a woman who lived in Oak Shadows. Mixon found that on the dates when Connie Warner was murdered and Randi Mebruer disappeared, Lee was out of prison. He was also out of prison on the dates when the serial killer murdered his victims in or near Baton Rouge. From this, Mixon concluded that despite the fact that Derrick Lee was black while the received wisdom was that the serial killer was white, he was the most likely suspect for the crimes.

To obtain the evidence needed to confirm his suspicions, Mixon applied to a judge in East Feliciana parish to issue a *subpoena duces tecum*, a judicial order that enabled him to obtain a DNA sample from Derrick Lee. This simple performance, which required a single swab of Lee's saliva to be taken from his mouth, was the breakthrough that finally cracked the case of the Baton Rouge killer: Lee's DNA matched the samples previously taken from the Baton Rouge crime scenes. Lee's sample was also linked to DNA discovered in Randi Mebruer's house in Zachary.

With that, the Zachary police, who had once been snubbed by the Multi-Agency Task Force, became the

Charlotte Murray Pace, 21, was killed by Lee on 31 May 2002 in her home in south Baton Rouge. He stabbed her more than 80 times and cut her throat.

heroes of the hour with congratulations heaped on McDavid and Mixon. Mixon, who insisted that he was 'just another flatfoot doing my job', received a special award.

Derrick Todd Lee was ultimately indicted for the homicide of seven women, but he was put on trial only twice: in August 2004 for the second degree murder of Geralyn de Soto, and the following October for the first degree killing of Charlotte Murray Pace. After the de Soto trial, Lee was sentenced to life imprisonment. But after the second trial he was sentenced to death by lethal injection, despite the efforts of his attorneys to convince judge and jury that his low IQ of less than 65 showed that he was too deficient mentally to understand what he had done. Derrick Todd Lee has been on Death Row in Louisiana State Prison ever since.

Angel Maturino Resendez
The Railway Killer

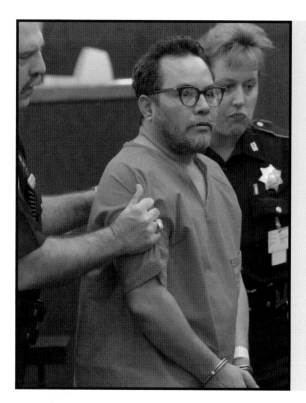

FULL NAME
Angel Maturino Resendez

DOB:
1 August 1959

DIED:
27 June 2006

NUMBER OF VICTIMS:
11 known victims

SPAN OF KILLINGS:
1997–1999

LOCATION OF KILLINGS:
Various locations across the USA, mainly near railway tracks

DATE OF ARREST:
13 July 1999

SENTENCE:
The death penalty (lethal injection)

Angel Resendez was a slightly built man, only 1.67m (5ft 6in) tall and an illegal immigrant from Mexico. He first tried to get into the United States in 1976, when he was 16 years of age. Deported several times, he constantly returned and committed various crimes – burglary, fraud, trespass – before he put the US railroad system to use as the network for his serial killings. Between 1997 and 1999, Resendez murdered 11 known victims, all of them diminutive, like himself. Most of them were killed in central Texas, but Resendez also reached as far as Florida, Kansas, Kentucky and Illinois, stowing away on freight trains and stopping off here and there to ply his trade.

Angel Resendez had no permanent home. As a child, he lived on the streets of Izucar de Matomoros in Puebla, Mexico, where he was born in 1959. He later took to hanging around the US–Mexican border, awaiting his chance to cross the Rio Grande to reach the American side of the river. After his first attempt in 1976 and subsequent deportation, he managed to get in undetected some three years later, and remained on American soil long enough to commit crimes in five US states – Maryland, Texas, Louisiana, Florida and New Mexico. These earned Resendez prison sentences totalling some 27 years, but parole saw to it that, between deportations, he served only nine of them in the 16 years up to 1995.

By then, he had established a method of getting around the United States for nothing by illegally stowing away on freight trains and leaving them, unseen, between stops along the way. After 1997, this became his preferred means of travel as well as a useful adjunct to his 'career' as a serial killer. He began to inhabit the railways of the United States, Canada and Mexico, 'earning' his living by burglary and also stealing the weapons he used on his murder victims: a tyre iron, a sledgehammer, a flat iron, gardening tools and, on one occasion, a shotgun. There was a pattern to his killings and a simple one: he committed his murders close to the railway tracks where there were few, if any, witnesses, then boarded the next freight train and was far away before – sometimes long before – the crime was discovered.

A Taste for Violence

Resendez committed his first two murders beside the rail tracks at Ocala, Florida, on 23 March 1997. Using an air hose coupling, he bludgeoned 19-year-old Jesse Howell to death. He then raped Howell's fiancée, Wendy von Huben, 16, and afterwards strangled and suffocated her. Jesse Howell was later found by the rail tracks where he fell. Von Huben was discovered buried in a shallow grave in Sumter County, Florida, some 48km (30 miles) from the murder scene.

Five months later, Resendez had moved on to Kentucky, where he claimed his third victim near the University of Kentucky at Lexington. On 29 August 1997, 21-year-old student Christopher Maier was strolling along by the rail tracks with his girlfriend, Holly, when Resendez leapt on them. He attacked

'There was a pattern to his killings and a simple one: he committed his murders close to the railway tracks where there were few, if any witnesses, then boarded the next freight train and was far away before the crime was discovered.'

Maier, bludgeoning him to death, and then raped Holly, beating her so savagely that she nearly died.

After that, Angel Resendez seemed to disappear for more than a year. He did not resurface until the evening of 4 October 1998, when he jumped off a train running on the Kansas City–Southern Rail Line and walked to the nearest house, some 46m (50yd) from the railway at Hughes Springs, Texas. He got in through a window and confronted the 81-year-old householder, Leafie Mason. Grabbing an antique flat iron, he beat her to death. Then, he was gone.

Lonely railway tracks curl through Weimar, Texas. Resendez visited here in May 1999, long enough to murder Pastor Norman J. Sirnic, and his wife Karen.

Resendez reappeared at West University Place in Texas some 11 weeks later, on 17 December 1998. His victim was Claudia Benton, 39, a pediatric neurologist who worked at the Baylor College of Medicine. Benton's house lay close to the Union Pacific St Louis Southwestern Railroad. She was raped, stabbed and repeatedly beaten. Although Resendez left no evidence of his involvement in her murder, he *did* make a bad mistake. He stole Benton's Cherokee Jeep and drove it to San Antonio. There it was found by police, who also found his fingerprints on the steering column. These were soon matched in the records of the Texas police to those taken several years back from the well-known drifter and illegal alien Angel Resendez. But amazingly enough, the warrant issued for his arrest was for burglary, rather than murder.

Nevertheless, the killing of Claudia Benton had consequences after 2 May 1999, when the bodies of Pastor Norman J. Sirnic, 46, and his wife Karen Sirnic, 47, were discovered bludgeoned to death with a sledgehammer in a parsonage belonging to the United Church of Christ in Weimar, Texas. The parsonage was adjacent to a railway and, once again, the victims' car, a red Mazda, was stolen. It was found in San Antonio three weeks later with his fingerprints on the steering column – a fact that linked the Sirnic deaths to the killing of Claudia Benton.

Extensive Investigations

Apart from the fact that Resendez was known to be Mexican, these were the first solid clues to his identity as the Railroad Killer. But where was he? He was like a will o' the wisp, never sighted near the murder scene, never spotted acting suspiciously, never recognized by anyone as a dangerous stranger. In these circumstances, the state and city law enforcement agencies resorted to every form of investigation in the book. Security in freight yards was increased. Freight trains were thoroughly searched. Hobos and other drifters were hauled off the streets and parks and sent for close questioning in local jails. The police staged raids on homeless shelters, soup kitchens, or blood centres where penniless idlers and tramps might try to make a little money by selling their blood – anywhere and everywhere loiterers and

The Trail of Murders

Ocala, Florida, 23 March 1997:
Resendez committed his first murder in Ocala, Florida, on 23 March 1997. His victims, as usual, were walking near the railway tracks. Jesse Howell, 19, was beaten to death with an air hose coupling and his fiancée Wendy von Huben, 16, was raped and strangled.

Lexington, Kentucky, 29 August 1997:
Riding a freight train far from his first murder in Florida, Resendez next struck in Lexington, Kentucky, on 29 August 1997. He bludgeoned to death Christopher Maier, 21, a University of Kentucky student, and severely injured his girlfriend, Holly Pendleton. She later testified against Resendez.

Texas, 1998–1999:
Resendez killed six people in Texas, the state adjoining his native Mexico. These included a pediatric neurologist who worked at the Baylor College of Medicine, a United Church of Christ minister and his wife in Weimar, a schoolteacher in Houston and two elderly victims.

Gorham, Illinois, 15 June 1999:
Resendez's last victims were killed in Gorham, Illinois, on 15 June 1999. George Morber, 80, was shot dead and Carolyn Frederick, 52, beaten to death in their home near a railway line. Resendez stole the woman's truck and was spotted driving it in Cairo, Illinois.

Key Resendez's victims

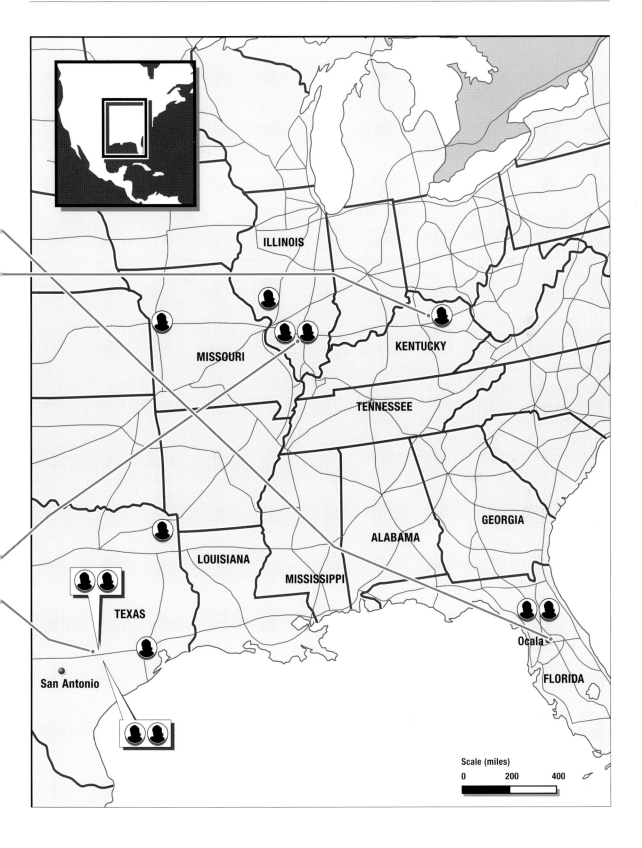

ILLINOIS

MISSOURI

KENTUCKY

TENNESSEE

LOUISIANA

MISSISSIPPI

ALABAMA

GEORGIA

TEXAS

San Antonio

Ocala

FLORIDA

Scale (miles)

0   200   400

Advocates against the death penalty in Texas gathered to demonstrate outside the prison in Huntsville, Texas, prior to Resendez's execution on 27 June 2006.

transients could be found. The Wanted posters that were displayed in the streets readily identified Resendez as Mexican, which meant that other Hispanics were scrutinized and – they claimed – harassed by the police and passers-by in the streets.

The description of Resendez circulated by the police went into remarkable detail, listing his height, weight of around 68kg (150lb), his black hair, brown eyes and colour of his skin (a mid-coffee unique to Mexicans). There were scars on the ring finger of his right hand, left arm and forehead, a snake tattoo on his left forearm and a flower tattoo on his left wrist. Resendez was also known to assume numerous aliases – Rafael Ramirez, for one – and use dozens of social security numbers. In addition, a hefty reward was offered, first $50,000, and later $125,000.

Yet with all this, Resendez remained at large and the killings continued. On 4 June 1999, Noemi Dominguez, 26, a schoolteacher at the Benjamin Franklin Elementary School in Houston, Texas, was hammered to death in her apartment, which was situated near a set of rail tracks. The same day, Josephine Konvicka, 73, was found murdered by a pointed garden tool in her farmhouse in Fayette County, Texas, near Weimar. Eleven days later, on 15 June, there were two murders: George Morber Snr, 80, was shot in the head and Carolyn Frederick, 52, was clubbed to death in their house in Gorham,

Illinois, which lay 91m (100 yards) from a railway line. This time, though, there was a witness who saw a man resembling Angel Resendez driving Frederick's red pickup truck in Cairo, Illinois, 96km (60 miles) south of Gorham.

In that same month of June, the Railroad Killer was placed on the Top Ten Most Wanted list issued by the Federal Bureau of Investigation. The FBI assigned some 200 agents to the case, who received over 1000 telephone tips, including a sighting in Louisville in north Kentucky, where John Matilda, director of the Wayside Christian Mission, also claimed that he had seen Angel Resendez. In fact, as the FBI had discovered, Resendez was elsewhere. He had fled to Ciudad Juarez on the US–Mexican border after the double murder on 15 June.

The Family Intervenes

His escape to Mexico was a complication, giving US law agencies less freedom to act. So, on 7 July, the FBI resorted to a more personal tack. It had located Resendez' common-law wife, Julietta Reyes, at her home in Rodeo, Mexico. Reyes came to Houston, bringing with her 93 items of jewellery, which her 'husband' had mailed her from various locations in the United States. She was certain that he had taken the jewels from his victims, and she was right. When relatives of Noemi Dominguez were shown the items, they identified 13 that had belonged to her. George Benton, Claudia Benton's widower, also recognized several pieces that had belonged to his wife.

Meanwhile, in early June 1999, Sergeant Drew Carter, a young Texas Ranger working with the FBI, had been pursuing an agenda of his own. Resendez had a sister, Manuela, whom he was reputed to idolize. Carter contacted Manuela, who lived in Albuquerque. New Mexico. She had, of course, been following the case and was afraid he was going to kill again, or that the FBI was going to kill him – or both.

Carter managed to convince Manuela that what the FBI wanted was to make a fair deal with her brother, guaranteeing his personal safety and regular visiting rights for his family when he was under arrest, and promising a psychological evaluation of his state of mind. The FBI enlisted the help of a relative who

ANGEL MATURINO RESENDEZ TIMELINE

1 August 1959: Angel Maturino Resendez born at Izucar de Matomoros in Puebla, Mexico.

23 March 1997: After spending several years, between 1976 and 1995, indulging in various crimes in the United States and being regularly deported back to his native Mexico, Resendez commits his first murders. He kills student Jesse Howell, 19, and his fiancée Wendy von Huben, at Ocala, Florida.

29 August 1997: At Lexington, Kentucky, Resendez kills university student Christopher Maier, and rapes and severely injures Maier's girlfriend, Holly Pendleton. She survives and later appears as a witness in Resendez's trial in 2000.

4 October 1998: Leafie Mason, 81, is murdered by Resendez in Hughes Springs, Texas, 45m (50yd) from the Kansas City–Southern Railroad line.

17 December 1998: Dr Claudia Benton, 39, is murdered by Resendez at West University Place, Texas. A warrant is issued for the arrest of Resendez for burglary.

2 May 1999: At Weimar, Texas, Pastor Norman J. Sirnic, 46, and his wife Karen, 47, are bludgeoned to death by Resendez with a sledgehammer in the parsonage of the United Church of Christ, a building adjacent to a railroad. Resendez steals the Sirnics' car and leaves his fingerprints on the steering column. After these killings, the FBI and other law enforcement agencies launch a widespread manhunt for the Railway Killer, as Resendez is now known. Nevertheless, the killings continue.

4 June 1999: Noemi Dominguez, a 26-year-old schoolteacher, is murdered by Resendez, who steals her car and again leaves his fingerprints on the steering column. The same day, in Fayette County, Texas, Resendez murders Josephine Konvicka, 73.

15 June 1999: Resendez commits the double murder of George Morber Snr, 80, and Carolyn Frederick, 52, at Gorham, Illinois. He then flees to Ciudad Juarez on the Rio Grande border between the United States and Mexico. In June, the Railway Killer is placed on the Top Ten Most Wanted list. The same month, Texas Ranger Sergeant Drew Carter contacts Manuela,

the sister Resendez adores, and enlists her help in finding her brother.

7 July 1999: Julietta Reyes, the common-law wife of Resendez, is contacted by the FBI. She hands over jewellery sent to her by her 'husband'. Several pieces prove to be the property of murder victims Noemi Dominguez and Dr Claudia Benton.

13 July 1999: Angel Resendez gives himself up to Sergeant Carter after Manuela persuades him to do so.

24 May 2000: The trial of Resendez for the premeditated murder of Claudia Benton culminates in a guilty verdict and death sentence. Six years of judicial appeals follow.

21 June 2006: The prolonged series of appeals ends when a judge in Houston pronounces Resendez of sound enough mind to be executed.

27 June 2006: Angel Resendez is executed by lethal injection in Huntsville, Texas.

had been in contact with Manuela, and who was now asked to transmit to Resendez the details of this deal. On 12 July, a message arrived from Ciudad Juarez to say that Resendez agreed to the deal.

On 13 July, Sergeant Carter and Manuela, who was accompanied by a priest, arrived at the bridge that connected Zaragosa, Mexico with El Paso, Texas. Shortly afterwards, Angel Resendez reached the bridge in a truck, disembarked and shook hands with Carter. Then, he calmly gave himself up.

At his trial, which took place in May 2000, Resendez was found guilty of the first degree premeditated murder of Claudia Benton and on 24 May he was sentenced to death. But the case still had a long way to run, for years of appeals and legal arguments lay ahead. The most important question to be answered was whether or not Resendez understood what he had done and could therefore be executed.

During those years, Resendez made several statements that seemed to show him to be delusional.

As one psychiatrist put it, 'delusions have completely taken over (his) thought processes.' Resendez described himself as half-man, half-angel and told psychiatrists that he did not believe he could die. 'I am eternal. I am going to be alive forever.' As a result, the forensic psychiatrist Dr Bruce Cohen diagnosed the killer as a schizophrenic who 'did not know his conduct was wrong.' He was suffering from the delusion that his victims were evil, Cohen maintained, so that he 'thought he was justified in his behaviour.'

But on 21 June 2006, a judge in Houston pronounced Resendez to be of sound enough mind to be executed for his crimes. The execution, by lethal injection, took place six days later in Huntsville, Texas.

'I want to ask if it is in your heart to forgive me,' Resendez declared in his final statement. 'I know I allowed the Devil to rule my life.... I deserve what I am getting.'

Angel Resendez was pronounced dead at 8.05 p.m. on 27 June 2006. He was 45 years old.

Andrew Cunanan

American Spree Killer

FULL NAME:
Andrew Phillip Cunanan

DOB:
31 August 1969

DIED:
23 July 1997

NUMBER OF VICTIMS:
Five

SPAN OF KILLINGS:
A three-month period in 1997

LOCATION OF KILLINGS:
Minneapolis, Minnesota, Chicago,
New Jersey and Florida, USA

DATE OF ARREST:
23 July 1997

SENTENCE:
Committed suicide when arrested

Andrew Cunanan appeared to have everything a young man required to make his mark in the world. He was handsome, charming, intellectually brilliant with an IQ of 147, and immensely self-assured – certainly assured enough to be open about his homosexuality. At least, that is how it looked on the face of it. Beneath Cunanan's urbane exterior, however, there lurked an instability that led him, and his victims, to disaster and death.

When Charles Podesta rang the 911 emergency number on 15 July 1997, he could hardly speak. The operator who took the call could barely hear what he was saying, for there was a woman screaming hysterically in the background. Eventually, though, Podesta managed to explain that the celebrated

Italian fashion designer Gianni Versace, 50, who employed him as a chef, had been shot at close range as he returned to his mansion on Ocean Drive in Miami, Florida, after his customary morning outing. When the shots were heard inside the house, staff rushed out to find Versace lying in a pool of blood, with half his face missing. Versace was still, if barely, alive by the time the police arrived, but he died in hospital minutes later.

The sudden, violent death of Gianni Versace made front-page headlines across the world. The sense of shock was immense, for his cutting-edge fashions had catered for royalty, aristocracy and the rich and famous. Versace's devotees included Diana, Princess of Wales, the supermodel Naomi Campbell, and rock stars Elton John and Sting, all of whom were among the 2000 mourners who attended his funeral in Milan on 22 July, a week after the shooting. By that time, the Miami police had already named their suspect, for ballistics tests had proved that the bullets that killed Versace came from the same .40-calibre handgun that had been used to slay two other victims, former US Navy officer turned businessman Jeffrey Trail and architect David Madson in Minnesota. Andrew Cunanan was already suspected of causing both those deaths, as well as two others – Lee Miglin, a wealthy property developer in Chicago, Illinois, and cemetery caretaker William Reese in New Jersey. By the end of July, the hunt was already on for Cunanan amid the fear, always intense in such cases, that the 27-year-old was not yet done with serial killing.

Life among Celebrities

Andrew Cunanan began his slide into psychosis in San Francisco, where he settled in 1990. At that stage, he was a personable 21-year-old who quickly attracted the attention of wealthy socialites, including several homosexuals of the Castro district, who became his lovers. Cunanan was in his element, for he had long

> **'He was handsome, charming, intellectually brilliant with an IQ of 147, and immensely self-assured – certainly assured enough to be open about his homosexuality. At least, that is how it looked on the face of it.'**

fancied that his proper place in life was among celebrities. It was here that he first met Gianni Versace and mixed with movie stars such as Hugh Grant and TV personalities such as *Friends* star Lisa Kudrow.

For a while, Cunanan relished the 'perks' that mixing in this rarified society brought him – the

Cunanan was placed on the FBI's 'Ten Most Wanted Fugitive' list after he murdered cemetery caretaker, William Reese in Pennsville, New Jersey, on 9 May 1997.

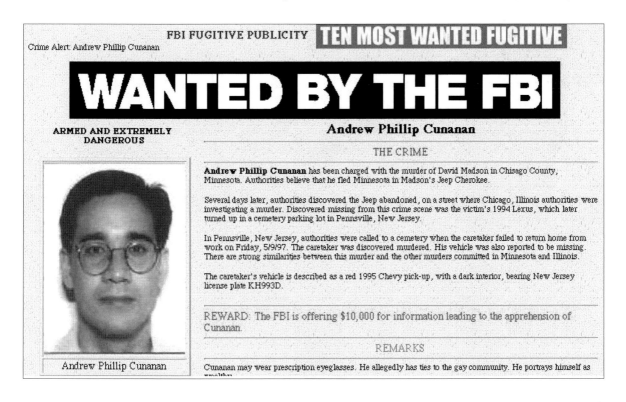

FBI FUGITIVE PUBLICITY
Crime Alert: Andrew Phillip Cunanan

TEN MOST WANTED FUGITIVE

WANTED BY THE FBI

ARMED AND EXTREMELY DANGEROUS

Andrew Phillip Cunanan

THE CRIME

Andrew Phillip Cunanan has been charged with the murder of David Madson in Chisago County, Minnesota. Authorities believe that he fled Minnesota in Madson's Jeep Cherokee.

Several days later, authorities discovered the Jeep abandoned, on a street where Chicago, Illinois authorities were investigating a murder. Discovered missing from this crime scene was the victim's 1994 Lexus, which later turned up in a cemetery parking lot in Pennsville, New Jersey.

In Pennsville, New Jersey, authorities were called to a cemetery when the caretaker failed to return home from work on Friday, 5/9/97. The caretaker was discovered murdered. His vehicle was also reported to be missing. There are strong similarities between this murder and the other murders committed in Minnesota and Illinois.

The caretaker's vehicle is described as a red 1995 Chevy pick-up, with a dark interior, bearing New Jersey license plate KH993D.

REWARD: The FBI is offering $10,000 for information leading to the apprehension of Cunanan.

REMARKS

Cunanan may wear prescription eyeglasses. He allegedly has ties to the gay community. He portrays himself as wealthy

Andrew Phillip Cunanan

WISCONSIN

MINNESOTA

IOWA

ILLINOIS

INDIANA

OHIO

PENNSYLVANIA

MISSOURI

KENTUCKY

VIRGINIA

NORTH CAROLINA

TENNESSEE

SOUTH CAROLINA

ARKANSAS

GEORGIA

LOUISIANA

ALABAMA

MISSISSIPPI

FLORIDA

Scale (miles)

0   200   400

The Trail of Murders

Minnesota, 29 April 1997:
Cunanan's first two murders happened in Minnesota. In a jealous rage over former gay lovers, he shot one, Jeffrey Trail, in Minneapolis on 29 April 1997. He drove away with the other, David Madson, on 1 May, shooting him two days later north of the city.

Chicago, 4 May 1997:
After his Minnesota murders, Cunanan drove on to Chicago, arriving on 4 May and killing a wealthy 72-year-old property developer. Cunanan spotted Lee Miglin in his front garden and forced him by gunpoint into his garage, where he tortured and killed him.

New Jersey, 9 May 1997:
On 9 May, only five days following his Chicago killing, Cunanan was in New Jersey driving his last victim's car. With the FBI now seeking him, Cunanan chose a Pennsville cemetery to hide in, but almost immediately he met and murdered the caretaker, William Reese.

Ocean Drive, Miami, 15 July 1997:
Cunanan's boldest murder was the shooting of the famed fashion designer Gianni Versace in front of his mansion on Miami's exclusive Ocean Drive. Cunanan gunned down the 50-year-old Italian in open daylight on the morning of 15 July 1997 and then escaped unseen.

Key

Cunanan's victims

expensive cars, the unlimited credit cards, the luxury hotel suites. But before long, his dark side took over and he was indulging in the bondage, orgies and pornography that underpinned the gay life. He even permitted a gang of men to torture him in a mass rape scene that was filmed for video.

Hammer Blows

Gradually, his charm and devil-may-care persona began to slip and he became an angry, wanton young man given to strange moods and weird fixations. He worshipped the Hollywood star Tom Cruise, turning his bedroom into a shrine to the actor. Cunanan excoriated Cruise's then wife, Nicole Kidman, whom he regarded as a 'bitch' because, he fancied, she blocked his 'access' to Cruise. On another occasion, he met the actor Hugh Grant at a gala and shortly afterwards tried for a walk-on part in Grant's current film: he failed to get it, and became convinced that Grant had personally ruined his chances.

By the time he had sunk this low, Cunanan was neglecting himself, growing his hair long and wild, putting on weight, resorting to alcohol and dressing in sloppy styles rather than the trendy fashions he had once preferred. His wealthy lovers began to reject him and, before long, he was friendless and broke with mountainous debts he could never hope to repay. Worst of all, he had reason to suspect that two of his lovers – Jeffrey Trail, 28, and David Madson, 33 – had started an affair of their own. Cunanan was consumed with jealousy, not least because Trail and Madson, who lived and worked in Minneapolis, Minnesota, were both successful – Trail as a business executive in Minneapolis, Madson as an architect. Furthermore, their families had accepted their homosexuality. The same was not true for Andrew Cunanan.

In late April 1997, Cunanan contacted Jeffrey Trail in Minneapolis and demanded to know if he was having an affair with Madson. Trail denied it, but Cunanan accused him of lying and warned him: 'I'm going to kill you!' Cunanan flew to Minneapolis, where David Madson picked him up at the airport. Friends in San Francisco had telephoned Madson, warning him about Cunanan's strange behaviour, but Madson felt he could handle it. He even invited

Jeffrey Trail to his apartment the following evening so that, together, they could convince Cunanan that there was nothing going on between them.

It did not work out that way. When Cunanan arrived, mere minutes passed before he was flinging insults and accusations at Trail, while Madson tried desperately to calm things down. Suddenly, Cunanan rushed into the kitchen, took a club hammer from one of the drawers and assaulted Trail. Over and over again, he smashed the hammer down on Trail's head, until blood and brains spattered the room and Trail collapsed battered and lifeless to the living room floor.

'With Miglin lying helpless and terrified in front of him, Cunanan proceeded to reproduce the tortures he had seen in the movie, first stabbing him several times in the chest with pruning shears.'

The opulent mansion of fashion designer Gianni Versace was in south Miami, Florida. Cunanan shot dead the renowned Italian as he unlocked the gate to his estate.

At this, Madson went into shock, but he managed to help Cunanan to roll the body into a Persian rug that lay on the floor and pushed it behind the sofa. Two days passed and Trail's corpse remained in a corner of the room. Colleagues at Madson's office became concerned when he failed to turn up for work, and his telephone went unanswered. One of them contacted Madson's landlord, who sent the building manager to investigate. Realizing that the truth was now out, Cunanan and Madson left Minneapolis in Madson's red Jeep Cherokee.

When the police arrived, they found a rucksack belonging to Cunanan, left behind in the rush to get away. It contained articles that identified him as Trail's killer together with a holster and cartridge, both of them empty. What David Madson did not know, as he and Cunanan sped away from the scene of the crime, was that Cunanan was hiding a .40 calibre handgun loaded with three bullets: another seven bullets were concealed in Cunanan's pocket. At a spot 76km

ANDREW CUNANAN TIMELINE (all dates are in 1997)

29 April: Andrew Cunanan murders his first victim: his lover Jeffrey Trail, 28, an ex-US Navy officer and businessman in Minneapolis.

1 May: Cunanan and David Madson, an architect and another former lover, who witnessed Trail's death, leave Minneapolis in a hurry after Trail's body is discovered.

3 May: Cunanan shoots Madson dead by a lake 76km (47 miles) north of Minneapolis.

4 May: Cunanan drives on to Chicago,

where he murders wealthy property developer Lee Miglin.

9 May: Abandoning David Madson's Jeep Cherokee, Cunanan takes Lee Miglin's Lexus and drives to Pennsville, New Jersey, where he kills cemetery caretaker William Reese and steals his pickup truck.

10 May: Cunanan arrives in Miami, where he vacations for two months before Italian fashion designer Gianni Versace returns to his Ocean Drive mansion after a tour of Europe.

15 July: After trailing Versace from his mansion to the News Café and back again, Cunanan shoots the designer in the back of the head. Fleeing the murder scene, Cunanan hides out in a private houseboat by the Indian Creek Canal.

23 July: Cunanan's hiding place is discovered and surrounded by police and FBI agents. After a three-hour siege, they assault the houseboat, only to find that Cunanan has killed himself.

(47 miles) north of Minneapolis, Cunanan pulled the Jeep Cherokee to the side of a lane that led to Duluth, drew out the handgun and shot Madson three times at point blank range.

Killing a Stranger

Cunanan's third victim died less than a week later. Lee Miglin, 72, was a wealthy Chicago property developer who had made his millions in the building boom of the 1980s. Unlike Trail and Madson, Miglin had no personal connection with Andrew Cunanan. He unfortunately happened to be in his front garden when Cunanan's automobile cruised by on the evening of Saturday, 3 May 1997. Cunanan stopped and approached Miglin, possibly with the intention of asking for directions. Cunanan still had his .40 calibre handgun and he produced it, motioning Miglin into the garage attached to his house.

Once there, Cunanan used duct tape to cover most of Miglin's face, apart from his nose. One of Cunanan's favourite films was *Target for Torture,* a so-called 'snuff' movie, depicting real-life torture and death without special effects. With Miglin lying helpless and terrified in front of him, Cunanan proceeded to reproduce the tortures he had seen in the movie, first stabbing him several times in the chest with pruning shears. He then reached for a hacksaw and proceeded to slice away at Miglin's throat. Presumably, hopefully, Lee Miglin was dead by this time. Cunanan stuffed his body into a sack, then

started up the property developer's Lexus 1994 and drove back and forth over the body several times until the corpse was virtually liquidized.

Miglin's wife Marilyn happened to be out of town at the time, which meant that Cunanan was now able to make free with the Miglin house. He helped himself to sandwiches, an apple and a glass of orange juice, viewed some videos, and spent the night sleeping in the Miglins' bed. There were some gold coins lying around in the house, and he stole them, together with US$2000, before driving off in Lee Miglin's Lexus. David Madson's abandoned Cherokee was later found by police, with photographs of Cunanan littering the front seat. It was as if the killer was intent on claiming the 'credit' for Miglin's death and daring the police to find him.

He made it even easier by using Miglin's mobile phone, which enabled the FBI, who were brought in on the case, to locate him. When Cunanan, now described as 'armed and dangerous', was approaching Philadelphia, police cars prowled the main roads, back roads and expressways, hoping to catch him, but he eluded them all. Eventually, Cunanan threw the mobile phone out of the car window and headed for what he believed would be the ideal hiding place: a cemetery. No one, he was sure, would think of looking for him there, even though an All Points bulletin had already been issued for his arrest.

The site Cunanan chose was Finn's Point Cemetery in Pennsville, New Jersey, which lay across the Salem River from Delaware. Soon after he arrived on the morning of 9 May 1997, he noticed that someone already lived there, for there was a pickup truck outside a house, which looked as if it might belong to the cemetery caretaker. Cunanan knocked on the door. It was opened by William Reese, 45, who took care of the cemetery, mowed and watered the lawns, trimmed the trees and generally kept the place looking immaculate.

When the door opened, Cunanan asked for a glass of water, but when Reese returned with it, he found himself facing a gun. 'Give me your truck keys!' Cunanan demanded. Reese readily complied – 'I don't want any trouble!' he said – but as he handed over the keys, Cunanan pulled the trigger and shot him in the head. Cunanan stole the pickup truck and then drove on to his next destination, Miami Beach in Florida.

After Reese's body was found and the police were called in, they found themselves with no clues, no fingerprints, no motive – only a great deal of speculation – and no idea where to look for Andrew Cunanan. Infuriatingly enough, Cunanan made a habit of leaving 'calling cards' at or near the scenes of his murders, which taunted the police for their failure to catch him. One such 'card' was the car involving Cunanan's last killing, which was left at the site of the next murder – David Madson's Cherokee, for instance, was abandoned a few blocks away from Lee Maglin's home in Chicago. Another was documentary evidence such as the photographs found by police in Madson's vehicle, or Cunanan's passport, which was discovered, together with bloodstained clothing, in

'At 8.15 a.m., the police began an assault. They shoved gas grenades through the houseboat windows while FBI agents burst into the interior, expecting to be met by a blast of gunfire. But all was quiet and still.'

the truck he stole from William Reese and abandoned on arriving at Miami Beach on 10 May 1997.

As for Cunanan's motives, there were, confusingly, a number of them: jealousy of and revenge against Jeffrey Trail; the need to silence a witness by killing David Madson; the thrill of random murder combined with theft in the case of Lee Maglin; and the need to steal another vehicle, which was the reason for shooting Reese. But Cunanan's next and last murder, the killing of Gianni Versace, was different from the others. For one thing, except perhaps for the murder of Jeffrey Trail, it was the only one that was premeditated. It may also have demonstrated a vicarious reason for murder: to kill a celebrity in order to become a celebrity.

Andrew Cunanan had, of course, already met Gianni Versace seven years earlier in San Francisco. Versace was now on an extensive tour of Europe, but Cunanan was in no hurry. For two months, Cunanan vacationed in Miami, sauntering along its lush beaches and lunching at smart beach-side salad bars. He danced at gay clubs, played tennis, visited bistros in the evenings, and from time to time took lovers back to his room at the Normandy Plaza Hotel for a one-night stand. Cunanan was by now 'America's Most Wanted', but somehow he eluded the manhunt that was going on all around him, living openly in Miami.

Eventually, though, he got down to business and homed in on his target and its setting: Gianni Versace and his mansion on Ocean Drive. On 12 July 1997, Versace returned from Europe, swathed in his entourage of agents, promoters and bodyguards. The designer planned to relax for a while after his hectic tour. Meanwhile, Cunanan had done his homework. He was familiar with Versace's daily routine and his favourite bars and clubs – The Twist, the KGB Club, Liquid or the News Café, where he drank his favourite Italian coffee every morning. Despite having a large retinue at his disposal, Versace usually made these excursions alone.

Avoiding Capture

On 15 July, Cunanan tracked Versace from his home to the News Café and back. Just as Versace was inserting his key into the lock on the scrolled gate of his mansion, Andrew came up behind him and fired two bullets into his head. By the time the police reached the scene, the killer had vanished, but Cunanan instantly became a number-one priority for the Miami force. In addition, hundreds of FBI agents were drafted in to comb the scene for clues, yet found nothing to pin down a killer who had deliberately publicized his presence across the country for the better part of three months and indulged in an almost non-stop murder spree.

It was, ironically, left to a Portuguese caretaker to unlock the problem. On the afternoon of 23 July, eight days after the Versace murder, the caretaker was checking out the private houseboat owned by his employer, the German millionaire Torsten Reineck, which was moored by the Indian Creek Canal. Reineck himself was away in Las Vegas at the time. The caretaker was alerted to something wrong when he noticed that a door on the houseboat was ajar. He investigated, found nothing suspicious in the living room, but on going upstairs, suddenly found himself face to face with a strange young man, who immediately took fright and ran into the nearby bedroom, slamming the door behind him. The

caretaker quickly concluded that he had found the fugitive for whom the police and FBI had been so diligently searching and at once alerted the police.

Within a few minutes, 400 FBI agents and police converged on the wharf at Indian Creek Canal, while snipers invaded the nearby apartment block and stationed themselves by the windows. Police boats crowded the canal. Helicopters patrolled up above. For three hours, Andrew Cunanan refused to answer calls to surrender and at 8.15 a.m., the police began an assault. They shoved gas grenades through the houseboat windows while FBI agents burst into the interior, expecting to be met by a blast of gunfire. But all was quiet and still.

They discovered the reason when they went upstairs. Andrew Cunanan lay on the floor of the bedroom, with a hole just above his right ear. It seems that in all the noise and furore of the attack on the houseboat, no one had heard the .40 calibre handgun fire its last shot into the serial killer's head.

Members of a SWAT team take up their positions around the Miami houseboat where Cunanan was trapped. Before they rushed in, he committed suicide.

Donato Bilancia

The Liguria Monster

FULL NAME:
Donato Bilancia

DOB:
10 July 1951

NUMBER OF VICTIMS:
17

SPAN OF KILLINGS:
1997–1998

LOCATION OF KILLINGS:
Liguria, Italy

DATE OF ARREST:
6 May 1998

SENTENCE:
14 terms of life imprisonment

The serial killings perpetrated by Donato Bilancia, who was born on 10 July 1951 at Potenza in southwest Italy, spanned more than one section of Italian society. He began with gamblers, went on to prostitutes and then embarked on a series of killings on trains, with his victims randomly chosen. Bilancia's 17 murders were all committed within the space of only six months, in 1997 and 1998. The killings on board trains earned him the nickname 'Monster of Liguria', and brought him countrywide notoriety through sensational TV and newspaper coverage.

Donato Bilancia began his career in crime as a thief and a burglar. He was not particularly successful, either. He fell afoul of the Carabinieri, the Italian police force, on two occasions in 1975 and in 1976,

and spent some time in prison before managing to escape.

Then, in 1982 a fearful tragedy struck the Bilancia family: Donato's brother Michele threw himself in front of a train on the Genoa–Ventimiglia line with his infant son in his arms. This appalling event had a profound effect on Donato Bilancia, and his mental state, already noticeably fragile, seemed to deteriorate. A car accident in 1990 that left him in a coma for several days exacerbated the problem: it was now that Bilancia became vicious and made the move to murder.

Impulse to Murder

First, though, he resorted to gambling. He later boasted that he had won and lost huge sums of money in a single night. Around this time, too, he began to exhibit a strange mixture of extreme violence and an almost puritan sense of rectitude. Bilancia regarded himself as an 'honest' gambler because he always paid the debts he incurred at the tables, and always kept his word. In the fall of 1997, Bilancia was playing at the gaming table with one Giorgio Centanaro when he realized – or thought he realized – that Centanaro was cheating him. This, Bilancia felt, cast a slur on his own honour and required retribution.

Killing for Profit

On 16 October 1997, Bilancia avenged himself when he called at Centanaro's house and strangled him with a roll of adhesive tape. Curiously enough, the Carabinieri could find no clues that revealed the death as suspicious, and Centanaro's demise went into the police record under 'natural causes'. But Bilancia was not finished yet. He suspected that Centanaro had

'He went round to the Parenti residence on 24 October 1997 and killed not only Parenti himself but his wife Carla Scotto as well. For good measure, Bilancia made off with US$9500 and several valuables.'

set him up as a 'fall guy' with Maurizio Parenti, a powerful figure in the Italian gambling underworld. This, too, demanded revenge. Bilancia exacted

Bilancia lived in Genoa, where his family moved in 1956. It is the capital of the Liguria region in Italy's northwest. Bilancia's entire murder spree happened there.

'She, however forestalled him, realizing what was about to happen, and managed to run away when two night security guards appeared on patrol in Novi Ligure. Bilancia, however, shot both guards.'

it when he went round to the Parenti residence on 24 October 1997 and killed not only Parenti himself but his wife Carla Scotto as well. For good measure, Bilancia made off with US$9500 and several valuables that had belonged to the Parentis.

Bilancia's next victims, Bruno Solari and his wife Maria Luigia Pitto, were killed purely for gain. They died on 27 October 1997 after Bilancia broke into their home with robbery in mind. On 13 November, Bilancia murdered Luciano Marro, a moneychanger in Ventimiglia, and again enriched himself, this time to the tune of US$33,000. Next, on 25 January 1998, Bilancia killed a night security guard, Giangiorgio Canu, in Genoa. After this, he changed tack, and began to concentrate on prostitutes.

An Albanian prostitute, Stela Truya, became the first of them when Bilancia shot her on 9 March 1998 in Varazze, a beach resort on the Italian Riviera. Nine days later, it was the turn of Ljudmyla Zubskova, a prostitute from the Ukraine, who was shot in the head in Pietra Ligure, another Riviera resort. Subsequently, Bilancia returned to Ventimiglia, where, on 20 March, he murdered another moneychanger, Enzo Gorni, after robbing him. Bilancia was seen by Gorni's brother-in-law as he fled from the murder scene in a black Mercedes. This vehicle would later become instrumental in bringing the Bilancia rampage to an end.

Leaving Behind Clues

Before that, though, Donato Bilancia made a mistake that would later turn out to be fateful. On 24 March

The Trail of the Murders

Genoa, 16 October 1997:
Bilancia initiated his string of murders in Genoa. These began on 16 October 1997 when he killed Giorgio Centanaro and eight days later added the lives of Maurizio Parenti and his wife, Carla Scotto. Bilancia believed that the two men had cheated him at the gaming table.

Ventimiglia, 13 November 1997 and 20 March 1998:
The Liguria Monster killed two moneychangers in Venitimiglia 130km (81 miles) southwest of Genoa. His victims were Luciano Marro on 13 November 1997 and Enzo Gorni on 20 March 1998. Gorni's brother-in-law saw the murderer's black Mercedes, leading to his eventual capture.

Italian Riviera resorts, March 1998:
Bilancia killed the first two prostitutes in resort areas. Stela Truya, from Albania, was shot dead on 9 March 1998 in the Italian Riviera beach resort of Varazze. Ljudmyla Zubskova, a Ukrainian, died the same way nine days later in another Riviera resort, Pietra Ligure.

Arma di Taggia, 21 April 1998:
Bilancia's last murder took place on 21 April 1998 in Arma di Taggia on the Italian Riviera near San Remo. He cornered Giuseppe Mileto, a petrol pump attendant, robbing and killing him. Less than a month later, police captured Bilancia by tracing his car.

Key
Bilancia's victims

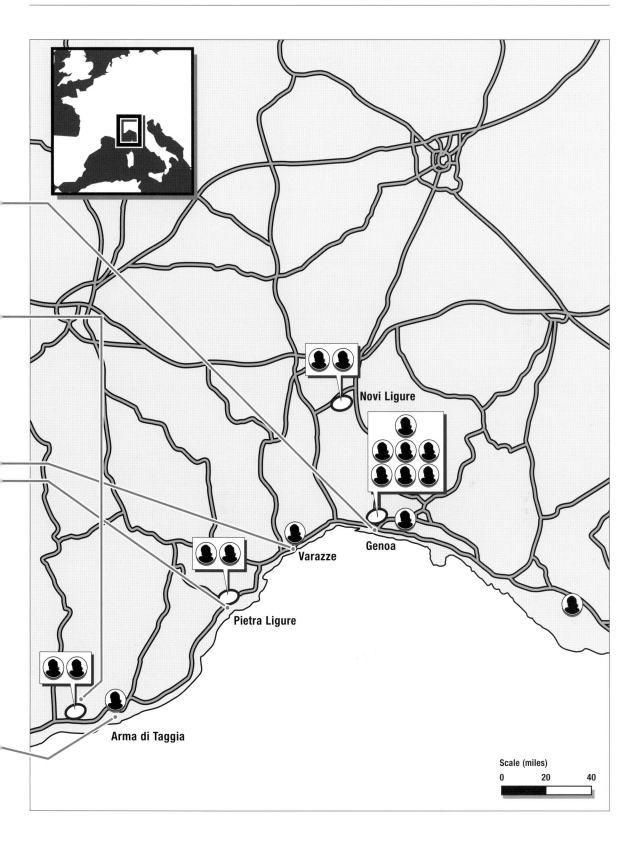

Novi Ligure

Varazze

Genoa

Pietra Ligure

Arma di Taggia

Scale (miles)

0   20   40

1998, he attempted to kill a transsexual named Lorena – formerly Julio – Castro. She, however, forestalled him, realizing what was about to happen, and managed to run away when two night security guards appeared on patrol in Novi Ligure. Bilancia, however, shot both guards, Massimiliano Garillo and Candido Rando, and then fired at Lorena, hitting her in the chest and leaving her for dead. Lorena survived and afterwards provided the Carabinieri with information to make an Identikit image of her assailant. The guards also survived, but in their case not for long. Bilancia soon finished them off, each with a bullet in the head.

Five days later, Donato Bilancia reverted to

Donato Bilancia is escorted by policemen after he is arrested in May 1998. His victims were killed in Liguria, giving him the nickname of 'The Liguria Monster'.

'The bullet retrieved from the body of Tessy Adobo was later found by police ballistics experts in Parma to match those that killed Stela Truya and another prostitute, Kristin Valla, murdered by Bilancia on a train.'

murdering prostitutes when he killed Tessy Adobo, a Nigerian woman, in Cogoleto, around 25km (15.5 miles) west of Genoa. For all his killings, Bilancia used a .38 Smith and Wesson revolver, which he had purchased, along with 50 bullets, in 1997. This, too, had far-reaching consequences. The bullet retrieved from the body of Tessy Adobo was later found by police ballistics experts in Parma to match those that killed Stela Truya and another prostitute, Kristina Valla, murdered by Bilancia on a train on 14 April. Two days earlier, on 12 April, on another train running along the Genoa–Ventimiglia line, Bilancia had killed a 32-year-old nurse from Milan, Elisabetta Zoppetti, who was on her way home by train on the La Spezia–Venezia intercity line, after spending a weekend on the Italian Riviera.

'I got on the train at Genoa,' Bilancia later told police. 'In first class, there was a woman. I waited until she went to the toilet, taking her bag with her.' Bilancia used his expertise as a burglar to pick the lock on the toilet door and open it. When he suddenly appeared, Bilancia went on, 'She screamed. I put her jacket over her head and fired. I had got on (the train) with the intention to kill.'

On 18 April, Maria Angela Rubina died at Bilancia's hands in the toilet of a train; she, too, was 32 years old. 'I did it like the last one, very quickly,' Bilancia afterwards explained. His last killing took place on 21 April 1998, at Arma di Taggia, near San Remo: the victim was Giuseppe Mileto, a petrol pump attendant, who was robbed before he died.

The black Mercedes Bilancia used to travel

DONATO BILANCIA TIMELINE

10 July 1951: Donato Bilancia born at Potenza in southwest Italy.

1982: Michele Bilancia, Donato's brother, commits suicide by throwing himself in front of a train on the Genoa–Ventimiglia line while carrying his infant son.

1990: Donato Bilancia is injured in a car accident and spends several days in a coma.

16 October 1997: Bilancia commits his first murder when he kills a fellow gambler, Giorgio Centanaro, for cheating him at the gaming table.

24 October 1997: Bilancia kills Maurizio Parenti, an influential gambler whom he suspects of being in league with Centanaro. He murders Parenti's wife Carla as well and steals US$95000 and a range of valuables.

27 October 1997: With robbery in mind, Bilancia breaks into the house owned by Bruno Solari and his wife Maria and kills both of them.

13 November 1997: Bilancia kills a Venitimiglia moneychanger, Luciano Marro and steals US$33,000.

26 January 1998: Giangiorgio Canu, a night security guard, is murdered by Bilancia in Genoa.

9 March 1998: The first of four prostitutes murdered by Bilancia, Stela Truya, an Albanian, is shot dead in Varazze, an Italian Riviera beach resort.

18 March 1998: Ljudmyla Zubskova, a prostitute from the Ukraine, is shot dead by Bilancia in Pietra Ligure, another Riviera resort.

20 March 1998: Moneychanger Enzo Gorni is killed by Bilancia in Ventimiglia.

24 March 1998: Bilancia's attempt to murder Lorena Castro, a transsexual, in Novi Ligure fails, though he does kill two night security guards, Massimiliano Garillo and Candido Rando. Lorena Castro later provides the Carabinieri with an Identikit image of her assailant.

29 March 1998: Reverting to prostitutes, Bilancia kills a Nigerian woman, Tessy Adobo, in Cogoleto, near Genoa.

12 April 1998: Bilancia murders Elisabetta Zoppetti, a 32-year-old nurse from Milan on a train on on the La Spezia–Venezia line.

14 April 1998: Another prostitute, Kristina Valla, is murdered by Bilancia on board a train.

18 April 1998: Maria Angela Rubina, 32, dies at Bilancia's hands on board a train.

21 April 1998: Bilancia's last victim, Giuseppe Mileto, a petrol pump attendant, is robbed and murdered at Arma di Taggia, near San Remo.

6 May 1998: Bilancia is arrested after being traced through the black Mercedes he has used to travel between murder venues.

15 May 1998: After nine days of questioning, Bilancia finally confesses to all 17 murders he has committed over the previous six months. His confession covers 14 pages.

12 April 2000: Bilancia is put on trial in Genoa and is given 14 life sentences for murder and another 14 years for attempting to kill Lorena Castro.

between murder venues had been a trial vehicle, which he failed to return to the dealer who owned it. Once the dealer tired of waiting, he reported it to the Carabinieri as effectively stolen. This enabled the Carabinieri to match up the driver, who had taken the Mercedes for a trial run but never come back, with the Identikit image provided by Lorena Castro. Lorena's description of the black Mercedes matched the missing vehicle, and further proof came from a tally between Bilancia's DNA – provided by cigarette butts and a coffee cup – and a sample found at one of the murder venues.

"'I waited until she went to the toilet, taking her bag with her."' Bilancia used his expertise as a burglar to pick the lock on the toilet door and open it. "She screamed. I put her jacket over her head and fired".'

Finally Arrested

Bilancia was arrested on 6 May 1998. He resisted questioning for a while, but a little over a week later, on 15 May, he gave in and admitted all the murders. His confession covered a lurid 14 pages and included the killing of Giorgio Centanaro, in which foul play had not originally been suspected. Bilancia went on trial in Genoa in the spring of 2000. On 12 April, he was sentenced to 14 terms of life imprisonment for murder, with 14 years added for the attempted killing of Lorena Castro.

The Beltway Snipers

AKA The Washington Snipers

FULL NAMES:
John Allen Muhamed and Lee Boyd Malvo

DOB:
31 December 1960 (Muhamed)
18 February 1985 (Malvo)

VICTIMS:
10 killed; three others seriously injured

SPAN OF KILLINGS:
2–22 October 2002

LOCATION OF KILLINGS:
Various locations around the Beltway
(ring road) circling Washington

DATE OF ARREST:
24 October 2002

SENTENCE:
Death penalty (Muhamed)
Six life sentences (Malvo)

S erial killing reached new heights of terror during the first three weeks of October 2002, when 10 people were killed and three others seriously injured in and around Washington DC in a series of shootings that came out of nowhere. Carried out at various locations around the Beltway (the ring road circling Washington), the murders prompted one of the most intensive investigations ever staged in the United States, involving some 400 agents from the FBI alone.

James Martin, a program analyst at the National Oceanic and Atmospheric Administration, became the first victim of the Beltway snipers – as the murderers were soon called – when he was crossing a grocery store parking lot at Wheaton, Maryland, in the northern suburbs of Washington DC. It was 6.30 p.m.

on 2 October 2002 and, as was later discovered, the killing tied in with two other earlier murders in 2002, one in Maryland, the other in Alabama: all had been perpetrated by John Allen Muhamed (née Williams), 41, and 17-year-old Lee Boyd Malvo.

Muhamed had changed his name a year earlier, when he joined the religious Black supremacist organization, the Nation of Islam, and together with Malvo, he carefully prepared their entry into the annals of American serial killings.

The Shootings Begin

First, the two men practised shooting at the stump of a tree in the backyard of the 3300 block in South Proctor Street in Tacoma, Washington State. They also sat through several showings of Oliver Stone's 1998 film, *Savior:* set in the Bosnian conflict of 1993, the film featured a cold-blooded sniper who shoots anyone crossing a bridge that joins the Serb and Muslim sectors of a Bosnian town.

After this, Muhamed and Malvo drove across the United States in their dark blue 1990 Chevy Caprice, and in September 2002 used their gun-handling skills on two victims. The first was killed on 5 September. Paul LaRuffa, 55, the owner of a pizzeria in Clinton, Maryland, was locking up his restaurant for the night when Muhamed and Malvo shot him six times at close range. He died instantly. Just over two weeks later, on 21 September, the killers appeared in Montgomery, Alabama, where they robbed a liquor store. Muhamed killed the store clerk, Claudine Parker, 52, with a Bushmaster XM-15 semi-automatic .223 calibre rifle: the bullet entered the base of her skull and a separate shot injured her assistant, 24-year-old Kellie Adams.

Customers in the liquor store witnessed the shootings and two men joined police in chasing Muhamed and Malvo as they fled. The two of them managed to get away and, 11 days later, reappeared in Maryland. After the murder of James Martin, they escalated the shootings. Next day, they killed five

'Muhamed killed the store clerk, Claudine Parker, 52, with a Bushmaster XM-15 semi-automatic .223 calibre rifle: the bullet entered the base of her skull and a separate shot injured her assistant.'

more victims, four in Maryland during the morning of 3 October and the other the same evening a few miles away, in the US capital itself.

The first to die on the second day of the Beltway murder spree was James L. Buchanan, 39, a landscape designer. He was shot at 7.41 a.m. while mowing the grass in Fitzgerald Auto Mall at Rockville, Maryland.

Pallbearers flank the casket of Conrad Johnson, shot dead on 22 October 2002 at Aspen Hill, Maryland. He was killed on the steps of the bus he drove.

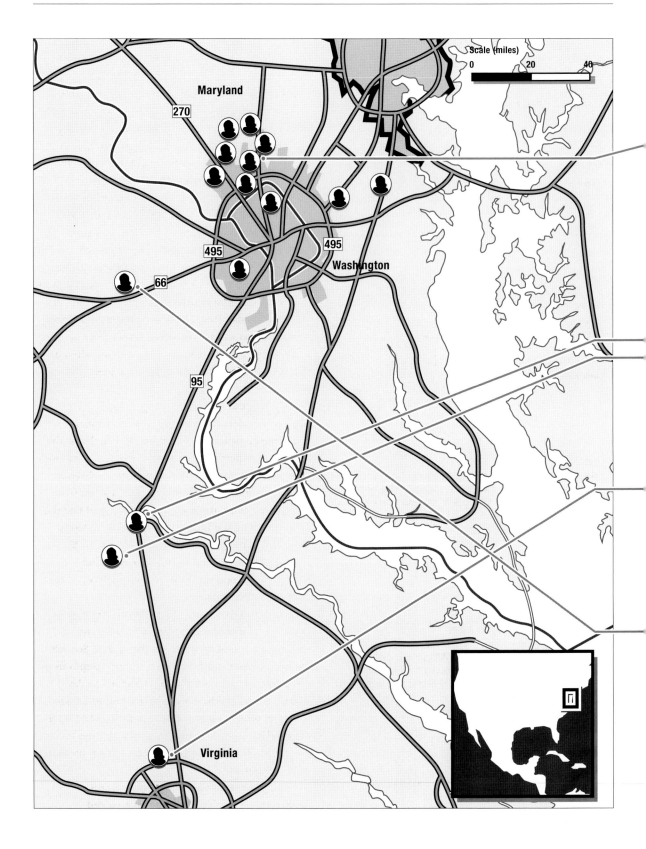

The Trail of Shootings

Maryland, 2 and 22 October 2002:
The first and last Beltway murders occurred in Maryland. The snipers killed James Martin in Wheaton on 2 October 2002 and, finally, Conrad Johnson at Aspen Hill on 22 October 2002. Four others were killed in Maryland and the schoolboy Iran Brown was wounded. It was later discovered that two murders earlier on in the year in Maryland and Alabama were attributable to Muhamed and Malvo.

Spotsylvania County, Virginia, 4 and 11 October 2002:
Muhamed and Malvo targetted two victims in Spotsylvania County, Virginia, in October 2002. Caroline Seawell was injured in a parking lot on the 4th and Kenneth Bridges died at a petrol station while filling his car on the 11th. Three others were murdered in Virginia.

Ashland, Virginia, 19 October 2002:
The snipers most southern trip out of the Beltway was to Ashland, Virginia, just north of Richmond. There on the night of 19 October 2002 they found Jeffrey Hopper, 37, standing in the parking lot of the Ponderosa Steakhouse. He was shot but survived.

Fairfax County, 14 October 2002:
Only one person was killed in Washington DC by the snipers. The Beltway, or Interstate 495, encompasses the District of Columbia's inner suburbs in Maryland and Virginia. The only Virginia victim in this area was Linda Franklin, an FBI analyst, who was shot dead in Fairfax County.

Key The Snipers' victims

Just over 30 minutes later, Premkumar Walekar, a 54-year-old taxi driver, was filling his tank at a Mobil station on the corner of Aspen Hill Road and Connecticut Avenue when he dropped dead, killed without warning, by a rifle shot that must have come from nearby. No one, however, saw exactly where it came from, or spotted the red dot projected onto targets by the Bushmaster by a sight that enabled shots to be fired at ranges of 45–90m (50–100yd).

This 'invisibility' was to become the prime terror factor in the killings that continued with another sudden death at 8.37 a.m. when Sarah Ramos, a babysitter, was shot dead while reading a book at a bus station. At 9.58 a.m., Lori Ann Lewis-Rivera, 25, was shot and killed while cleaning out her Dodge Caravan at a Shell station in Kensington, Maryland. The last victim of the day, Pascal Charlot, a 72-year-old retired carpenter, was walking along Georgia Avenue at Kalmia Road, Washington DC, at 9.15 p.m. when he, too, was shot, and died about an hour later.

A City in Fear
The five murders that took place on 3 October established a pattern. The shootings were clearly the work of an expert marksman, who was able to kill with a single bullet, fired with chilling accuracy. No one saw the gunman, who must have used his gun from cover and at a fair distance. Police suspected that the killer was using the Beltway around Washington to move from one murder scene to the next, for the killings of Lewis-Rivera and Charlot had been committed on opposite sides of the ring road, some 23km (14 miles) apart.

In just two days, the murder statistics for the Washington area had escalated by 25 per cent, spreading a pall of dread across the capital. Schools banned outdoor sports and even stopped pupils from going into playgrounds during breaks in the day. Parents whose children normally walked home from school or took the school bus were now picked up in the car. Holidaymakers took to scurrying from their hotels onto the tour coaches that took them on tours of the capital.

Filling car tanks was soon identified as a dangerous occupation. Some stations placed

tarpaulins around the awning above the pumps to make customers feel safer. Customers also sought safety by walking quickly round their cars, hoping to give the sniper a more difficult target to strike.

After 3 October, Muhamed and Malvo widened their area of operations and shot their first victim in Virginia the following day. Fortunately, 43-year-old Caroline Seawell was only injured as she loaded her car in the parking lot of Michaels Craft Store in Spotsylvania County, Virginia on 4 October. Iran Brown, 13, also survived being shot as he arrived at the Benjamin Tasker Middle School in Bowie in St George's County, Maryland.

It was after the Iran Brown shooting that police managed to retrieve some useful clues. A shell casing was found and a Death card from a Tarot pack was left behind, inscribed with a message: 'Dear Policeman, I am God!' This was one of many Tarot cards left at the murder scenes. At other sites, police found long,

Christine Goodwin points to a diagram of the crime scenes as she testifies during one of the snipers' trials which were held in both Virginia and Maryland.

handwritten letters, one of which demanded a $10 million ransom. Another contained threats to the lives of children living in the surrounding area. One particularly chilling missive, later released to the press by Montgomery County Police Chief Charles Moose, read: 'Your children are not safe, anywhere, at any time.'

Calls to the Police

The next shooting followed two days later, at 9.18 p.m. on 9 October. Dean Harold Meyers, 53, shared the fate of Premkumar Waleker six days earlier when he was shot and killed while filling his car at a Sunoco gas station on Sudley Road in Virginia's Prince William County. The third man to die while filling a vehicle was Kenneth Bridges, 53, who was shot at 9.30 a.m. on 11 October at an Exxon station off Interstate 95 in Spotsylvania County.

Arlington County, Virginia, became the next crime scene when Linda Franklin, an intelligence analyst for the Federal Bureau of Investigation, was killed at 9.15 p.m. on 14 October: she had just finished shopping at a Home Depot in Fairfax County. Subsequently, a witness to the shooting came forward, but it later transpired that he had been inside the Home Depot at the time and could not have seen anything. When it turned out that he had made up his 'evidence', he was arrested for obstructing the police investigation.

The next incident took place on 19 October, when Jeffrey Hopper, 37, was shot and wounded at 8.00 p.m. in the parking lot of the Ponderosa Steakhouse in Ashland, Virginia, near Interstate 95, some 145km (90 miles) south of Washington. The Beltway killers briefly returned to Maryland for their next killing, which followed three days later at 5.56 p.m. on 22 October: Conrad Johnson, a bus driver, was killed as he was taking a break, standing on the steps of his bus in Aspen Hill.

Muhamed and Malvo made several telephone calls to the police, taunting them for their lack of success in catching them and boasting about their exploits. In one call, one of the snipers made a mocking reference to the still unsolved liquor store robbery and murder of 21 September. The police managed to trace the call to a payphone in Henrico County, Virginia. However, by the time squad cars reached it, Muhamed and

THE BELTWAY SNIPERS TIMELINE

5 September 2002: Pizzeria owner Paul LaRuffa shot while locking up his pizzeria in Clinton, Maryland. It was later discovered that this killing was carried out by the Beltway murderers.

21 September 2002: Muhamed and Malvo rob a liquor store in Montgomery, Alabama, killing Claudine Parker and injuring Kellie Adams. It was later discovered that this was carried out by the Beltway murderers.

2 October 2002: After shooting practice in the yard of a building in Tacoma, Washington State, Muhamed and Malvo drive east to commit the first of the 'Beltway murders'. James Martin is shot in the parking lot of a grocery store in Wheaton, Maryland.

3 October 2002: Muhamed and Malvo commit multiple murders, four in Maryland and one in Washington DC.

4 October 2002: Caroline Seawell is injured in a parking lot in Spotsylvania County, Virginia.

7 October 2002: Schoolboy Iran Brown, 13, is injured as he arrives at school in Bowie, Maryland. A shell casing and a Tarot Death card bearing the message 'I am God' are found at the scene. This is one of several cards and letters containing threats and demands left behind by the Beltway killers.

9 October 2002: Dean Harold Meyers shot dead while filling his car at a station in Prince William County, Virginia.

11 October 2002: Kenneth Bridges is killed while filling the tank of his car.

14 October 2002: Linda Franklin is shot dead after shopping in Fairfax County, Virginia.

19 October 2002: Jeffrey Hopper is killed in the Ponderosa Steakhouse parking lot at Ashland, Virginia.

21 October 2002: Although police knew that Muhamed's dark blue Chevy Caprice had been registered in his name and its New Jersey licence plate NDA-21Z was issued to him, rumours and reports of a white van as the killers' vehicle proved a distraction. On 21 October, police arrested two men, one with a white van, who turned out to be illegal immigrants and unconnected with the Beltway murders.

22 October 2002: Conrad Johnson, a bus driver, shot dead at Aspen Hill, Maryland.

23 October 2002: Police find the shooting practice site in Tacoma, Washington State, together with bullets, shell casings and a tree trunk used as a target by the Beltway killers.

24 October 2002: Muhamed and Malvo are arrested in the Chevy Caprice where they had been sleeping.

24 November 2003: After a month-long trial in Prince William County, Virginia, John Muhamed is sentenced to death for murder. In August, he is extradited to Maryland to face further charges there.

10 March 2004: Found guilty of murder of Linda Franklin after a trial at Chesapeake, Virginia in December 2003, Malvo is formally sentenced to the penalty recommended by the jury: life imprisonment without the chance of parole.

27 October 2004: Malvo agrees to a deal that enables him to avoid the death penalty for the murder of Kenneth Bridges and instead accept a second sentence of prison for life without parole.

30 May 2006: In Montgomery County, Maryland, Muhamed is convicted on six counts of murder and is again sentenced to death.

10 May 2008: Muhamed decides to lodge an appeal against his conviction and death sentence with the federal government of the United States.

Malvo had gone, having departed the scene only a few minutes earlier.

Meanwhile, gossip and rumour proliferated in and around Washington, encouraged by massive TV coverage of every Beltway attack. The subject occupied hours of screen time, which was meant to enlist the help of the public in tracking down the killers, but resulted in overkill. Hotlines set up to elicit public help in the investigation were flooded and the special post office box was filled to the brim with often spurious information. One message concerned a 'crazy white guy armed with an AK-47 Kalashnikov sub-machine gun', who was driving around in a 'boxy white van'. Another white van, carrying dark lettering, was reported to have sped away from the Leisure World shopping centre with two men inside. Before long, the Maryland police were pulling over virtually every white van and truck on the road.

The white van story led, in fact, to a mistake that was, in its way, fruitful. On 21 October, police arrested two men outside a petrol station. One of them had the now expected white van, but both turned out to be illegal immigrants. They were handed over to the Immigration and Naturalization Service.

Despite this error, the police investigation made substantial advances on 23 October. The practice ground Muhamed and Malvo had used in Tacoma, Washington was located, and there the police used metal detectors to discover shell casings and bullets, the debris left behind by the killers. This was added to

Police examine the Chevrolet Caprice after arresting Muhamed and Malvo sleeping in it. The snipers had cut a gap into the truck to aim their rifle at victims.

the 14 bullets recovered by the police from the sites of earlier attacks. They also found the tree stump that was thoroughly shot up after the killers' practice sessions. In addition, after examining the bullet that had killed Conrad Johnson, ballistic experts were able to confirm him as one of the victims, the tenth murdered in the Beltway shootings. It turned out that he was also the last.

Caught Napping

On the night of 23 October, Muhamed and Malvo parked the Chevy Caprice at a reststop in Maryland off Interstate 70 near Myersville and went to sleep inside. The police had already identified the Caprice as the car – licence plate NDA-21Z – purchased in New Jersey by John Muhamed. It had been observed by radio patrol cars parked close to several shooting sites and its details were well publicized. But the almost obsessive police focus on white vans had prevented them from investigating more closely.

Now, though, this vital clue was about to come into its own. At 11.45 p.m., the Caprice was noticed and reported by Ron Lanz, a truck driver. He used his massive truck to block the exit to the parking lot and so prevent escape, while Maryland State police, Montgomery County SWAT officers and agents from the Hostage Rescue Team descended on the reststop, where they found the Beltway killers still asleep. They were immediately arrested and gave in without a fight.

Now the authorities were able to discover how the Beltway killings had been achieved. A gap large enough to allow the Bushmaster .223 calibre rifle to poke through and the scope to be used for taking aim had been cut in the trunk just above the licence plate. This enabled shots to be fired from inside the automobile and at the same time hid the sniper from detection. With the metal sheet at the back of the passenger compartment removed, it was possible to get into the trunk without getting out of the car. The police also found maps of the crime scenes and getaway routes on a stolen laptop computer, a digital voice recorder and walkie-talkies. The Chevy Caprice was, in fact, a mobile operations room.

The two Beltway killers went on trial in Virginia and Maryland and both were found guilty of murder. John Muhamed received the death sentence, but Lee

'A gap large enough to allow the Bushmaster .223 calibre rifle to poke through and the scope to be used for taking aim, had been cut in the trunk just above the licence plate. This enabled shots to be fired from inside...'

Malvo escaped the same penalty because of his youth. Instead, he was twice sentenced to six consecutive terms of imprisonment without possibility of parole.

A firearms expert demonstrates how the defendants operated their Bushmaster .223 calibre rifle from their car. The gun had a range of 45–90m (50–100yd).

Daniel Gonzalez
The Freddy Krueger Killer

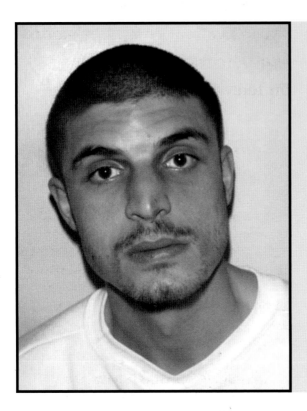

FULL NAME:
Daniel Gonzalez

DOB:
1980

DIED:
9 August 2007

VICTIMS:
Murdered four people and injured two others

SPAN OF KILLINGS:
Three days in September 2004

LOCATION OF KILLINGS:
London and Sussex, United Kingdom

DATE OF ARREST:
17 September 2004

SENTENCE:
Six life sentences

Lesley Savage wrote to her Member of Parliament, asking, 'Does my son have to commit murder before he can get help?'. The question was meant to be rhetorical. Tragically, it proved prophetic. In September 2004, 24-year-old Daniel Gonzalez, who had been diagnosed as a psychopath and paranoid schizophrenic, terrorized parts of London and seaside resorts along the English south coast. Driven on by his own psychoses, as well as by drink and drugs, Gonzalez murdered four elderly people and injured two others – and highlighted the shortcomings of the police and social services, who, as his mother feared, waited for him to kill before they did anything to stop him.

Daniel Gonzalez was a sad, bored loner with no job, no friends and nothing to do but spend his days taking drugs, playing violent computer games and watching horror films on television. These films became his world, peopled by fictional characters such as Freddy Krueger, the undead serial killer in the *Nightmare on Elm Street* movie series, and Jason Voorhees, the machete-wielding mass murderer of the *Friday the Thirteenth* slasher pictures, who went about his deadly business wearing a hockey mask. Gonzalez also admired, and doubtless longed to emulate, the two 17-year-olds who perpetrated the Columbine High School massacre in Colorado in 1999, when 12 students and one teacher were killed and another 23 people were injured.

In this world of ghastly images, grisly murders and fear-filled suspense, where murderers were heroes and slaughter an achievement, Daniel Gonzalez conceived a terrible ambition, which he later confessed to the police: he wanted to be remembered as a famous serial killer. He also longed to be Freddy Krueger for a day and carry out the killings of 'at least ten people'.

His mother, Lesley Savage, was well aware of her son's murderous delusions long before they were revealed to the British police and lawcourts. But although he underwent seven years of hospital treatment for his mental problems, his condition failed to improve and, according to Ms Savage, the medical authorities failed to take his case seriously.

'Every time we asked for help for Daniel or Daniel did himself,' she commented, 'we were told we would have to wait for a crisis to occur before he could get the help he needed.' The help Gonzalez needed, his mother asserted, was to be detained under the Mental Health Act 1995, but the aid she sought, despite her many efforts, was not forthcoming.

Ultimately, when the crisis occurred in 2004, it shocked the nation, sent tabloid newspapers into a frenzy, cost the lives of two men and two women, and terrified a couple in their 50s who were injured but managed to survive. It also embarrassed the British police, who already had a file on Gonzalez for weapons offences, mental health problems and threats against their officers. The latest proof that Gonzalez was not right in the head was dated 13 September 2004, only two days before he embarked on his killing spree. That day, police received no less than seven reports that a man was running around naked in front of schoolchildren and their parents at Knaphill in Surrey. But no arrest was made.

Initial Failure

The murder campaign started on 15 September 2004, when Gonzalez took a steak knife from his mother's kitchen drawer and took a train from his home in Woking, Surrey, to Portsmouth, Hampshire, on the south coast of England. He arrived at Hillsea station at 11.12 a.m. Not far from the station, Gonzalez encountered Peter King, 61 and his wife, who were out exercising their dog on the sea front. Gonzalez confronted King and told him, quite frankly, that he intended to kill him. King, fortunately, was made of stern stuff and kicked Gonzalez away. Gonzalez fled.

'Daniel Gonzalez was a sad, bored loner with no job, no friends and nothing to do but spend his days taking drugs, playing violent computer games and watching horror films on television.'

The would-be killer took a train along the south coast until he reached Worthing in Sussex. In the struggle with Peter King, he had lost his knife, so he now purchased another. Moving further along the coast, Gonzalez reached Southwick, 5km (3 miles) west of Brighton. There, he encountered Marie Harding, 73, a well-known local figure who sold tickets for Brighton and Hove Albion football club. She was walking along a country path near her home when Gonzalez, wearing a Jason Voorhees hockey mask, approached her and stabbed her. She suffered deep wounds in the neck and back and died almost at once.

Gonzalez visited Highgate in north London to kill pensioners Derek and Jean Robinson. During the attack, a worker fled and called police.

'"I had to do it", Gonzalez later explained to the police, adding that voices in his head were telling him to act like Freddy Krueger and kill someone.'

After that, Gonzalez travelled to London, where he spent 10 hours drinking at public houses in the fashionable West End. He thought over the murder of Mrs Harding, which, as he later confessed, he had enjoyed carrying out.

'A proper bloodbath ...' Gonzalez later wrote. 'It felt really, really, really good. One of the best things I've done in my life ...'

Choosing His Victims

On 16 September 2004, having made up his mind to go on killing, he took a bus to Tottenham, in north London, and prowled around looking for a victim. By then, Gonzalez was armed with two kitchen knives that he had stolen from a local store.

The first person in his search for someone, anyone, to kill, was Kevin Molloy, 46, the landlord of a public house in Tottenham. He was later found dead in the street with several deep stab wounds in his neck, chest and abdomen.

'I had to do it,' Gonzalez later explained to the police, adding that voices in his head were telling him to act like Freddy Krueger and kill someone.

Gonzalez was not so greatly in thrall to his voices that he was unable to deploy a degree of cunning. As he plotted his next killing, he realized that one street murder at a time was enough, and that another might attract too much attention. So, instead, he decided to head for the nearby district of Hornsey, where he broke into a house on Frobisher Road owned by Koumis and Christina Constantinou. It was 7 a.m., and the couple, both in their 50s, were still asleep at the time. They were suddenly terrified awake as Gonzalez launched a frenzied attack on them. Mrs Constantinou attacked Gonzalez with a pair of slippers and then ran out into the street, screaming

Trail of Murders

Southwick, near Brighton 15 September 2004:
Gonzalez's first murder was in Southwick near Brighton. His victim was Marie Harding, 73, a popular local woman who sold tickets for the Brighton and Hove Albion football club. Wearing a hockey mask, Gonzalez found her alone on a country path and stabbed her.

Tottenham, London, 16 September 2004:
Gonzalez's first London murder occurred in the district of Tottenham on 16 September 2004. After stealing two kitchen knives, he took a bus there and roamed the streets until he met Kevin Molloy, 46, the landlord of a local public house. Gonzalez stabbed him to death.

Highgate, London, 17 September 2004:
A double murder occurred in the north London district of Highate when Gonzalez killed an elderly married couple. These proved to be his last murders, since police closed in and arrested him that day after he visited a hospital for treatment.

Hornsey, London, 17 September 2004:
In the London district of Hornsey, Gonzalez broke into the home of Koumis and Christina Constantinou while they were sleeping. They survived his attack, and Koumis fought back, inflicting injuries on the assailant. Those injuries forced Gonzalez to seek treatment at a nearby hospital, after which police arrested him.

Key   Gonzalez's victims

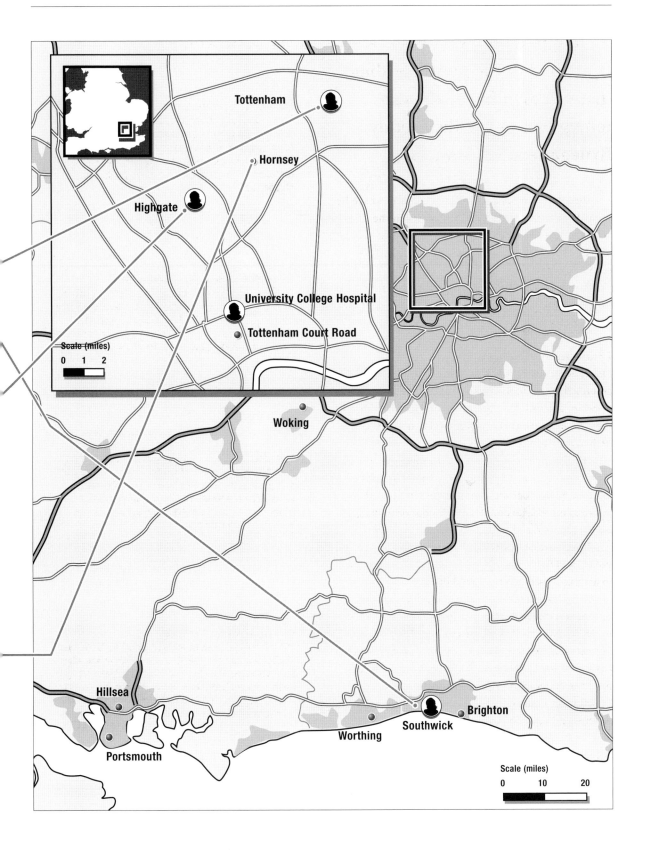

Tottenham

Hornsey

Highgate

University College Hospital

Tottenham Court Road

Scale (miles)
0   1   2

Woking

Hillsea

Brighton

Southwick

Worthing

Portsmouth

Scale (miles)
0   10   20

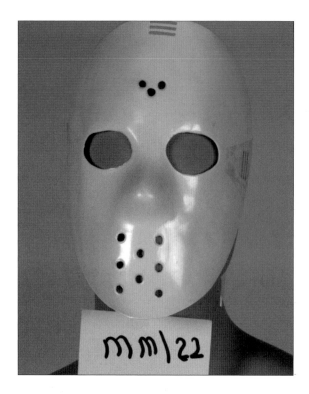

Presented as evidence during Gonzalez's trial was his Jason Voorhees hockey mask. He wore it to kill Marie Harding, 73, as she walked near her home in Southwick.

for help. Meanwhile, her husband kicked and punched Gonzalez and, despite being stabbed in the arms and chest and bitten on the hand, managed to fight him off. For good measure, the valiant Constantinou bit his younger assailant on the neck.

Gonzalez moved to another district, Highgate in north London, where he made himself conspicuous by running from house to house along Makepeace Avenue, randomly ringing doorbells. Unfortunately for two pensioners, retired paediatrician Derek Robinson, 75, and his 68-year-old wife Jean, they let Gonzalez into their flat after opening the front door.

A few minutes later, a decorator who was working on the Robinsons' flat arrived. He found the couple dead in spreading pools of blood, the walls smeared with blood, and Daniel Gonzalez, also covered in blood and stark naked, apparently preparing to take a shower. Doubtless fearing that he might be next, the decorator ran from the flat and called the police.

While he was away, Gonzalez ransacked the Robinsons' flat for cash, and by the time the police arrived, he was gone.

Gonzalez made his way to the Accident and Emergency department at University College Hospital, where he gave a false name and received treatment for injuries inflicted by Constantinou: deep cuts on his hands and a cut lip, which, he said, had been caused by broken glass. But the police had located him, possibly through a tip-off from the hospital. Later, they caught up with Gonzalez at the Tottenham Court Road underground station, where they arrested him. The killer told officers that the experience of murdering the Robinsons had been 'orgasmic'. Killing, he also commented, was the next best experience to taking drugs.

Of Highest Risk

In October 2004, Gonzalez was taken for assessment to Broadmoor at Crowthorne, Berkshire, the most famous of the three high-security psychiatric hospitals in Britain. He arrived surrounded by a mass of prison of officers, all of whom were wearing protective riot gear. Once inside Broadmoor, Gonzalez was placed in the highest risk assessment category and two nurses were assigned to watch him round the clock: one of their instructions was to be within arm's length of Gonzalez at all times. These precautions were not considered excessive by one of the hospital's psychiatric consultants, Dr Edward Petch. It was already known that Gonzalez had caused violent scenes at the police station where he was first taken after his arrest, and again at the prison where he was

'...a decorator who was working on the Robinsons' flat arrived. He found the couple dead in spreading pools of blood, the walls smeared with blood and Daniel Gonzalez, also covered in blood and stark naked'

DANIEL GONZALEZ TIMELINE

13 September 2004: Daniel Gonzalez is reported for running around naked in front of schoolchildren and their parents. He is not arrested.

15 September 2004: Gonzalez travels to Portsmouth, Hampshire, where he tries to kill Peter King, 61, and his wife. King fights him off. He goes on to Worthing and Southwick, near Brighton in Sussex, where he kills Marie Harding, 73.

16 September 2004: Travelling next to London, Gonzalez spends 10 hours drinking in the fashionable West End, then takes a bus to Tottenham, in north London, where he kills Kenneth Molloy, 46, the landlord of a public house.

17 September 2004: Gonzalez attacks Koumis and Christina Constantinou at their house in Hornsey, also in north London. Though injured, Constantinou fights the intruder off having inflicted some damage on his assailant. In Highgate, another north London district, Gonzalez kills two pensioners, Derek Robinson, 75, and his 68-year old wife, Jean, but is interrupted by a decorator who runs outside and calls the police. Gonzalez goes to University College Hospital, where he is treated for injuries inflicted by Constantinou. After leaving the hospital, Gonzalez is followed and is arrested at Tottenham Court Road underground station.

October 2004: Gonzalez is assessed at Broadmoor Psychiatric Hospital, at Crowthorne, Berkshire, and is pronounced a dangerous schizophrenic. He twice attempts, but fails, to kill himself.

26 February 2006: The trial opens at the Old Bailey in Fleet Street, London. Gonzalez pleads Not Guilty to murder but Guilty to manslaughter and attempted murder.

17 March 2006: The defence plea of diminished responsibility is rejected by the jury, who find Gonzalez guilty of murder. He is sentenced to six life terms in prison, with no parole.

9 August 2007: After being returned to Broadmoor, Gonzalez commits suicide in his cell.

kept before being transferred to Broadmoor. The staff at Broadmoor were therefore taking no chances. They were also taking seriously the peril Gonzalez represented to himself and others. They understood what his desperate mother had known for years, that Daniel Gonzalez was an extremely dangerous and unpredictable young man.

'It is not rocket science to say that he is at risk of extreme, unprovoked and unpremeditated violence without warning,' Dr Petch later told the court at the trial of Gonzalez in 2006. 'He would lunge, attack and punch and sometimes do himself harm.'

Suicide Attempts

While he was in Broadmoor, Gonzalez twice attempted to kill himself by biting his arm. On the first occasion, he bit so hard that it not only drew blood but penetrated almost to the bone. As warders were cleaning him up, Gonzalez attacked them, punching one of them in the face. After this, Gonzalez was transferred to a specialist care unit, the most secure facility of its kind in Britain.

At his trial, where the jury was sworn in on 27 February 2006, Gonzalez was flanked by medical staff as he sat in the dock at the Old Bailey in London's Fleet Street. He pleaded Not Guilty to murder, but admitted the manslaughter of his four victims and the attempted killing of Peter King and Koumis Constantinou. His defence attorneys entered a plea that Gonzalez was suffering from 'auditory hallucination' – voices that urged him to kill. Dr Petch appeared for the defence and told the court that in his opinion Daniel Gonzalez was schizophrenic, which meant that he did not appreciate what he was doing.

None of this was good enough for the prosecution, who refused to accept the principle of diminished responsibility. On 17 March 2006, after a trial lasting nearly three weeks, the jury took just over an hour to pronounce a Guilty verdict. Consequently, Judge Ann Goddard handed down six life sentences and told Gonzalez that there was no chance of parole or amnesty, because in his case 'life meant life.' She also refused to permit him to appeal against his sentences.

Afterwards, Daniel Gonzalez was returned to Broadmoor Hospital, where he was treated as one of the Berkshire institution's most dangerous patients. He was constantly watched, kept away from other inmates and knew, of course, that he would never be released. At some time over the next 17 months, he decided to end it all. Despite the intensive surveillance that surrounded him, he was found dead in his cell at Broadmoor on 9 August 2007. He was 27 years old. The verdict this time was suicide.

SERIAL KILLERS OF RECENT TIMES

NAME	COUNTRY	TIMESPAN	MURDERS (includes suspected victims)
Teofilo Varon	Colombia	1948–1963	592
Harold Shipman	United Kingdom	1975–1998	218
Luis Garavito	Colombia	1992–1998	172
Miyuki Ishikawa	Japan	1944–1948	103+
Javed Iqbal	Pakistan	1996–1999	100
Delfina and Maria de Jesus Gonzalez	Mexico	1955–1964	91
Daniel Barbosa	Colombia	1986–1988	72
Giuseppe Greco	Italy	1977–1985	58+
Woo Bum–Kon	South Korea	1982	57
Pedro Lopez	Colombia	1978–1980	57
André Chikatilo	Russia	1978–1990	53
Anatoly Onoprienko	Ukraine	1989–1996	52
Gary Ridgway	United States	1982–2000	48
Andrew Kehoe	United States	1927	45
David Burke	United States	1987	43
Charles Sobhraj	Vietnam	1975–1976	42
Moses Sithole	South Africa	1994–1995	38
Donald Harvey	United States	1970–1987	36
Serhiy Tkach	Ukraine	1984–2005	36+
Martin Bryant	Australia	1996	35
Vera Renczi	Romania	1920s–1930s	35
Ted Bundy	United States	1974–1978	35
John Wayne Gacy	United States	1972–1978	33
Charles Cullen	United States	1988–2003	32
Karl Denke	Germany	1903–1924	31

SERIAL KILLERS OF RECENT TIMES

NAME	COUNTRY	TIMESPAN	MURDERS (includes suspected victims)
Mutsuo Toi	Japan	1938	30
Camo Elias Delgado	Colombia	1986	30
Dean Korll	United States	1970–1973	27
Fritz Haarman	Germany	1919–1924	27
Cedric Maake	South Africa	1996–1997	27
Robert Pickton	Canada	1995–2001	26+
Marcel Petiot	France	1926–1944	26
Leonard Lake and Charles Ng	United States	1982–1985	25
William Bonin	United States	1979–1980	21
James Huberty	United States	1984	21
Patrick Kearney	United States	1965–1977	20
Donato Bilancia	Italy	1997–1998	17
Randy Steven Kraft	United States	1969–1983	16
Angel Resendez	Mexico	1997–1999	15
Richard Ramirez	United States	1984–1985	14
Peter Sutcliffe	United Kingdom	1975–1980	13
Volker Eckert	Germany	1994–2006	12
Henry Lee Lucas	United States	1960–1983	11
Joachim Kroll	Germany	1955–1976	8
Kenneth Erskine	United Kingdom	1986	7
Ivan Milat	Yugoslavia	1992–1994	7
Derrick Todd Lee	United States	1985–2003	7
David Berkowitz	United States	1996–1997	6
Tommy Lynn Sells	United States	1980–1999	6
Aileen Wuornos	United States	1989–1990	6
Lawrence Bittaker & Roy Norris	United States	1979	5
Andrew Cunanan	United States	1997	4

INDEX

Photo Credits

Amber Books: International edition front cover, bottom (Natascha Spargo)
Alamy: Front cover, top (Jack Carey)
Corbis: Back cover (Lexington Herald-Leader/Sygma),15 (Bettmann), 32 (Kapoor Baldev/Sygma), 36 (Bettmann), 37 (Bettmann), 41 (Bettmann), 42 (Bettmann), 43 (Bettmann), 50 (Bob E. Daemmrich/Sygma), 51 (Bettmann), 55 (Bettmann), 58 (Bettmann), 67 (Bettmann), 72 (Epix/Sygma), 79 (Epix/Sygma), 80 tl & tr (Bettmann), 84 (Bettmann), 86 (King County Sheriff/Reuters), 87 (Matthew McVay), 92 (Anthony Bolante/Reuters), 94 (Bettmann), 99 (Bettmann), 101 (Bettmann), 115 (Scott Lituchy/Star Ledger), 119 (Ed Murray/Star Ledger), 121 (Steve Klaver/Star Ledger), 130 (Gleb Garanich/Reuters), 141 (Megan Lewis/Reuters), 158 (Sygma), 162 (Stephane Cardinale), 172 tl (Reuters), 172 tr (Brendan McDermid/Reuters), 176 (Dave Ellis/Pool/CNP), 178 (Reuters)
Getty Images: 28 (Tekee Tanwar/AFP), 44 (Thomas Lohnes/AFP), 45 (Thomas Lohnes/AFP), 48 (AFP), 57 (Pam Francis/Liaison), 73 bl & br (Terry Smith/Time Life Pictures), 76 (Terry Smith/Time Life Pictures), 78 (Terry Smith/Time Life Pictures), 91 (Elaine Thompson-Pool), 114 (John Wheeler), 122 (Florida DOC), 123 (Acey Harper/Time Life Pictures), 128 (Acey Harper/Time Life Pictures), 143 (Patrick Riviere), 144, 145 (Mario Villafuerte), 148 (Mario Villafuerte), 150 (Erik S. Lesser), 151 (Baton Rouge Police Department), 159 (AFP), 165 (Roberto Schmidt), 173 (Shawn Thew/AFP), 179 (Dave Ellis/AFP)
Mirrorpix: 61, 64, 65
Photoshot: 6/7 (UPPA), 11 (UPPA), 16 (UPPA), 17 (Imagebrokers), 20 (UPPA), 23 (UPPA), 34 (Xinhua), 59 (UPPA), 63 (UPPA), 129 (UPPA), 167 (World Pictures), 180 (UPPA), 181 (UPPA), 184 (UPPA)
Press Association Images: 8 (Marta Lavandier/AP Photo), 9 (AP Photo), 10 (AP Photo), 22 (AP Photo), 27 (AP Photo), 56 (Dan Sheehan/AP Photo), 81 (AP Photo), 100 (Lacy Atkins/AP Photo), 102 (AP Photo), 103 (Chris Johnson/AP Photo), 106 (Eric Gay/AP Photo), 112 (PA), 136 (AP Photo), 137 (AP Photo), 142 (Rick Rycroft/AP Photo), 152 (David J. Phillip/AP Photo), 153 (Pat Sullivan/AP Photo), 156 (Tony Gutierrez/AP Photo), 170 (Italo Banchero/AP Photo)
Rex Features: 29, 35, 66 (Courtesy of the Everett Collection), 126 (Sipa Press), 131 (Sipa Press), 134 (Sipa Press), 166 (Sipa Press)
Stock.xchng: U.S. edition front cover, bottom (Pablo Rios)
TopFoto: 70, 108 (PA), 109 (PA)